THE STORY OF THE UNSINKABLE
TITANIC

THE STORY OF THE UNSINKABLE TITANIC

MICHAEL WILKINSON AND ROBERT HAMILTON

Daily Mail

Trans Atlantic Press

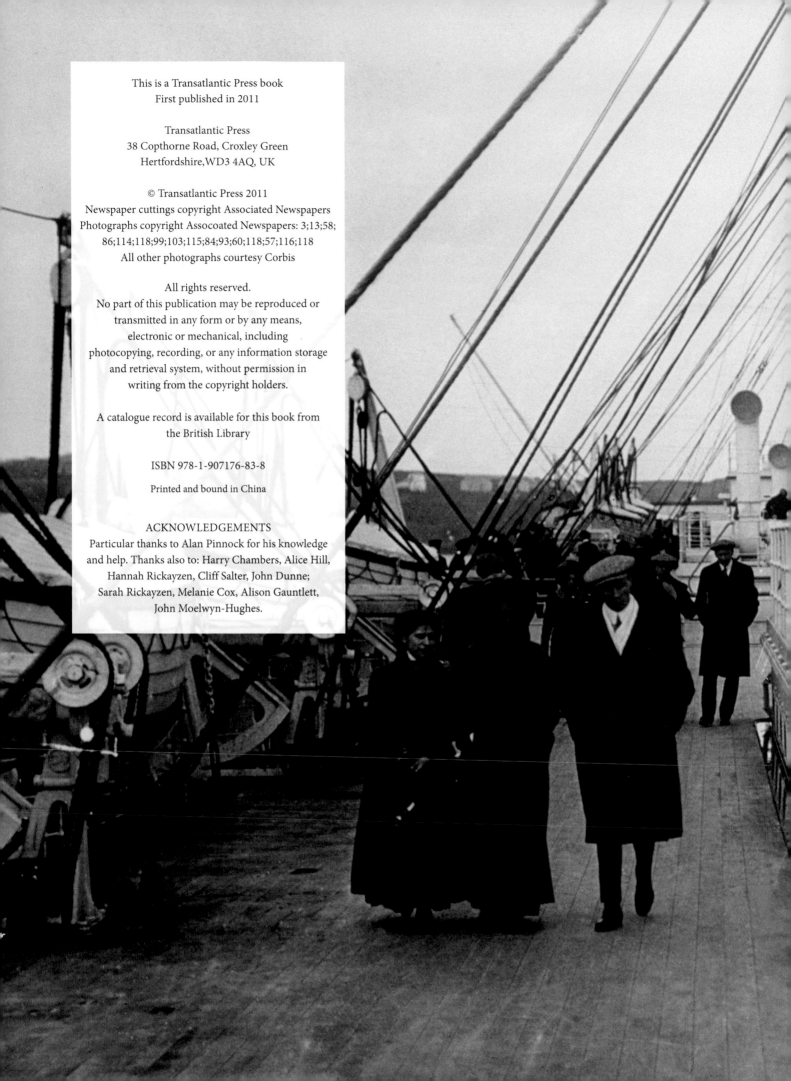

This is a Transatlantic Press book
First published in 2011

Transatlantic Press
38 Copthorne Road, Croxley Green
Hertfordshire, WD3 4AQ, UK

A catalogue record is available for this book from
the British Library

ISBN 978-1-907176-83-8

Printed and bound in China

ACKNOWLEDGEMENTS
Particular thanks to Alan Pinnock for his knowledge
and help. Thanks also to: Harry Chambers, Alice Hill,
Hannah Rickayzen, Cliff Salter, John Dunne;
Sarah Rickayzen, Melanie Cox, Alison Gauntlett,
John Moelwyn-Hughes.

Contents

The World's biggest ship

With the death of Millvina Dean in 2009, the last direct connection with White Star liner RMS Titanic was broken. She was nine weeks old when her family set out for the fresh pastures of opportunity in the New World in April 1912. Dean's father planned to open a tobacconist's shop in Kansas, a tale of migratory hope replicated many times over among the ship's third-class and steerage contingent. The well-heeled end of the passenger list included John Jacob Astor, one of the world's richest men, White House advisor Major Archibald Butt, businessman Benjamin Guggenheim, Isidor Straus and his wife – co-founders of Macy's department store - and British aristocrat Sir Cosmo Duff-Gordon, accompanied by his couturier wife 'Lucile'. It was they and their ilk who earned Titanic the 'Millionaire's Special' label in the press.

White Star chairman and managing director J Bruce Ismay was happy to see all strata of society on his flagship vessel, either soaking up the gracious living the premium tickets bestowed, or corralled into the less salubrious steerage quarters. Titanic, along with her sister ship Olympic, represented a £3 million investment to White Star, a bold move aimed at establishing a competitive advantage over its Cunard rival. The company founded by Ismay's father in 1868 had been in the doldrums, as had its parent concern, International Mercantile Marine. American financier and industrialist J P Morgan had formed IMM in 1902 with a view to becoming the dominant player on the lucrative transatlantic routes. White Star became a subsidiary that year, with Ismay installed as IMM president in 1904.

The thorn in Ismay's flesh was the British Government-backed Cunard Line, which remained outside the IMM syndicate. Cunard upped the stakes considerably with its sibling giants Lusitania and Mauretania. Both entered service in 1907, both capable of a 25-knot cruising speed that saw them trade the coveted Blue Riband until 1909, when Mauretania set a transatlantic record that would stand for 20 years. The 790-foot-long Mauretania was slightly the larger vessel; both broke the 30,000-ton barrier.

Luxury over speed

White Star's response was to build two ships that would dwarf even Cunard's behemoths, with a third to follow. They would be 90 feet longer, and in tonnage terms 50 percent bigger than anything afloat. Rather than place the emphasis on speed, it was decided that opulence and comfort should inform the design. Although only three funnels were needed to carry the engine exhaust gases, a fourth 'dummy' was incorporated to match the imposing look of Cunard's finest. They would be built in Belfast at Harland and Wolff, whose chief designer Thomas Andrews drew up plans that were finalised in 1908. Then commenced a three-year construction period in which a workforce of thousands brought the vision to life. Vertiginous gantries, heavy machinery and a deafening cacophony made for dangerous working conditions. Hundreds were injured, nine killed.

Titanic was modified in a number of ways following the launch of her sister ship. More first-class staterooms were added, while the trellised Café Parisien, in the style of a chic pavement bistro, extended the fine-dining facilities. Some of the promenade area was also enclosed to protect it from the elements. With these in place, she completed her sea trials on April 2, 1912 and immediately embarked on the first leg of her maiden voyage, the 570-mile trip from Belfast to Southampton. A coal strike threatened the scheduled onward departure, but fuel commandeered from other White Star ships ensured that the 159 furnaces, serving 29 boilers, were adequately supplied. Titanic's triple-screw propulsion system – the two outer propellers were 23 feet in diameter and weighed 38 tons - consumed around 700 tons of coal per day.

As she left Southampton harbour on Wednesday, April 10, Titanic had a near escape when the suction generated by her huge propellers drew the steamer New York towards her, the latter's mooring ropes snapping 'like a piece of cotton', according to one eyewitness. A burst of port-engine power averted a collision, Titanic's wash stopping the approaching ship dead when it was within six feet. Captain Edward J Smith, White Star's most senior commander, took the incident coolly in his stride.

Achilles' heel

Titanic's final ports of call before heading out into the Atlantic were Cherbourg and Queenstown. Even as the southern tip of Ireland receded into the distance, several of the factors that would contribute to the tragedy were already in play. One was the design itself, which had an Achilles' heel. 15 transverse bulkheads divided the ship into compartments that could be sealed off at the flick of a switch. Andrews calculated that two adjacent sections could be flooded without compromising the ship's integrity. It could even stay afloat if the forward four compartments shipped water. However, these compartments were not capped. The bulkheads all rose at least as far as E Deck, around 10 feet above the waterline. But should the ship sink low enough, water could pour over the top of one bulkhead and flood its neighbour. Bulkheads had been incorporated into ship design for decades, their height representing a trade-off between safety and practicality.

BELOW: Construction work taking place on the ship's prow. The Titanic was conceived in 1907, the brainchild of J. Bruce Ismay, the managing director of White Star Line and Lord Pirrie, chairman of Harland & Wolff, a Belfast shipbuilding company. Transatlantic travel was rapidly increasing and with it, the competition to build bigger, faster and more luxurious ships. Designs for the Titanic, the Olympic and the Gigantic (later named the Britannic) were drawn up the following year with a team headed by Lord Pirrie, Thomas Andrews, a naval architect at White Star and the Right Honourable Alexander Carlisle, the chief draughtsman at Harland & Wolff.

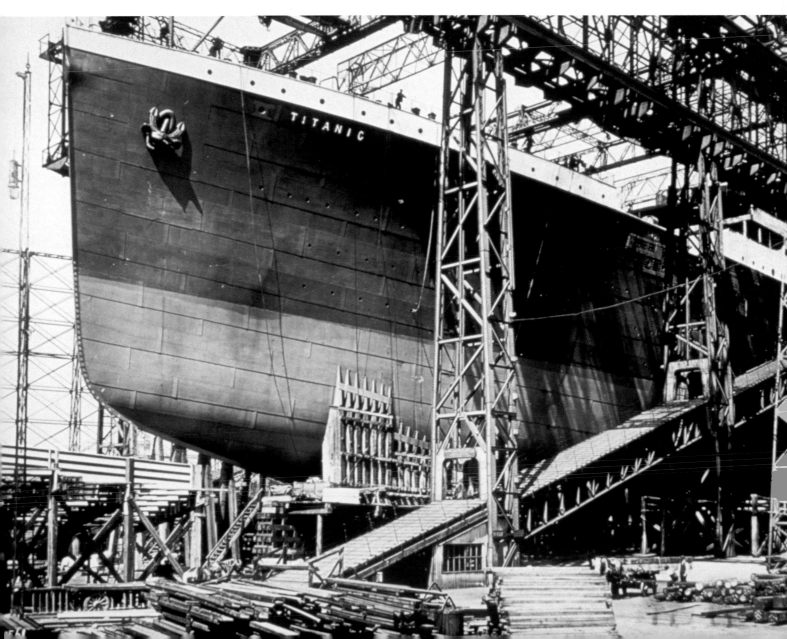

The three million rivets that held Titanic's superstructure together would also come under the microscope - quite literally. Metallurgists have examined rivets recovered from the ocean bed and found iron containing impurities that would have made them fail at much lower pressures. Had higher-grade iron been used, or steel, Titanic's ability to withstand an impact would have been significantly enhanced. Superior steel rivets were already widely used – indeed, Titanic herself had them in her central section of the hull, but not at the bow or stern.

Another crucial issue was lifeboat capacity. Long-standing Board of Trade regulations stipulated that 16 lifeboats were enough for 10,000-ton vessels or larger. Ismay overruled the original design, which stipulated a higher specification, and stuck to the minimum requirement. To Ismay, lifeboats impinged on space and spoiled the outlook for his premium passengers. That view left the Titanic with lifeboat capacity for around 1,170 people. Even when the collapsible emergency craft were taken into account, the lifeboats could accommodate only half of those on board. It was widely held that, in extremis, Titanic would remain afloat long enough for help to arrive. With cutting-edge wireless telegraphy now standard on White Star liners, summoning assistance in a busy shipping lane was a straightforward matter. In short, if an emergency arose Titanic would act as her own lifeboat. That notion had been reinforced by an incident three years earlier involving White Star liner Republic, which stayed afloat for over 30 hours after colliding with another ship in heavy fog off Nantucket. By the time it went to the bottom, the Marconi system had proved its worth, and no lives were lost beyond the initial impact.

100 MILES OF ICE.

Phenomenal Conditions in the Atlantic.

NEW YORK, Monday.

The liners Carmania and Niagara also encountered ice fields.

The former had a perilous time threading her way through.

The Niagara was less lucky, and had two holes knocked in her bottom and several plates bent.

The ice was encountered on the westbound track, off the Grand Banks.— Reuter.

Reuter's Agency is informed that the Canadian Pacific liner Empress of Britain, which arrived at Liverpool from Halifax (Nova Scotia) yesterday, reported the presence of an immense quantity of ice in the Atlantic.

Last Tuesday, when three days out from Halifax, she encountered an ice field a hundred miles in extent with enormous bergs, and steered a wide course, which delayed the vessel.

The Empress of Britain had previously received a wireless message from the Allan liner Virginian warning her of the presence of ice.

The extent of the ice was regarded as phenomenal, and the bergs appeared to be joined to the ice field, which appeared as an enormous white line on the horizon.

Ice warnings

A late personnel reshuffle aboard Titanic also had important ramifications. It left Second Officer David Blair surplus to requirements, but in his haste to disembark at Southampton he took with him the key to the cabinet containing binoculars used by the crow's nest crewmen. When reports of field ice, bergs and low-lying 'growlers' started to arrive from ships in the vicinity, the look-outs had to rely solely on their eyesight. A flat calm – such as it was on the night of Sunday, April 14 – didn't help matters, for there were no readily observable breaking waves on the treacherous bergs.

It was a hit-and-miss affair as to whether the ice warnings from other ships reached the bridge. One such, from Boston-bound cargo ship Californian, was received at 11.00 pm. Advised that Californian had stopped because the ship was 'surrounded by ice', Titanic wireless operator Jack Phillips hammered out a terse reply. He and his junior colleague Harold Bride may have been on White Star's payroll but they were Marconi employees whose bread-and-butter was passenger correspondence. Phillips had a backlog to deal with – hence his brusque response, which in turn prompted his opposite number on the Californian to shut up shop for the night.

It may be that the ice warnings that did reach the bridge were heeded, for Titanic was travelling further south than was normal for the time of year. Not far enough, though, for in 1912 ice reached latitudes beyond the norm.

At 11.40 pm Frederick Fleet spotted an iceberg dead ahead from his crow's nest vantage point. On receiving the alert, First Officer William

OPPOSITE PAGE TOP: An advertisement issued by White Star Line in 1912 demonstrated the sheer size of the Titanic against existing buildings. The designs specified that her overall length was to be 882 feet 9 inches (269.1m), the breadth 92 feet (28.0m), with a tonnage of 46,328 GRT and a height of 59 feet (18m) from the water line to the boat deck. The 29 boilers were fired by 159 coal burning furnaces and she was designed to reach a top speed of 23 knots (26mph). The project was funded by John Pierpoint Morgan, an American who owned the International Mercantile and Marine Company and construction began at Harland & Wolff's Belfast site on March 31, 1909.

OPPOSITE PAGE BOTTOM: The hull of the Titanic photographed in the water at Belfast after the initial launch. She was then towed to the Thompson outfitting wharf where more than 3,000 tradesmen set to work fitting out the interior of the ship. A day of sea trials was held on April 1, 1912 with 120 crew members on board and Titanic was then deemed seaworthy, granted its Board of Trade certificate and left Belfast arriving in Southampton at about midnight on April 3.

The White Star Line's New Triple-screw Steamers
"OLYMPIC" ☆ "TITANIC"
LARGEST AND FINEST IN THE WORLD
(SEE OVER)

(SEE OVER)

Murdoch issued a hard-to-port and full-astern order. Understandable though they were, his instructions may have unwittingly helped seal Titanic's fate. Slowing the ship down impacted on its turning capability; had forward momentum been maintained, contact might have been avoided. It is generally thought even a head-on collision would have been survivable. In the event, less than 40 seconds after the warning was given, Titanic was struck a glancing blow that tore a gash in the hull extending to almost one-third of her length. Rivets popped. Steel buckled. Andrews soon delivered the grim news to Captain Smith that six of the forward watertight compartments had been breached. Titanic was doomed.

CAPE RACE.

The Ancient Beacon of the North Atlantic Coast.

Cape Race, the nearest point of land to the spot of the disaster, is the "beacon" of the North Atlantic route to America— the objective point to which, for nearly four hundred years, all westward bound ships aimed to make a landfall.

In recent years the large and powerful liners have lain their course by a more southern route, but Cape Race is still the most important headland in North America.

In a map of the year 1500 the cape appears under the name of Cavo de Ynglaterra, but for hundreds of years it has figured under the name of Cape Raso, Rasso, Ras, Raz, or Race—all derived from the Latin "rasus," and meaning "the flat cape," because it is lower and more level than the adjacent headlands.

For a long period the British Government maintained a lighthouse there, but in 1880 it was taken over by the Dominion of Canada.

"S.O.S."

The wireless signal for "assistance wanted" is now "S.O.S.," the more familiar letters "C.Q.D." having been abandoned because they led to confusion with other code signals.

INSURED FOR £2,500,000.

Underwriters will lose heavily in the event of the Titanic becoming a total loss.

A director of Muir, Beddall and Co., the well-known insurance brokers, states that insurances to the amount of £2,500,000 have been effected on the vessel's cargo and hull.

The vessel, which cost £1,250,000 to build, is insured for one million, the remainder covering the cargo.

The company, it is understood, effected their insurances at the rate of 1 per cent. per annum.

Re-insurances were effected at Lloyd's this morning at the rate of 50 guineas per cent.

TITANIC DESCRIBED.

How She Sucked a Liner from Her Moorings on Departure.

A floating town would be an adequate description of the Titanic. She cost nearly a million and a quarter of money to build. To inspect her thoroughly a walk of four and a half miles would be necessary.

On her spacious decks, connected with each other by electric lifts, a stroll of two miles is possible. So easy is it to get lost within the ship that plans of her galleries and cabins have been placed in each of her decks.

She was built at Belfast by Messrs. Harland and Wolff for the White Star line, the keel being laid on March 22, 1909, and the vessel launched on May 31 last year.

Her displacement—46,328 tons—is over 1,000 tons more than that of her sister ship Olympic.

Figures, however, convey but a poor suggestion of her enormous bulk; a more vivid illustration was the incident which occurred when the liner left Southampton last Wednesday.

Near to where she was berthed lay the Oceanic and the New York, great vessels in their day, but now dwarfed to comparative insignificance.

POPULATION OF 3,000.

Directly the huge screws of the Titanic began to revolve the suction caused the seven great stern ropes of the New York to snap like wisps of cotton, and the American liner's stern swung round into midstream.

For a moment it was feared that there must be a collision. The Titanic's screws had to be stopped, and then the New York was towed back to safety.

The Titanic's full complement of passengers and crew was more than 3,000 persons, made up as follows:—

Saloon passengers	750
Second-class passengers	500
Steerage passengers	1,100
Crew	800
Total	3,150

The cost of a trip across the ocean on the Titanic ranged from £7 15s to £870, the latter figure being the price charged during the height of the season for either of the two parlour suites with private promenade deck.

BELOW: At the stroke of 12 noon on April 10, 1912 the Titanic finally set sail from Southampton. With different classes of accommodation available and a wide spectrum of passengers the travel costs varied between £3 for a third-class ticket to £870 for the most expensive first-class suite.

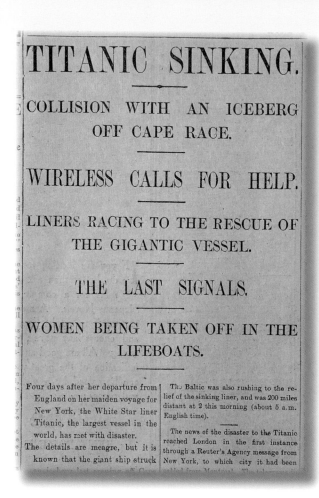

TITANIC SINKING.

COLLISION WITH AN ICEBERG OFF CAPE RACE.

WIRELESS CALLS FOR HELP.

LINERS RACING TO THE RESCUE OF THE GIGANTIC VESSEL.

THE LAST SIGNALS.

WOMEN BEING TAKEN OFF IN THE LIFEBOATS.

Four days after her departure from England on her maiden voyage for New York, the White Star liner Titanic, the largest vessel in the world, has met with disaster. The details are meagre, but it is known that the giant ship struck

The Baltic was also rushing to the relief of the sinking liner, and was 200 miles distant at 2 this morning (about 5 a.m. English time).

The news of the disaster to the Titanic reached London in the first instance through a Reuter's Agency message from New York, to which city it had been

Undermanned lifeboats

The impact did not register with many passengers, some of whom slumbered on as the starboard hull ground against the iceberg. Those who noted the juddering didn't appreciate the dire consequences for some time. No general alarm was sounded, Captain Smith perhaps fearing the panic it would create. Shortly after midnight, he ordered the Marconi operators to put out a CQD distress signal, Harold Bride suggesting they also try the new SOS call. Smith also ordered the lifeboats to be made ready for launching, knowing they could accommodate but a fraction of the passengers and crew. Titanic's only other hope was to attract attention by firing rockets. Lights were spotted in the distance that might have been from a masthead, and a number of distress rockets were fired between 12.45 am and 1.45 am. Attempts to make contact were also made using Morse signals. These elicited no response. Visual contact was then lost and the legend of the 'mystery ship' was born.

Before the listing of the ship made the outcome all too obvious, and with potential salvation on the horizon, passengers showed little enthusiasm for swapping the solidity of the world's largest liner for a flimsy lifeboat, especially since both air and sea temperature were hovering around freezing. Such reluctance, allied to the fact that the boat drill planned for earlier that day had been cancelled, meant that the evacuation operation was anything but a model of efficiency. When the first lifeboat was winched down at around 12.45 am, it carried 28 people, less than half its capacity. Another had just 12 occupants when it could have housed 40. In all, fewer than 700 took to the 20 lifeboats, which could have accommodated almost 1,200 people.

BELOW: Titanic narrowly avoided collision on the way out of Southampton harbour after her wake caused another ship, the New York, to break away from her moorings. She drifted out into the path of the liner and it was only the prompt action by the master of a tug that prevented an accident. Titanic finally sailed clear of the harbour after an hour's delay and set off on a course to Cherbourg in France. Two purpose built tenders then ferried further passengers onto the ship that evening while also collecting some who only planned to travel as far as France. She then set sail again just before 8.00pm rounding Land's End before crossing the St. George's Channel and heading towards Queenstown in Ireland.

MAIN IMAGE: Titanic arrived in Queenstown (now called Cobh) at 11.30am the following morning and anchored two miles offshore. More passengers and 1,385 sacks of mail were loaded while a few disembarked. One of these was an amateur photographer called Frances Browne who carried with him the last surviving photographs to be taken aboard.

INSET: The final radio message sent from the ship by First Operator Jack Phillips and Second Operator Harold Bride. They worked constantly first sending the message 'Come Quick Danger' and later on the SOS signal which had only been introduced 4 years earlier. Both were eventually relieved of their duties just before the ship finally sank. They managed to board the upturned lifeboat No. 12 but Phillips died just before the rescue.

OPPOSITE PAGE ABOVE AND BELOW: Titanic left Ireland for the last leg of her journey with 1317 passengers on board. The sky was clear, there was little wind and passengers quickly settled into the routine of life aboard ship. During Thursday the ship built up a speed of 21.5 knots and by Sunday she was averaging 22.5 knots.

LINERS RACING TO THE RESCUE.

Titanic's Wireless Call for Help.

COLLISION WITH AN ICEBERG.

Last Signal Blurred and Ends Abruptly.

NEW YORK, Monday.

A telegram received here from Montreal says:—

The liner Virginian reports in a wireless communication that the liner Titanic, which is reported to have been in collision with an iceberg, has requested assistance.

The Virginian is hastening to her aid. —Reuter.

LATER.

A telegram from Cape Race says: The wireless telegraph operator on board the Titanic reported the weather calm and clear, the position of the liner being then 41.46 north, 50.14 west.

The Virginian at midnight was 170 miles west of the Titanic, and is expected to reach her at ten o'clock (American time) this morning.

The Olympic at midnight was in 40.32 north latitude, 61.18 west longitude. She is also in direct communication with the Titanic, and is hastening to her.—Reuter.

3.30 a.m.

The liner Baltic has also reported herself within two hundred miles of the Titanic and says she is speeding to her help.

The last signals from the Titanic came at 12.27 this morning. The Virginians operator says that these were blurred and ended abruptly.—Reuter.

The Titanic is one of the White Star liners.

NO. 9,501. [Thirty-First Year.] LONDON: MONDAY, APRIL 15, 1912. ONE HALFPENNY.

The Biggest Shipwreck in the World.

THE TITANIC COLLIDES WITH AN ICEBERG NEAR CAPE RACE.

LINERS RACE TO THE RESCUE.

ALL PASSENGERS SAFELY TAKEN OFF BY THE LIFEBOATS.

WIRELESS MESSAGES FROM SHIP.

CRIPPLED VESSEL STEAMING TO HALIFAX.

THE WHITE STAR LINER TITANIC.

The biggest ship in the world, the Titanic, has met with disaster on her maiden voyage.

She collided with an iceberg last evening, 270 miles from Cape Race, and was reported in a sinking condition.

Not till after two o'clock this afternoon was the tense anxiety in London relieved by the news that all the passengers had been put off in lifeboats, and that the liner Virginian was standing by her. The sea was calm.

Later, it was reported that the Titanic was still afloat, and making her way to Halifax.

Only last Wednesday the Titanic, the pride of the White Star Line, and the very last word in ship-building, sailed majestically from Southampton for New York, crowds of people watching her stately progress. "A floating

White Star Line; Colonel J. J. and Mrs. Astor, Mr. Noramn Craig, M.P., and Mr. W. T. Stead.

HOW THE NEWS CAME.

STORY OF A SERIES OF WIRELESS CALLS.

(FROM OUR OWN CORRESPONDENT.)
NEW YORK, Monday.

A wireless message from the Titanic received at Cape Race, Newfoundland, at 10.25 on Sunday night reported that the liner had "hit iceberg; badly damaged," and asked for assistance.

Thirty minutes later another wireless message reported that women were being put off in the lifeboats, and that the Titanic was sinking bow first.

The wireless then ceased abruptly.

The weather was calm and clear. The Allan liner Virginian, which sailed from Halifax on Sunday morning, received the new from Cape Race, and answered,

at 4.30 this morning stated that most of the passengers from the Titanic had been put in the lifeboats, and that the sea was calm.

The White Star officials here state that the Virginian is standing by the Titanic, and that there is no danger of loss of life.—Exchange Telegraph Co.

HALIFAX, Monday.
All the passengres were safely taken off the Titanic at 3.30 (8.30 English).—Exchange Telegraph Company.

NEW YORK, Monday.
A wireless message received here from Cape Race from the Allan liner Virginian states that the last word received from the wireless operator on board the liner Titanic was at 3.35 a.m., and in that message he reported that the women and children were being taken off the liner and that the sea was calm.

This message was questioned, but the Virginian's operator insisted that it was as he received it.

The message, he added, was interrupted in the middle, and this is believed here to mean that either the Titanic's engines had ceased working or that her wireless apparatus had failed owing to some local cause.

Soon afterwards the Virginian was in uninterrupted communication with the shore stations.—Exchange Telegraph Company.

NEW YORK, Monday.
The Montreal Star reports from Halifax

two holes knocked in her bottom and several plates bent.

The ice was encountered on the westbound track, off the Grand Banks.—Reuter.

Reuter's Agency is informed that the Canadian Pacific liner Empress of Britain, which arrived at Liverpool from Halifax (Nova Scotia) yesterday, reported the presence of an immense quantity of ice in the Atlantic.

Last Tuesday, when three days out from Halifax, she encountered an ice field a hundred miles in extent with enormous bergs, and steered a wide course, which delayed the vessel.

The Empress of Britain had previously received a wireless message from the Allan liner Virginian warning her of the presence of ice.

The extent of the ice was regarded as phenomenal, and the bergs appeared to be joined to the ice field, which appeared as an enormous white line on the horizon.

UNLUCKY CAPTAIN.

In Command of the Olympic When In Collision With Cruiser.

It is a remarkable coincidence that Captain E. J. Smith, R.N.R., who is in command of the Titanic, should have been captain of the Olympic when, in September last, she was in collision with

ment maintained a lighthouse there. In 1880 it was taken over by the Do of Canada.

"S.O.S."

The wireless signal for "assistance wanted" is now "S.O.S.," the more f letters "C.Q.D." having been aba because they led to confusion with code signals.

INSURED FOR £2,350

What the Loss of the Titanic Will to the Underwriters.

Underwriters will lose heavily event of the Titanic becoming a tot

A director of Muir, Beddall and well-known insurance brokers, stat insurances to the amount of £2,3 have been effected on the vessel's ca hull.

The vessel, which cost £1,250, build, is insured for one million, bearing the first £150,000 of any a the remainder covering the cargo.

The company, it is understood, their insurances at the rate of 1 p per annum for the hull.

Re-insurances were effected at to-day at the rate of 50 guineas pe

It is stated that there is a lar signment of diamonds on the Titan

In addition to the loss the unde will sustain owing to the damage hull and cargo there may be a ve siderable sum owing to personal acci surance, as it is the custom among

Heroes and villains

Amid the chaos and dawning realisation that many faced a watery grave, there were incidents of great heroism and nobility. In some cases, less attractive qualities came to the fore. Bruce Ismay, who took his place on one of the collapsible boats, would be vilified, particularly in the American press, by mere dint of the fact that he survived the ordeal. 'Women and children first' had been the guiding principle. Ismay took his seat some 20 minutes before Titanic entered her death-throes, when he might easily have offered it up in accordance with the rules of the sea. The actions of those aboard Lifeboat No. 1, who rowed away in a craft less than half full, were also called into question. At least one man attempted to flout the unwritten rule by donning women's garb. Officers fired several warning shots to enforce the code and maintain order.

OPPOSITE PAGE: The ship was designed with four signature funnels measuring 62 foot (19m) high to make it look more impressive, although only the front three were actually functional. The fourth was used purely to provide ventilation ducts.

ABOVE: A line of the Titanic's lifeboats designed to be lowered by moveable davits using a system of pulleys, cranks and gears.

WHO'S WHO ON BOARD.

Notes About Some of the Passengers.

First class	350
Second class	305
Steerage	800
Crew	903
Total	**2,358**

The above figures show the number of passengers and crew on the Titanic, including the Cherbourg passengers.

The total mail on board was 3,418 sacks.

In addition to the names in the official list *The Evening News* New York correspondent states that Mr. Norman Craig, M.P. for the Isle of Thanet, was on board.

A list sent out by the London News Agency includes also Lord Ashburton, his Excellency Manuel de Lizardi, the Hon. and Mrs. L. Grove Johnson, Mr. Alfred Vanderbilt, and Mr. Gustave Scholle (Secretary of Legations at Madrid).

The Countess of Rothes was on her way to America to meet the Earl of Rothes.

Mr. C. M. Hays is president of the Grand Trunk Railway.

Major A. W. Butt is aide-de-camp to President Taft.

Mr. Benjamin Guggenheim is a member of the banking family.

Mr. J. Bruce Ismay is chairman of the White Star Line. He was carrying out his usual practice of sailing on the maiden voyage of the company's new liners.

Mr. W. T. Stead, editor of the *Review of Reviews*, was on his way to attend the convention which is to close the "Man and Religion Forward Movement," which has been operating in America for some months.

Mr. Isidor Straus is a member of Congress.

Mr. George D. Widener is a son of the millionaire who bought "The Mill."

Colonel J. J. Astor is cousin of Mr. Waldorf Astor.

Lord Ashburton is a member of the family of Baring, and he married, a few years ago, Miss Frances Donnelly, an American actress.

Mr. J. B. Thayer is president of the Pennsylvania Railroad.

Mr. Washington Roebling is the millionaire president and director of John A. Roebling's Sons Co., iron and steel wire and wire-rope manufacturers. He it was who directed the construction of Brooklyn Bridge.

Jonkheer von Reuchlin is joint managing director of the Holland America line.

Mr. Christopher Head, of Messrs. Head and Co., Cornhill, is Mayor of Chelsea.

Major Archibald Butt is aide-de-camp to President Taft.

Mr. Frank D. Millet is an American artist who has a house at Broadway, in Worcestershire.

Among the passengers are two well-known Welsh boxers, Leslie Williams, of Tonypandy, and Dai Bowen, of Treherbert, who were going to America to fulfil a year's contract.

Mr. Isidor Straus, who lives in Broad

UNLUCKY CAPTAIN.

In Command of the Olympic When In Collision With Cruiser.

It is a remarkable coincidence that Captain E. J. Smith, R.N.R., who is in command of the Titanic, should have been captain of the Olympic when, in September last, she was in collision with the cruiser Hawke off Cowes.

He is one of the best known shipmasters on the North Atlantic. He has been in the service of the White Star Line for many years, and has been chosen to command the biggest ships launched by the company.

A native of Staffordshire, he is sixty years of age, and served his apprentice-

Captain E. J. Smith.

ship to the sea with Gibson and Co., of Liverpool.

He joined the White Star Line as fourth officer, and has been one of the company's commanders since 1887.

He was a member of the executive council of the Mercantile Marine Service Association prior to his removal to Southampton to take over the command of the Oceanic when the White Star moved their big service to the Channel.

He holds an extra master's certificate. Captain Smith is one of the most popular figures on the Atlantic route.

THE EVENING NEWS. MONDAY. APRIL 15. 1912.

The Perils of the Iceberg.

This diagram is drawn to show how an iceberg floats in the sea, and gives an excellent idea of the enormous mass of the submerged portion of the berg.

The lower picture represents the breaking away of the bergs from the parent glacier.

AN iceberg is one of the arch-enemies of the sailor. A skilled seaman is aware of the location of rocks and other perils that combine to make his calling one of great responsibility. The know-ledge of these dangers makes him careful, and unless some accident occurs over which he has no control, it can be reason-ably supposed that the craft which he is sailing will come into port all right.

An iceberg, however, is another matter, and even the most careful seaman can be pardoned if he finds himself "betrayed" by one of these "sea curses." The pre-sence of an iceberg constitutes a grave danger, as can be seen by the picture of one which we reproduce on this page.

To meet a floating mass of ice broken from the end of a glacier or from an ice sheet varying in length up to sixty miles means the doom of any ship, no matter how big, if a collision occurs. In the daytime, of course, it can be avoided, but under cover of darkness or during a fog the captain is more or less helpless.

Only one-ninth of the iceberg stands out of the water, the remainder is sub-merged. The structure of the iceberg varies with its origin, and is always that of the glacier or ice-sheet from which it was broken. The breaking-off of the ice-sheet from a Greenland glacier is called locally the "calving" of the glacier. The lower picture illustrates this process. The constantly renewed material from which the icebergs are formed is brought down by the motion of the glacier. The ice-sheet cracks at the end, and masses break off, owing to the upward pressure of the water upon the lighter ice which is pushed into it.

As stated above, icebergs vary con-siderably in size. In 1893 Captain Patti-son' of the clipper ship Loch Torridon, sighted a berg standing 1,500 feet out of the water off Cape Horn. This was the record until November, 1904, when the Zinita passed an ice island quite as high, and seven miles long. Another mass of floating ice sighted by the Loch Torridon, also in 1893, was no fewer than fifty miles long, but it did not approach the others in height.

Probably one of the largest icebergs seen in recent years near the track of ocean-going steamers was in 1910. It was sighted by the liner Oravia as she passed the Falklands Islands in the South Atlantic on her way to Liverpool.

An officer of the ship, in describing this iceberg said: "It was a huge mass 500ft. high partly covered with mist. When the moon appeared the sight was one never to be forgotten. We gazed upon what appeared to be a floating city of ice as large as Liverpool, with its towers, its temples, its tapering monuments shoot-ing up fantastic architecture shimmer-ing in the moonlight like polished silver."

Packs That Look Like White Ripples on the Sea.

"There is nothing astonishing in the character of the accident to the Titanic," said Captain J. H. Baxter, of the Nautical School, Leadenhall-street, to an *Evening News* representative.

"Sometimes an ice pack is all white, like a field of snow, and you can quite easily mistake it for white ripples in the water. So you keep on your course, and you strike before you know where you are.

"Then there are sometimes conditions of moonlight which are very puzzling; the berg may be practically invisible till you are on it."

"Yes," said another expert who was pre-sent, "and a ship like the Titanic goes at a very high speed. When I saw an iceberg last, I was on a sailing vessel, and we had time to get out of the way. But that's not easy when you are doing from eighteen to twenty-two knots an hour."

"People say that you can fell the chill from the berg at some distance," Captain Baxter said, "but that's only true when you are in water through which the iceberg has just passed. Water is a very bad conductor.

"Sometimes they whistle on board ship with the notion of getting an echo from any berg that may be near. But then in many cases the berg shows very little above the water, and there wouldn't be any echo.

"And, of course, there may have been a thick fog where the Titanic struck; then they would have had no chance of seeing the iceberg."

The general opinion of Captain Baxter and his friends seemed to be that the iceberg constitutes one of those dangers of the sea, against which no precaution or set of precau-tions is absolutely infallible.

OPPOSITE PAGE: Mrs. Benjamin Guggenheim (centre), wife of the wealthy American businessman who lost his life aboard the Titanic.

Titanic's folk-lore musicians

More heartwarming was the poignant story of Mrs Isidor Straus, who chose to remain with her husband instead of taking her place in one of the lifeboats. Neither survived. Benjamin Guggenheim dressed up in his finery, helped others into the lifeboats and said he was ready to go down like a gentleman. Then there was the case of 36-year-old Edith Evans, who selflessly gave up her place in the last lifeboat for a friend who had children. Of the 156 women and children travelling first class, 145 survived. Statistically, this was the category that fared best, though Edith Evans numbered among the 11 victims.

The five postal clerks began feverishly transporting packages and letters onto the upper deck when the mail-room started shipping water soon after impact. All were lost. Wireless operator Jack Phillips carried on signalling while there was still power to transmit, even after he was relieved of his duties. His last message was recorded at 2.17 am, just before Titanic went under. 'I will never live to forget the work Phillips did for the last awful 15 minutes,' said his junior colleague Harold Bride. He survived, Phillips perished.

The story of Titanic's musicians has gone down in folk-lore. Under bandleader Wallace Hartley, the eight-strong ensemble played right to the end, lively tunes initially to raise the spirits, then hymns in keeping with the solemnity of the occasion. None survived. They would get their own special memorial in Southampton Library, a replica of which was unveiled in 1990 on the same site after the original was destroyed in World War Two.

"UNSINKABLE SHIP."

How the Designers Tried to Avert Loss of Life.

(FROM OUR OWN CORRESPONDENT.)
BELFAST, Monday.

Interviewed this afternoon, a representative of Harland and Wolff, the builders of the Titanic, stated that if the liner was sinking the collision must have been of great force, for the aim of Lord Pirrie and his colleagues had been to make the vessel practically unsinkable.

All the beams, girders, and stanchions in the Titanic's framework were specially forged and constructed, the deck and shell-plating were of the heaviest calibre, so as to make the hull a monument of strength.

The Titanic's transverse bulkheads number fifteen, extending from the double bottom to the upper deck at the forward end, and to the saloon deck at the after end, in both instances far above the load water line.

The builders state that any two of these compartments might be flooded without in any way involving the safety of the ship.

Relative to the closing of watertight doors, the official description issued by the White Star Line when the Titanic was launched states these are electrically controlled.

Those giving communication between the various boiler-rooms and engine-rooms are arranged on the drop system—Harland and Wolff's special design.

Each door is held in the open position by a friction clutch, which can be instantly released by means of a powerful electric magnet controlled from the captain's bridge, so that in the event of accident the captain can by imply moving an electric switch instantly close the doors throughout, practically making the vessel unsinkable.

Precaution floats are provided beneath the floor level which, in the event of water accidentally entering any of the compartments, automatically lift, and thereby close the doors opening into that compartment if they have not already been dropped by those in charge of the vessel.

A ladder or escape is provided in each boiler-room, engine-room, and similar watertight compartments, in order that the closing of the doors at any time should not imprison the men, though the risk of this is lessened by electric bells placed in the vicinity of each door, which ring prior to their closing, and thus give warning to those below.

LONDON

The Titanic Sunk

8 Pages.

ONLY 650 PASSENGERS AND CREW SAVED.

SURVIVORS' NAMES.

PATHETIC SCENES AT THE COMPANIES' OFFICES.

WAITING FOR NEWS.

Poignant Scenes at the London Offices.

WEEPING WOMEN.

Sorrowful Stream of Inquirers of All Classes.

The scenes at the White Star offices in Cockspur-street to-day were pitiful beyond description.

To the officials this April 16, when the spring sun seemed to mock the agony of sleepless men and distraught women, will

in Two Miles of Water.

8

ENING NEWS' CIALCABLES.

S LATEST NEWS FROM NEW YORK.

EN & CHILDREN FIRST."

OUR OWN CORRESPONDENT.)
NEW YORK, Tuesday.

t a crowd of anxious relatives
s of the passengers on the lost

THE TITANIC DISASTER IN FIGURES.

Number of souls on board (passengers 1,200, crew 900)	2,100
Number saved	650
Number drowned	1,450
Value of the ship	£1,250,000
Value of the cargo	£1,000,000

CAPTAIN'S FATE

Commander

It is reported

CITY
6.1 Lona
Martin, 10-

MANAGER'S STATEMENT.

Will Publish Nothing Officially Until Advised From New York.

I waited (writes an *Evening News* representative) for nearly an hour at the White Star offices to-day to obtain a word with Mr. Parton, the manager, who received many callers himself.

He was working as hard as the clerks, and even in the course of a minute's conversation, was interrupted to answer the telephone.

"As soon as the names of survivors can be given out," he said, "they will be cabled to our Liverpool office and also to London.

"An agency is sending out a list of survivors, but I do not know how it has been obtained.

"We shall publish nothing officially until we are advised from New York."

Mr. Parton, who remained at the office till close on midnight, had the telephone at his bedside all night to answer enquiries, and was back at five o'clock to-day.

The first caller arrived immediately after, and many others were in the office before 6.30.

"Since seven," said Mr. Parton, "the telephones have been going incessantly. We are quite ready to see enquirers, and give all the information we can, but at present we can only wait, and hope for better news.

OPPOSITE PAGE: A bird's eye view of the crowds waiting for news outside the White Star Line offices the morning after the Titanic sank. Due to the crush below members of staff gave out information from the fourth floor balcony. Initially, the mood was optimistic until later in the evening a message sent from the Olympic to White Star confirmed the number of dead.

ABOVE: As anxious relatives waited, rumours were circulating around the world. Bruce Ismay, who had survived and was aboard the Carpathia, was finally persuaded by Captain Rostron to send a telegram to New York confirming the disaster. It read 'Deeply regret to advise you Titanic sank this morning after collision with iceberg, resulting in serious loss of life. Full particulars later, Ismay.'

A FATHER'S LOSS

As details of the disaster were being thrown on the *New York Times* bulletins shortly before midnight, a well-dressed man, on the arm of a friend, wedged his way through the crowd, and, glancing at the bulletins, fell fainting on the pavement.

He moaned:

My God! My two brothers and little daughter were on the ship. I lost my wife and other child in the San Francisco earthquake, and have been waiting seven years for the return of my little daughter and my brothers.

It was C. J. E. Clayton, whose brother-in-law, George A. Brayton, was saved.

AN M.P.'s ESCAPE

Always on occasions like these, there are discovered fortunate individuals who, by altering their plans and deciding not to travel upon a particular train or steamer, have preserved their lives.

A leading instance in the present case is that of Mr Norman Craig, M.P. for Thanet, whose name was actually among the list of passengers, but who at the last moment had changed his intentions, and remained at home.

ADEQUATE LIFEBOATS

"The lifeboats on board the Titanic were equal to twice the number of passengers actually on the liner," was the statement of an official of the White Star line to an *Evening News* representative. All the life saving apparatus was passed by the Board of Trade and the boats had a capacity equal to the accommodation of the vessel had she been full. The first and second class accommodation was only about half full in each case.

There is a fear that some of the boats were sucked under water by the liner when she sank.

It is said that one of the reasons of the difficulty in obtaining information is the fact that so many "amateur" wireless telegraphists are dispatching messages, thereby delaying important news, and also disseminating much that is inaccurate.

"WOMEN & CHILDREN FIRST"

All night a crowd of anxious relatives and friends of the passengers on the lost Titanic was massed in front of the White Star's offices in Broadway.

Up to midnight not a word of definite information had come from the Carpathia to relieve the tension.

The list of rescued began to come all too slowly over the wires about two in the morning.

The Carpathia flashed the wireless messages to Cape Race, and, as the names, mainly those of women, appeared, one searched in vain for those of famous persons aboard the liner.

Then came the name of Mr J. Bruce Ismay, chairman of the White Star Company.

The *New York American* states that Col. Astor's body has been recovered. Mrs Astor was saved.

Among the women rescued were Mrs George D. Widener, Philadelphia; Mrs H. B. Harris, wife of the well-known theatre manager.

The New York American states that Colonel Astor's body has been recovered. Mrs Astor was saved.

The front pages of the Chicago Daily Tribune and The New York Times on Tuesday, April 16th, 1912, headlined the disaster.

EXTRA The Chicago Daily Tribune. **EXTRA**

THE WORLD'S GREATEST NEWSPAPER

VOLUME LXXI—NO. 92.   TUESDAY, APRIL 16, 1912—TWENTY-EIGHT PAGES.   PRICE ONE CENT

LINER TITANIC SINKS; 1300 DROWNED, 866 SAVED

GIANT OF SEA RAMS ICEBERG IN ATLANTIC

Women and Children Taken Into Lifeboats While Men Remain.

RESCUE SHIPS TOO LATE

Wireless Calls Summon Help, but It Arrives After Disaster.

Women and Children Saved.

THE TITANIC AND ITS CAPTAIN.

Boston, April 16—(2 a.m.)

The New York Times.

NEW YORK, TUESDAY, APRIL 16, 1912

TITANIC SINKS FOUR HOURS AFTER HITTING ICEBERG; 866 RESCUED BY CARPATHIA, PROBABLY 1250 PERISH; ISMAY SAFE, MRS. ASTOR MAYBE, NOTED NAMES MISSING

Col. Astor and Bride, Isidor Straus and Wife, and Maj. Butt Aboard.

"RULE OF SEA" FOLLOWED

The Lost Titanic Being Towed Out of Belfast Harbor.

PARTIAL LIST OF THE SAVED.

CAPT. E. J. SMITH.

AND THEN . . . SILENCE.

One of the most mysterious and tragic incidents in connection with the disaster is the sudden flickering out of the wireless messages which were being flashed out by the Marconi operator on the doomed liner.

The operator was a highly skilled telegraphist, and it is stated that his messages, up to that which announced the lowering of the lifeboats full of women and children, were sent perfectly clearly and distinctly. The key was being tapped by a hand which to the receiving operators showed no trace of nervousness or haste.

And then . . . then came a few flickering, blurred signals, and after that silence absolute and complete.

The launching of the boats must still have been in progress when something happened, something, surely, tragically sudden and complete, that cut off the only means of communication with the outside world.

What that something was we may, perhaps, know before long, or it may be that we shall never know; but at present the evidence points to an unexpected ending which robbed the operator of any chance of telling of the fate that was overtaking himself and his comrades.

Colonel Astor's Body.

Captain E. J. Smith is believed to have gone down with the ship. Colonel J. J. Astor's body has been picked up. Mrs. Astor is in the list of saved.

Mr. W. T. Stead is said to be amongst the victims.

The relatives of Mr. W. T. Stead have so far had no definite news as to his fate. He was going to New York to speak at a convention at which President Taft was to appear on the same platform.

Mr. Thomas Andrews, jun., a director of Messrs. Harland and Wolff, was on the big vessel built by his firm.

Mr. and Mrs. Alfred G. Vanderbilt were reported to have booked passages on the Titanic, but *The Evening News* is informed that they were not on board, and had never contemplated making the trip.

Mr. Ryerson, who is saved, together with his wife, two daughters, and a son, was (says *The Evening News* New York correspondent) making the journey from England to attend the funeral of a daughter in Philadelphia.

Amongst the saved are Mr. and Mrs. Henry S. Harper. He is grandson of the founder of the famous publishing house.

TITANIC DISASTER.

Continued from Page 1.

LIST OF SAVED.

Recovery of Colonel Astor's Body.

MR. STEAD MISSING.

Lists of survivors are being published, but the New York correspondent of *The Evening News* points out that they are by no means complete.

In the rush, moreover, it is evident that many of the names have been misspelt, and do not conform to the official list. No doubt they will be recognisable.

It is feared that many of the well-known passengers have perished. A significant feature of the list of saved is the fact that in nearly every case the wife was rescued and the husband apparently lost.

This indicates that every effort was made to get away the women and children.

The list of passengers already published represents the state of the bookings a day or two before the boat sailed.

A number of people made plans to join her at Cherbourg.

Karl H. Behr, one of America's leading lawn tennis players, who escaped, defeated Larner at Newport, and in 1907 competed in the All-England championships at Wimbledon.

The Countess of Rothes and Mr. J. Bruce Ismay (chairman of the White Star Line) are amongst those reported to be saved.

Lord Ashburton, it transpires, was not on the Titanic, but is a passenger on the Olympic.

An Exchange telegram from New York says that the missing passengers include Mr. Isidor Straus, bank director and importer of pottery and glassware; Major Butt, aide-de-camp to President Taft; and Mr. Benjamin Guggenheim, the well-known banker.

Mr. Chas. Hays, who is also believed to be lost, is president of the Grand Trunk Railway; Mr. Frank D. Millet, an American painter; Mr. Henry B. Harris, theatrical manager, and son of the owner of several New York theatres; Mr. Jacques Futrelle, author and journalist; Mr. J. B. Thayer, president of the Pennsylvania Railroad; and Mr. W. T. Stead, London, journalist.

OPPOSITE PAGE: At 9.00am on Sunday April 14, a warning had come over the wireless from the Cunard-owned Caronia warning of 'bergs, growlers and field ice'. The previous winter had been very mild causing ice to break away from Arctic ice cap. Further warnings also came through from other sources although it is not clear whether the information reached the bridge.

LEFT: The front pages of the Chicago Daily Tribune and The New York Times on Tuesday, April 16, 1912, headlined the disaster.

Carpathia to the rescue

Titanic received a number of responses to her distress calls. These included her sister ship Olympia - too far distant to be of any practical assistance – Frankfurt, Virginian and Cunard steamer Carpathia. Captain Arthur Rostron, Carpathia's master, set an immediate course for the stricken vessel 58 miles away. His engineers managed to squeeze 18 knots from the ship instead of the usual 15, negotiating many ice hazards along the way and putting his own ship at risk. But that still equated to a three-and-a-half-hour mercy dash. The call was received at around 12.30 am, Carpathia arriving on the scene at 4.00 am, almost two hours after Titanic went to her final resting place 12,500 feet down on the Atlantic floor. It was after 8 o' clock before the rescue operation was complete. Even some of those in lifeboats failed to survive exposure on that timescale. Carpathia brought several lifeless bodies aboard; one succumbed later that day. For those left to take their chance in the water, a lifejacket was of little use in 28-degree temperatures, where survival time could be reckoned in minutes.

ABOVE: J Chief Purser McElroy (left) and Captain Edward Smith aboard the Titanic. Captain Smith was the senior commander of the White Star Line and in this capacity always took each new ship on its maiden run. By the time the ship set sail from Southampton there were 891 crew members on board of which only 214 ultimately survived.

OPPOSITE PAGE: A view of the ship's prow on the sea bed.

VOYAGE OF THE SURVIVORS.

CARPATHIA AMONG THE ICE.

SWIFT SHIP SENT TO MEET HER.

FROM OUR OWN CORRESPONDENT.

NEW YORK, Tuesday.

The Titanic lies two miles deep at the bottom of the sea, probably some 420 miles east south-east of Sable Island.

The Carpathia, with the 800 odd survivors, is now steaming towards New York through a perilous field of ice. "Lat. 41deg. 45min. north, long. 50deg. 20min. west. Am proceeding to New York unless otherwise ordered with about 800," runs the message received this morning from Captain Rostron, of the Carpathia, who adds, "After consulting with Mr. Ismay and considering the circumstances with so much ice about, we consider New York the best. There is a large number of icebergs and twenty miles of field ice with bergs among it."

The fact that the Titanic apparently drifted some thirty miles from the time she struck until she sank gave rise to the hope that some lifeboats might have drifted too, but this hope was dissipated by the repetition of the intelligence that all the lifeboats that were not damaged by the collision were picked up, and by definite reports from the liners Virginian and Parisian that they found no survivors.

In contradiction of various statements published yesterday the Virginia to-day informed the Allan agents that she arrived on the scene of the disaster too late to be of any assistance, and could not say if any bodies or survivors were amid the mass of wreckage covered a large area of the sea. In the improbable event of any of the ill-fated passengers and crew being adrift on rafts, the piercing cold and heavy weather in all probability long ago ended their sufferings, for according to the weather reports heavy fogs lay off Nova Scotia and a violent thunderstorm broke in that neighbourhood last night.

The Leyland liner Californian, however, is still cruising in the forlorn hope of making further rescues in the neighbourhood of the catastrophe. The Virginian has resumed her voyage eastwards.

APRIL 17, 1912.

LAST SIGNALS.

WIRELESS RECORD OF THE DISASTER.

MIDNIGHT SCENES.

Titanic Struck	:	10.25 p.m. Sunday
Wireless Failed	-	12.27 a.m. Monday
Titanic Sank	- -	2.20 a.m. Monday

The bewildering reports published in New York of wireless messages received concerning the collision have befogged even the scanty details obtainable. The wireless messages printed below are those of the authenticity of which there can be no possible doubt.

They show that the Titanic struck on Sunday night at 10.25 at a point roughly 360 miles from Cape Race, Newfoundland, the nearest land, 1,070 miles from New York, and 2,020 miles from Southampton. The sea at the place is 12,000 feet deep.

The women were placed in the lifeboats at once, and wireless appeals for help were sent out. At 12.27 a.m., two hours and two minutes after the collision, the last wireless signal from the Titanic was received, showing that the dynamos were then flooded.

After that there was an interval of one hour and fifty-three minutes' waiting in the dark before the Titanic sank.

She went down by the bows, and the 1,490 people lost were probably gathered together in the stern, which sank last, while the lifeboats, all of which are accounted for, pulled away to avoid the whirlpool caused by the sinking ship. The sea was quiet and the weather clear. The Carpathia arrived at daybreak.

The first authentic message was that from the wireless station at Cape Race. It ran:

CAPE RACE, Monday.

10.25 p.m. yesterday Titanic reports by wireless struck iceberg and calls for immediate assistance. At 11 p.m. she reported sinking by head. Women being put off in boats. Gave position as 41.46 N., 50.14 W. Steamers Baltic, Olympic, and Virginian all making towards scene of disaster. Latter was last to hear Titanic signals at 12.27 a.m. to-day. Reported them then blurred and ending abruptly.

The next authentic message, published exclusively in yesterday's *Daily Mail*, was only received when the Olympic, with her powerful wireless installation, was able to take the Carpathia's messages and forward them to the land. It read:

CAPE RACE, Monday Afternoon.

The Olympic reports that the Carpathia reached the Titanic's position at daybreak.

She found boats and wreckage only.

The Titanic had foundered about 2.20 a.m. in 41deg. 16min. North, 50deg. 14min. West.

All her boats are accounted for.

About 675 souls are saved of the crew and passengers, the latter nearly all women and children.

The Leyland liner Californian is remaining searching the position of the disaster.

The Carpathia is returning to New York with the survivors.

The fact that the Titanic apparently drifted some thirty miles from the time she struck until she sank gave rise to the hope that some lifeboats might have drifted too.

A New York Exchange message adds that wireless communication with the Carpathia has been established, via Sable Island, and definite news is momentarily expected.

TITANIC DISASTER GREAT LOSS OF LIFE
EVENING NEWS

ABOVE: As newspapers reported on the disaster the Carpathia was gradually able to send through the lists of passengers who had survived. Harold Bride, who had been carried onto the ship due to frostbitten feet worked alongside the Carpathia's wireless operator Harold Cottam to send out information as quickly as possible.

OFFICERS
OF THE TITANIC SAVED

OLYMPIC MESSAGE

A message from Cape Race says that Captain Haddock, the commander of the Olympic, has sent the following wireless message:-

Please allay rumours that the Virginian has any of the Titanic's passengers.

The Tunisian also has none, and I believe the only survivors are those on board the Carpathia.

The second, third, fourth and fifth officers and the second Marconi operator are the only officers reported to have been saved.—Reuter.

THE SURVIVORS

Carpathia Coming Into the Wireless Range Again

The Carpathia is now coming into communication with the wireless station at Sable Island, and more definite reports of the accident may be expected.

The report that the Allan liner Virginian was putting into St. John's, Newfoundland, is incorrect.

No communication has been received at Halifax from her, and she is believed to be on her way to Liverpool, as previously stated, without picking up any survivors of the Titanic.

Up to a late hour last night the names of 323 survivors of the disaster had been officially announced by the White Star Company.

It was stated by Reuter late last night that a further 483 names of rescued were expected from the Carpathia as soon as she comes into wireless range again.

This will leave 62 more survivors still to come.

A New York Exchange message adds that wireless communication with the Carpathia has been established, via Sable Island, and definite news is momentarily expected.

NEW YORK,
Tuesday (9.10pm)

A revised list of names of those saved is now coming in and is practically the same as that telegraphed this morning.

It contains the name of Mr J. Bruce Ismay but does not mention Mrs Ismay. No mention is made of Mr Charles M. Hays, but the list contains the names of his wife and daughter. Mr John J. Astor is not on the list, but Mrs Astor and maid are.

It is confirmed that Sir Cosmo and Lady Duff Gordon have been saved.—Reuter.

MESSAGE FROM THE KING.

SYMPATHY WITH THE BEREAVED.

TELEGRAM TO WHITE STAR LINE.

The White Star Line have received the following telegram from the King and Queen :—

Sandringham,
Tuesday, 6.30 p.m.

The Managing Director,
White Star Line,
Liverpool,

The Queen and I are horrified at the appalling disaster which has happened to the Titanic and at the terrible loss of life.

We deeply sympathise with the bereaved relatives, and feel for them in their great sorrow with all our hearts.

GEORGE R.I.

Queen Alexandra telegraphed to the White Star Line :

Sandringham, Tuesday.

It is with feelings of the deepest sorrow that I hear of the terrible disaster to the Titanic and of the awful loss of life. My heart is full of grief and sympathy for the bereaved families of those who have perished. **ALEXANDRA.**

HONEYMOON COUPLES.

YOUTHFUL BRIDE SAVED— HUSBAND MISSING.

There were no happier persons in the Titanic before disaster befell her than Mr. and Mrs. D. W. Marvin, a newly married American couple, aged nineteen and eighteen, who were returning to New York from a three weeks' honeymoon in England. Mrs. Marvin's name appears in the list of survivors, but her husband apparently has not yet been accounted for.

Mr. Marvin was the son of the head of one of the largest cinematograph organisations in America and was being trained as an engineer. Mr. A. Hamburger, a director of the Dover-street Studios, London, who knew Mr. D. W. Marvin intimately, said yesterday: "He was a splendid specimen of American youth—strong, athletic, and well-set-up. Mrs. Marvin is an extremely pretty and vivacious girl. They were both of them full of the joy of life and affection for each other and when in England behaved just like two happy school children on a holiday. They spent most of their time sight-seeing and going to parties, dances, and the like. Everyone made much of them. The girl's parents are wealthy, and she had received £2,000 from her mother as a wedding present."

BELOW: Passengers pass the line of lifeboats as they stroll along the boat deck. In the early stages of planning Carlisle had recommended a system that would allow the Titanic to carry 64 wooden boats giving a capacity of 4,000 passengers. However White Star had decided to reduce it to only 16 with 4 collapsibles, giving a much smaller capacity of 1,178. This complied with the existing Board of Trade regulations at the time which stated that a ship of her size carry a minimum of 16 wooden lifeboats.

Had the Titanic Sufficient Boats?

TITANIC'S BOATS.

Did She Carry Only Twenty on Board?

BOARD OF TRADE RULES.

"Unsinkable" Passenger Ship a Dream.

The Titanic was carrying 1,293 passengers (316 saloon, 279 second class, and 698 third class), according to figures supplied at the offices of the White Star Company in London.

She had a crew of 903. Embarkations at Cherbourg and Queenstown made up the total to 2,358 souls on board.

She had a lifeboat accommodation of 970 persons.

It would have been no more had the ship been full, and if full she would have carried 3,080 persons.

We are informed, says The Daily Mail, that she had only twenty lifeboats, capable of carrying 970 persons. Their total capacity was 9,702 cubic feet, and by Board of Trade regulation 10 cubic feet of capacity is required for each person.

She had a few collapsible boats—probably half a dozen. A collapsible boat approved by the Board of Trade may be able to carry about fifty persons in calm weather.

On the most favourable reckoning the boats could not have carried much more than half the population of the ship.

There was at least one lifebelt for every person. Probably the Titanic had 5,000 of these on board. There may have been rafts, but as to this no information is obtainable in London.

ROOT OF THE TROUBLE.

The root of the trouble is the antiquated Board of Trade regulations, the revision of which is now under consideration. The rules made when a 10,000-ton ship was a huge vessel still obtain.

In a copy of them obtained at the Board of Trade yesterday the highest line in the table showing the "minimum number of boats to be placed under davits and their minimum cubic contents" was "10,000 tons and upwards, minimum number of boats sixteen, minimum cubic contents 5,500 feet."

That meant provision for 550 persons.

Another authority of the White Star Line declares that the Titanic had thirty-two lifeboats, each capable of carrying sixty persons, or a total of 1,920.

This estimate leaves over 1,000 persons of her full complement unprovided for.

Although ships have grown until they reach the huge proportions of nearly 50,000 tons, no more boat accommodation is required of the owners than if they remained at 10,000 tons. This fact is well-known in shipping circles.

Californian arrives

As Carpathia was plucking the last survivors from the ocean, the Californian arrived on the scene. The ship whose wireless operator had received a sharp rebuff from his Titanic counterpart the previous night had laid up for the night, possibly a mere 10 miles away. It was just before 6.00 am when that sole radio operator returned to duty and learned of the disaster that had unfolded close by overnight.

Captain Rostron and his crew were highly praised in the subsequent inquiry, receiving a monetary token of appreciation for their valiant efforts. The Californian, by contrast, came in for heavy censure. It was said Titanic's distress rockets were seen and misinterpreted. The doomed vessel's closest neighbour failed to act until it was too late. But was Californian really the closest neighbour? What of the 'mystery ship' sighted by those aboard Titanic as she foundered; a ship within range to prevent the unfolding calamity?

TITANIC WARNED.

French Liner's Wireless Message About the Icebergs.

The Paris correspondent of *The Daily Mail* says the *Presse* publishes a telegram from Havre, stating that the French liner Touraine, which has arrived at that port, entered the ice field last Wednesday night just after midnight. The ice was lying very low in the water.

The Touraine was in commuication by wireless with the Titanic from the afternoon of Friday, April 12, until about nine nine o'clock in the evening, and her captain warned the Titanic of the position of the icebergs.

Captain Smith replied by wireless, thanking the French captain for the information.

SOME OF THE SURVIVORS IN THE CARPATHIA.

Sir COSMO DUFF-GORDON.   Lady DUFF-GORDON ("Lucile.")   Mr. BRUCE ISMAY (of the White Star.)   COUNTESS OF ROTHES.

PASSENGERS IN THE TITANIC.

Mr. J. J. ASTOR (Missing.)   Mrs. J. J. ASTOR (Saved.)   Mr. W. T. STEAD (Missing.)

The Cunard liner Carpathia which picked up survivors from the Titanic.
[Bassano, Langfier, Topical, Syren.]

Mr. D. MARVIN. (Aged 19. Missing.)   Mrs. D. MARVIN. (His wife, aged 18. Saved.)
Mr. and Mrs. Marvin were returning home from their honeymoon.

SEARCH ABANDONED.

From Our Own Correspondent.

St. John's, Newfoundland, Tuesday.

Everything indicates that the loss of life is about 1,500. The Carpathia, the first liner to arrive, rescued all the survivors in boats. Most of them are woman and children.

Other liners have found no survivors in their searches on the scene of the wreck and are now continuing their voyages.

MASSES OF WRECKAGE.

New York, Tuesday.

The Leyland Company have instructed the captain of the Californian by wireless to remain near the scene of the wreck and to render whatever aid is possible until he is relieved or until his coal supply runs low.

A telegram from Montreal states that notwithstanding the reports to the contrary the officials of the Allan Line still cling to the hope that the Parisian may have on board some survivors from the Titanic. This assumption is apparently based upon the fact that the Parisian is heading for Halifax, although her original destination was Philadelphia.—Reuter.

Halifax (Nova Scotia), Tuesday.

The Parisian steamed through much ice looking for survivors. No life rafts or bodies were sighted among the floating wreckage, which covered a large area. The weather was cold, and even if persons had been on the wreckage they would in all probability have perished from exposure before they could have been picked up. The Parisian is expected to reach here to-morrow.—Reuter.

MILLIONAIRE'S SON.

With swollen eyelids they thronged the corridors, ever coming and going, listening, where they dared not ask, for a word of the safety of kin or friends, and now and then breaking into hysterical inquiries. At an early hour an official of the White Star Line was called up on the telephone by Mr. William Vincent Astor, the son of the great millionaire. The official informed him that Mrs. John Jacob Astor and her maid had been saved. "But what of my father?" cried the boy, and made no effort to choke back his sobs when the faltering reply came, "No word has been received of the fate of Colonel Astor."

Grief such as his has visited hundreds of families, and wealthy women and poor awaited news side by side. With a tall woman in blue velvet Mr. Cornell, a popular magistrate, elbowed his way into the offices to get some word of his wife and two sisters, Mrs. E. D. Appleton and Mrs. Murray Brown, of Boston. No sooner had he gained the counter than the tall woman fainted. She was revived and said that she was Mrs. Weir, and that her husband was in the Titanic. When told that there was no news of him she fainted again, and was carried to her motor-car by policemen.

Mr. Cornell's face went ghastly white when he was told that his sisters were safe but that there was no word of his wife. "I can't understand it," he cried, "they were all in the same cabin. They had been abroad for only a week just to attend the funeral of their sister." Later, to his intense relief, the name of Mrs. Cornell was included in the list of survivors.

Later, to his intense relief, the name of Mrs Cornell was included in the list of survivors.

OPPOSITE PAGE: All quiet on the Boat Deck. Just after 11pm on the Sunday evening the lookouts noticed a large object ahead. Despite repeated attempts to contact the bridge the ship did not change course until it was directly reported to Murdoch. By the time the bridge was ordered to turn 'hard a-starboard' and the engine room was told 'Stop: Full Speed Astern', the ship was only 800 yards away and struck the iceberg on the starboard side.

The Mystery of the Titanic.

On Monday the world knew the dreadful fact that the biggest ship in the world was in collision with an iceberg and was feared to be sinking. There followed reassuring messages, the origin of which is at present a mystery, but in the very early hours of Tuesday morning came black tidings of disaster. The Titanic was sunk in two miles of water, and the loss of life was known to be appalling.

From that hour to the moment of writing we are without any certain knowledge of how the disaster took place. We have received, indeed, the most important matter of all, the names of the survivors, or, at any rate, the great bulk of them, but despite the use of wireless telegraphy the story of the sinking of the Titanic remains untold.

One thing that has rendered the task of the newspapers exceptionally difficult has been the receipt of wireless messages in America purporting to come from vessels which have subsequently denied all knowledge of them. Bearing in mind the sources from which these messages were issued, we are bound to believe that they were received, and that they were sent with some deliberate purpose from private stations. What that purpose was we can only conjecture.

Under such circumstances, it is the duty of a newspaper to lay such information as it has at its disposal before the public, together with such comment as may be needful, so that, in the case of an evening paper, its readers may at the end of the day know exactly what news has arrived and how that news is regarded. Such comment, throwing grave doubts on the authenticity of the message, was attached by "The Evening News" to the story of the disaster which was cabled to this country as having appeared in the "New York Herald." We do not question that this story was inserted by the "Herald" in good faith, but it subsequently turned out to be pure invention.

The wireless messages announcing the safety of the Titanic fall, however, into another category, and the public both here and in America will not rest until every effort has been made to trace these heartless and cruel fabrications to their source.

Demographic death toll

The divisions between the classes were rigidly enforced during Titanic's first three days at sea, and the stark survival statistics suggest that those who paid most for their tickets fared best when calamity struck. The inquiry found no evidence of discrimination, yet one steward testified that third-class male passengers were kept below decks as late as 1.15 am. Notwithstanding the high-minded gestures of Benjamin Guggenheim and his like, more men with first-class tickets survived than children from third-class. Proximity to the boat deck may have been a factor, and that favoured first and second-class passengers. There were also reports of closed stairways impeding the path to possible safety for those with the cheapest tickets. But class awareness, either conscious or subconscious, may have played a part. One officer was heard to direct a woman from second class to the lifeboats on the deck that matched her passenger status. Another eyewitness said: 'It was only in the very last desperate moments that third-class passengers were given any chance to reach safety'.

Separation occurred from the moment passengers arrived on board, the elite admitted into a reception area resembling a five-star hotel lobby before being escorted to their quarters. Who can say the extent to which such divisions obtained in a time of crisis? These were more deferential times and there was no great outcry when the ratios became known.

Let the figures speak for themselves. 60% of the 329 first-class passengers survived the ordeal, a proportion that would have been even higher but for some noteworthy acts of selflessness. 119 survived from second-class, representing around 42% of the total. The highest death toll was among third-class passengers, 536 of the 710 on board losing their lives. Of those, 417 were men, equating to 86% of that sub-group.

It is worth noting that the Titanic story abounds with conflicting reports and inconsistencies; unsurprisingly, perhaps, given the speed with which a floating luxury hotel became a watery grave for two-thirds of its population. Even the total number of passengers and crew varies somewhat among the many sources that have examined the events surrounding one of the darkest days in maritime history.

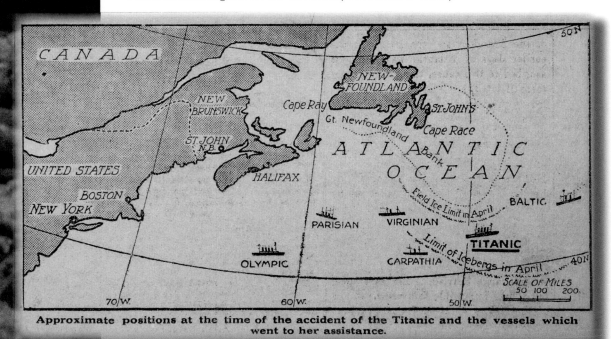

Approximate positions at the time of the accident of the Titanic and the vessels which went to her assistance.

LEFT: The wreck of the Titanic lies in 3,800 metres of water approximately 750 kilometres southeast of Newfoundland. It was finally discovered 73 years after it sank by Dr Robert Ballard and Captain Jean-Louis Michel who were leading a team of scientists. Using the unmanned submersible Argo they obtained their first images of the Titanic on September 1, 1985.

THE NIGHT VIGIL AT SOUTHAMPTON.

Woman Who Had Eight Relatives on the Liner.

(FROM OUR SPECIAL CORRESPONDENT.)
SOUTHAMPTON, Thursday.

The third hopeless dawn has broken over Southampton, and hundreds of hearts are still heavy and sad.

No news of the crew has yet arrived to allay anxiety, and the usual crowd is beginning to gather again outside the White Star office.

The officials are weary with long watching. All night long they awaited news which they might post on the illuminated board outside.

The crowd which thronged the streets throughout yesterday thinned as the night wore on.

Hundreds dropped out from sheer fatigue, and after a sympathetic little speech by a local councillor from the steps of the office, advising a few hours rest, the others gradually departed.

There was a pathetic scene before the long night closed.

EIGHT YOUNG ORPHANS.

A poor woman, distraught with anxiety, fell into a dead faint at the very steps of the office when she heard for the hundredth time that no news had yet arrived.

She was hurriedly taken inside. A doctor was summoned, and presently she was led away, a pitiful sight, by friends almost as distracted as herself.

The sight of all this helpless suffering is heartrending. Instances of the misery caused by the disaster multiply with pathetic monotony.

There was one woman, whose husband was a third-class passenger. She had seven children. Yesterday her eighth was born, and the mother now lies dead. Eight young orphans must now seek charity.

Another woman has been sorely stricken. No fewer than eight of her relatives were among the Titanic's crew: her husband, two brothers, son, and four cousins.

WIDOWED BRIDES.

In neighbouring streets there are two young widows who have only been married a month or so. One of the husbands was making his first voyage since his honeymoon.

In another case a man, after being out of work for some time, was making one trip on the Titanic before returning to a berth on a yacht.

His wife only came out of hospital, after an operation, a day or two ago, and her condition under the double blow is serious.

IN TOUCH.

Parisian Speaks to Titanic as Late as Sunday Night.

HALIFAX, Wednesday.

The Allan liner Parisian arrived to-night with no news of the Titanic beyond what it obtained at second hand by cross-messages.

Captain Hains declined to make a statement as to the purport of these messages, but gave other facts which he felt at liberty to disclose.

An interesting thing, he said, was that at half-past ten on Sunday night his Marconi operator was in touch with the Titanic, and got that ship to relay a message via Cape Race to his owners. That message was forwarded by the Titanic.

The Parisian never heard the signal from the Titanic for help, the reason being that the operator, having been busy all day, had retired for the night.

The Parisian, Californian, and Masaba had all been trying to pick up another steamer which was adrift without coal, but she was eventually picked up by the Asian from New York.

Captain Hains believes that when the Titanic struck the iceberg he was 150 miles to the west of that vessel. The Carpathia and Californian were much nearer.

The bergs, he added, were thick in that vicinity, and the Titanic must have struck so that the whole side of the liner was ripped out.

The first he heard of the accident was at four o'clock on Monday morning. He received no communication from the Titanic, the only message being the one previously referred to.

It is remarkable that not one of the Parisian's passengers knew of the disaster until informed of it when the boat reached here.

The sole possessors of the tragic news were the captain and the wireless operator.—Reuter's Special.

The official lists prove that women third-class passengers took precedence over millionaires.

A LABOUR CANARD.

A Groundless Accusation That Wealthy Passengers Had Preference.

The *Labour Leader* suggests that there was "obeisance to wealth even in the hour of danger and death," and that first-class passengers of the Titanic were given preference in the lifeboats.

Mr. Ben Tillett is circulating a resolution passed by the executive of the Dock, Wharf, Riverside, and General Workers' Union, protesting "against the wanton and callous disregard of human life and the vicious class antagonism shown in the practical forbidding of the saving of the lives of the third-class passengers."

[All the latest information goes to show that of those saved a strictly fair proportion were third-class passengers; and the official lists prove that women third-class passengers took precedence of millionaires, a number of whom are drowned.]

LEGISLATION FORESHADOWED.

WASHINGTON, Wednesday.

Mr. Taft and the members of the Cabinet are taking a personal interest in the determination of the leaders in Congress to impose upon the steamship companies regulations calling for the provision of further safeguards for the lives of passengers.

Government officials are also bent on obtaining legislation restricting the operations of amateur wireless telegraph operators.

It is stated that Congress will be able to provide for the refusal of clearance papers to foreign vessels failing to comply with new and more stringent rules.—Central News.

MAIN PICTURE: Rusted gears from the ship. In July 1986 Ballard, along with Martin Bowen and Ralph Hollis returned on the Atlantis II to conduct the first manned dives to the wreck using the three-man submersible Alvin.

LIMITED LIABILITIES.

POSSIBLE COST OF £830,000 TO THE WHITE STAR.

The disaster to the Titanic will entail upon the White Star Company heavy liabilities in the matter of compensation.

Under the Workmen's Compensation Act, in the case of those of the crew who have been drowned, their dependents can claim either a sum equal to the seaman's earnings during the three previous years or £150, whichever be the larger amount. In no case, however, is more than £300 to be paid, and the relatives making the claim must have been wholly dependent on the seaman's wages. This loss is understood to be covered by a mutual insurance club of which the large Liverpool and London shipping companies are members. The higher ranks are not provided for by the Act.

In the case of injury to or loss of life by passengers and damage to baggage, the White Star Company by their form of contract exclude liability, when the cause of the loss or injury is "an act of God," stranding, collision, or peril of the sea.

The company's liabilities are further limited by the provisions of the Merchant Shipping Act of 1894, which restricts the total sum payable for compensation in respect of loss of life, damage to vessels, goods, merchandise, and other things, to an aggregate amount not exceeding £15 per ton of the ship's dimensions.

In this case the extreme possible loss of the company would be £690,000 (i.e., 46,000 tons at £15 per ton). For loss of or damage to vessels, goods, and merchandise there is a limit of £8 per ton, which in this case would be £368,000.

Thus under the Act, assuming that the White Star Company were held liable, it might conceivably be called upon to pay:

For damage to baggage, etc. £368,000
For loss of life or personal injury to passengers £332,000

Assuming that 700 of the crew whose relatives can claim have been lost, and that the compensation reaches an amount of £200 a head on the average, that would involve a further £140,000.

It will be observed that while the liability of railway companies is unlimited in the matter of compensation for accidents, that of shipping companies is strictly limited, and the aggregate amount payable has to be divided up, pro rata, according to the claims.

THE LOST LETTERS.

The Titanic carried the whole of the British letter mails for the United States and Canada, and for certain places in Central and South America. There were about 3,418 mail bags, containing some 400,000 ordinary letters and 200,000 newspapers and magazines.

Among the British mails there were rather more than 3,000 registered letters, but as the values are not declared on registration the authorities have no means of knowing the total amount of the loss.

The Post Office does not undertake any insurance on letters for either America or Canada.

The Strange Silence

NO RESPONSE TO INQUIRIES.

MESSAGES IGNORED.

EVEN MR. TAFT GETS NO

parture from New York should be postponed from to-day till to-morrow so that she may take them to England.

A CENSORSHIP?

Mystery of the Carpathia's Reticence.

NO "O.K." SIGNAL.

FOR THE W AND FATHER

Lord Mayor's

"So is this great and there go the ships, there i which Thou hast suffere These wait all upon Thee which Thou givest them th openest Thine hand, the good. Thou hidest Thy

of the Carpathia.

WIRELESS MYSTERY MESSAGES.

WHO SENT THE "PASSENGERS SAFE" TELEGRAM?

A NEW TERROR ON THE HIGH SEAS

mesage to a source within reasonable range —and that is wide enough—and there seems no chance of the time-origin of his Marconigram being discovered.

He could fling out his ball into the great ocean of the æther, making it as plausible as possible; the stations or the ships within the lines of the pear-shaped curves of the radio-current would receive the message; operator would pass on the lie to operator; and a few hours belief of the false intelligence might amply suffice to upset the commerce of the world.

It is clear that in the wireless system there are infinite possibilities of evil as well as of good use and benefit; the message beginning "Pairsian reports Carpathia picked up twenty boats of Titanic passengers" may well be but the first chapter in a very strange history that is yet to be told.

FEWER SURVIVORS

ONLY 705 SAID TO BE ON BOARD THE CARPATHIA.

The latest telegrams giving the number of the survivors from the Titanic place them at 705 instead of 868.

It is hoped, however, that this number refers only to the passengers rescued apart from the crew, but nothing definite has yet been learnt on that point.

The Carpathia, with the survivors on board, is expected to reach New York between eight to-night and midnight (1 a.m. and 5 a.m. to-morrow by English time).

The number of missing is now stated to be 1,653.

It is now definitely known that the Titanic carried twenty boats, providing accommodation for about 1,200 persons.

There were actually on board her nearly 2,200 men, women, and children, but her twenty boats were in excess of the minimum provision required by the Board of Trade rules.

These rules, in spite of the great increase in the size of ships during recent years, have not been revised since 1894.

OPPOSITE PAGE: The RMS Carpathia, a Cunard-line transatlantic passenger steamship was en route from New York City to Fiume in Austria Hungary when the radio operator Harold Cottam picked up the distress signal from the Titanic just after midnight. He immediately woke Captain Arthur Rostron, the ship's captain, informing him that they were approximately 58 miles from the Titanic's last known location.

ABOVE: A 1958 photograph of Captain Rostron of RMS Carpathia. After hearing the news Rostron immediately diverted the ship, cutting off the heating and hot water to maximise the steam available for the engines. His prompt actions led to the rescue of 710 passengers and were later celebrated with a congressional gold medal from the U.S Congress. He was also presented with a gold medal and a loving cup by Mrs J.J. Brown, the Lady President of the Survivors' Committee.

Conflicting reports

'The Titanic sank at 2.20 this morning. No lives were lost.' This Reuters report was one of many misleading releases that reached the public domain in the hours following the disaster. Stories abounded of her limping into port or being towed to safety. One said that Titanic was sinking slowly and would be beached if a suitable spot could be reached before she foundered. News agencies tried to meet the demand for information when few hard facts were known. The rumour mill went into overdrive to take up the slack. In the days that followed there was much press criticism regarding the wilful misuse of wireless telegraphy, namely, 'the reckless dissemination of false news', as The Times put it.

Phillip Franklin, White Star's top executive at their New York office, made reassuring noises on the morning of 15 April, attempting to quash suggestions that there had been major loss of life. Disbelieving that the Company's state-of-the-art flagship could have gone down so quickly, Franklin focused on the positive reports, including one that said all passengers and crew had been safely transferred to the Virginian. Or, alternatively, that Titanic was being towed to Halifax by that vessel. Even as Franklin began making arrangements to transfer passengers and crew overland from Halifax to New York, the picture took on a bleaker hue. It was announced that 'Carpathia, with several hundred passengers from the Titanic, is now on her way to New York'. By early evening White Star officials were finally admitting that there had been a terrible death toll.

ABOVE: A re-enactment of the scene in the wireless room of the RMS Carpathia where the liner's distress signals and later the lists of survivors were picked up by radio operators who were on duty at the Wanamaker Radio Station in New York City.

OPPOSITE PAGE: One of the lifeboats is drained of water and hoisted onto the Carpathia. Titanic's crew successfully launched 18 out of the 20 lifeboats before the ship sank with an estimated 705 people carried to safety. The ship had been equipped with 3500 lifebelts but these were ineffective when passengers were falling into water that was 2° Celsius, with most freezing to death rather than drowning.

"The Titanic sank at 2.20 this morning. No lives were lost."

> *"In answer to your question we state that the Titanic had life-saving appliances for all passengers and boatage accommodation in excess of the Board of Trade requirements."*

TITANIC'S BOATS.

BOARD OF TRADE AND SAFETY PRECAUTIONS.

VIEWS OF ADVISORY COMMITTEE.

SUBJECT TO BE RAISED IN HOUSE OF COMMONS TO-DAY.

The managing director of the Wellins Davits and Engineering Company last night issued a statement to the effect that the Titanic carried fourteen lifeboats and two cutters aggregating a capacity of 9,702 cubic feet, which is in excess of that required under the present rule.

Mr. Shelley, of the White Star Line at Liverpool, said yesterday:

In answer to your questions, we state that the Titanic had life-saving appliances for all passengers and boatage accommodation in excess of the Board of Trade requirements. Beyond that we will not go.

THE NUMBER OF BOATS.

Difficulty of Lowering Them After Mishap to Ship.

The Parliamentary correspondent of *The Times* writes to-day that the Advisory Committee to the Marine Department of the Board of Trade have for some time past had under consideration the need for increasing the number of boats carried in large passenger and emigrant steamers.

The Committee is composed of representatives of the shipowners, marine engineers, shipbuilders, and seamen.

Various expedients have been considered by the Committee, and it is understood that before the disaster to the Titanic occurred the opinion had been formed that more safety provisions were necessary in these large ships.

But one vital consideration, it is felt, must govern the increase in the number of boats. The number of the boats must not be increased to such an extent as to lead to clashing and confusion in lowering them.

It is thought better, for obvious reasons, that it would be well to have an insufficient number of boats, which would take only a proportion of those on board the vessel, rather than boats to take all on board if from the number and close proximity of these boats they could not be launched in an emergency in safety.

When as many boats are provided as can be launched with safety, the official view is that if more provision is needed other apparatus must take the place of additional apparatus, such as collapsible boats, deck raftage, etc.

ON THE DECK LEVEL.

It is pointed out by shipowners that much of the difficulty with the boats lies in the fact that the passengers must get into them on the deck level before they are lowered—a distance in the case of the Titanic of probably fifty or sixty feet.

Passengers cannot swarm down ropes attached to the guy between the davits as seamen do in rough weather.

Full boatloads have to be lowered, and it would be disastrous to have full boatloads one above the other in layers, for lowering, or to lower three at a time, if they were close enough to clash. And when a vessel has a list on her the boats as they are lowered may clash against the vessel on one side.

The recent catastrophe is thought in official circles to point to the complete failure of the deck raftage.

But sufficient data are not yet to hand. In the meantime, despite the good intentions of the Board of Trade and the Advisory Committee, it appears that no step was taken, and that the present regulations, which were framed on the assumption that liners would not exceed a tonnage of 10,000, have not been revised for years.

Last December an old pilot wrote to Mr. John Ward M.P., making serious statements about the lack of proper provision for boats on board liners and emigrant ships.

After considering the matter Mr. Ward put a question to the President of the Board of Trade on December 12 last, asking whether regulations were being prepared for the testing of the lifeboats, and whether the Board would insist that all passenger ships should possess sufficient seaworthy lifeboats to carry at least a reasonable percentage of the passengers and the crew.

MR. BUXTON'S REPLY.

Mr. Buxton's reply was as follows:—

Under the provisions of the Merchant Shipping Act, 1894, and the instructions issued by the Board of Trade, the boats of every passenger steamer are inspected by the Board surveyors at each survey of the vessel for passenger certificate, and at other times as opportunities occur.

"The boats of emigrant ships are also inspected at the survey which takes place before a vessel is allowed to clear as an emigrant ship from a British port.

"It is the custom of the surveyors to require, whenever practicable, a number of the boats to be lowered into the water, and in the case of emigrant ships they are frequently manned and rowed about for five minutes.

"The owners and masters of all British ships are also responsible, under the Merchant Shipping Act, 1894, for seeing that the life-saving appliances are kept so as to be at all times fit and ready for use; and the masters are required to keep a record in the official log of every occasion on which boat drill is practised and the life-saving appliances are examined.

"The Board of Trade has reason to believe that this is regularly performed on passenger and emigrant steamers. It is also required by the statutory rules that means shall be provided for launching ships' boats as quickly as possible, and attention is always paid to this point by the Board's surveyors.

"The Board of Trade are carefully considering at present the question of the number of boats required to be carried by large passenger and emigrant steamers, and also the question of the seaworthiness of ships' boats."

Mr. Ward, adds the writer, will put the following question to Mr. Buxton on Monday:—

"Whether his attention has been called to the alleged absence of proper and sufficient lifeboat accommodation on board British passenger ships, and whether his Department are now in a position to take action in accordance with his statement on December 11 last."

This and other aspects of the subject will be raised at question time in the House of Commons to-day.

BELOW: A shipping register entry from April 10, 1912, logged the first and final departure of the Titanic from the Southampton port.

ABOVE: The children's playground was located on the Saloon Deck. The ship's passenger list included the names of 109 children who were aged 13 years or under but only 57 of these survived. The majority of those who died were in the third class section of the boat with many families perishing together when unable to find their way up to the Boat Deck.

SAVED BY A DREAM
CAUSE OF A CANCELLED PASSAGE

A confession that a dream prevented him from sailing in the Titanic was made yesterday by the Hon. J. C. Middleton, vice-president of the Akron-Canton Railway of Ohio. Mr Middleton told the dream to his friends ten days before the tragedy, and this fact is vouched for by several well-known people, one of whom gave Mr Middleton a signed "affidavit" to that effect.

Mr Middleton says : "I booked a cabin in the Titanic on March 23. I felt unaccountably depressed at the time, and on April 3 I dreamt that I saw the Titanic capsized in mid-ocean and a lot of the passengers struggling in the water. The following night I dreamt exactly the same dream The next day I told my wife and several of my friends, and afterwards, on receiving cable advice from America that my business did not necessitate my crossing at once, I decided to cancel my passage."

Both Mr J. H. Curling, the pigeon-shooting champion, and Mr Feddon, to whom Mr Middleton told his dream, confirmed his statement yesterday.

FATE OF A FAMILY
PARENTS AND
NINE CHILDREN IN TITANIC

On board the Titanic were eleven residents of Peterborough, Mr and Mrs John Sage, of Gladstone Street, and their nine children, whose ages ranges from twenty-two to five years.

Mr Sage, who is a Londoner, went to Peterborough from Lynn about two years ago, and for a time had a shop at the corner of Gladstone Street and Hankey Street. He, however, disposed of the business, and with his eldest son George went to Canada and spent some time on a farm in Saskatchewan. He returned to England about three months ago, and, intending to go in for fruit farming, purchased a farm at Jacksonville, Florida. He was proceeding to his new home with his family in the Titanic. On Saturday a postcard was received in Peterborough with the Queenstown postmark from Mr Sage, who stated that they were getting on well.

Among those who were waiting at the White Star London office in Cockspur Street last night was a German, who said he had three sisters on board the Titanic when she sailed. He had waited at the office for news without sleep since the first messages regarding the disaster arrived. Another man said he had four sisters and three brothers in the ship.

Titanic

131428

Liverpool 2183

ABOVE: Isidor Straus, the co-owner of Macy's department store also went down with the ship. He was travelling with his wife Ida who refused to be loaded onto a lifeboat, wishing to remain with her husband. He was offered a place due to his age but refused, letting his wife's maid have it instead. The inseparable couple were last seen sitting on deckchairs holding hands before they were washed overboard.

THE KAISER'S MESSAGE TO THE KING.

The Kaiser has sent a telegram from Corfu to the King expressing his sympathy in connection with the Titanic disaster. His Majesty has charged the German Ambassador to express his sympathy to the British Government. His Majesty has also telegraphed to the White Star Line as follows:—

I am deeply grieved at the news of the terrible disaster which has befallen your line. I send an expression of deepest sympathy with all those who mourn the loss of relatives and friends.

THE FRENCH PRESIDENT.

PARIS, Wednesday.
President Fallières has sent the following telegrams to King George and to President Taft:—

To his Majesty George V., King of the United Kingdom of Great Britain and Ireland and of the British Dominions beyond the Seas, Emperor of India, London.
I am anxious to express personally to your Majesty the profound grief with which I learned of the horrible Titanic disaster, and I beg you to accept my most heartfelt and sincere condolences.
A. FALLIÈRES.

To his Excellency Mr. Taft, President of the United States of America, Washington.
It was with profound affliction that I learned of the terrible Titanic catastrophe which plunges so many American families into mourning, and I am anxious to address to you my most sincere condolences. I beg to assure your Excellency that I share your anxiety regarding the fate of your aide-de-camp and friend Major Butt.
A. FALLIÈRES.
—Reuter.

ANGER IN NEW YORK.

QUESTIONS FOR THE WHITE STAR.

ACTION IN CONGRESS.

FROM OUR OWN CORRESPONDENT.
NEW YORK, Wednesday.
All hopes that some eminent men, passengers of the Titanic, whose names were not mentioned in the list of survivors, might still be alive, were crushed to-day when Commander Decker, of the scout cruiser Chester, sent the following wireless message, via Portland, Maine, to Washington:—

"Carpathia states that the list of the first and second class passengers and crew has been sent to shore. The Chester will forward the list of third class names when convenient to the Carpathia."

The Carpathia is expected to reach here either late to-morrow night or early on Friday morning.

The iceberg which sent the Titanic down is declared by Captain Ferrie Wood, of the Etonian, Leyland Line, which arrived here to-day, to have been probably the largest of any in the field of ice, 100 miles in length.

Captain Wood, who passed close to it in latitude 42deg. N., longitude 49deg. 50 min. W., describes it as being at least 500 feet long and 100 feet high. Captain Wood is of the opinion that under water the berg was seven times greater in bulk than above.

Flags on public buildings to-day are flying half-mast, and all ships in the harbour will observe the same signs of mourning to-morrow.

The Olympic finished sending to the Marconi station at Cape Race the list of survivors at 2.15 this morning. She remained in wireless communication with the station for another hour without offering any more names, and then signalled "Daylight has come." Shortly after she passed beyond the range of the wireless instruments.

The fast cruiser Salem is hurrying toward the Carpathia at the rate of 24 knots, and it is hoped that during to-night she will be in a position to report the full list of survivors.

WHITE STAR REPORTS.

Meanwhile, comment on the secrecy that was observed regarding the disaster on Monday is assuming an acrid character. The Associated Press has been asked if it can discover the origin of the false reports circulated throughout Monday to the effect that the Titanic was afloat at eight o'clock in the morning, that three vessels were standing by the disabled liner, and so forth. The manager, Mr. Melville Stone, has replied that all the reports issued by the Associated Press under its own authority were correct, but that statements given out from other sources acquired an importance too great to be ignored, and that consequently they were given with all due reserve as being rumours circulating in Halifax, Boston, and other places.

It is suggested that many of the false rumours originated with amateur wireless stations, which have become a pest to seafaring men on this side of the Atlantic. The Marconi stations, however, state that their apparatus was not interfered with by the amateur wireless brigade.

On referring to Monday evening's newspapers, I find the following recorded:—

"At eleven o'clock this morning Vice-President Franklin said at the White Star offices that he had received the following version of the Montreal despatch:— 'Titanic slowly proceeding for Halifax under own steam.'

"Shortly before noon the following wireless despatch was received from Captain Haddock, of the Olympic:— Parisian and Carpathia are in attendance on Titanic. Carpathia has already taken off twenty boatloads of passengers. Baltic is approaching, Olympic 230 miles away.'

"Mr. Franklin, in making public his message from the Olympic, declared that the Titanic would be safely towed to port and the passengers would be landed at Halifax. At one o'clock in the afternoon the White Star officials received the following bulletin from Boston:— 'Allan Line, Montreal, by telephone confirms report that Virginian, Carpathia, and Parisian are in attendance. Mitchell, White Star agent at Montreal, telegraphs he is not responsible for report credited to his office that Titanic is sunk. So far as he knew, Titanic is still afloat and making for Halifax under own steam.'"

DELAY OF FATEFUL MESSAGE.

The mystery seems all the more inexplicable in view of the following wireless from Mr. Louden Charlton, a passenger in the Olympic, dated yesterday, to the Associated Press:—"Olympic received the news at midnight on Sunday that Titanic had struck ice. She started immediately for the scene, but resumed her course eastward at five o'clock in the morning, hearing that the Titanic had sunk at 2 a.m. The only details known are that 670 persons were saved, mostly women and children. All the crew, except those manning the boats, are believed to have been lost."

What people here are asking is why, if the Olympic knew of the sinking of the Titanic at 5 a.m., she was unable to add to her message, received shortly before noon, the fact that the Titanic had sunk? According to Mr. Franklin, the message from Captain Haddock, of the Olympic, telling of the awful calamity, reached him (Mr. Franklin) about 7 p.m. on Monday (New York time). Before that hour he had no idea that the Titanic had sunk.

The information contained in Captain Haddock's despatch I sent to *The Daily Mail* before eight o'clock, but a long time elapsed before Mr. Franklin issued it to the reporters waiting at his office.

Mr. Marconi this afternoon displayed considerable irritation when questioned concerning the reports circulated on Monday that the Titanic was being towed slowly into port.

"Good gracious," said Mr. Marconi, "has not wireless done enough in this instance to free it from complaints? If you can prove that one of our operators either sent or gave out that message I will take off my hat to you. This sort of thing happened before there was any wireless. Look at the confused and false reports which were circulated at the time of the Spanish War."

STRUGGLE FOR A RAFT.

Mr. John R. Joyce, a banker, of Carlsbad, New Mexico, said:

"In response to the wireless call, when we got to the scene of the wreck eighteen boats and one raft were floating around.

"The Carpathia picked them all up. Four of the people on the raft were dead.

"They were buried at sea from the Carpathia on the way to New York.

"On the raft were about thirty-five people. They said about thirty-five others had tried to get on.

"These others were either lost off the raft or while trying to get to it.

"Some of the women refused to go first. The men had to push them into the boats.

"Many of the men were in dinner jackets and evening dress.

"One of the survivors I talked with said that when he was stepping into the last boat that left the Titanic he saw Mr. Isidore Straus was pushing his wife toward the boat, and she was insisting on remaining with him."

"I saw Mrs. Astor come aboard the Carpathia," one of the survivors said to me, "and I saw Mr. Astor drown.

"Some of the people jumped from the Titanic and were immediately drowned. They did not hit a lifeboat at all."

CHIEF STEWARD.

DISASTER NOT AT FIRST REALISED.

NEW YORK, Friday.

Edward Wheelton, the chief steward in the Titanic, gave the following account of the disaster:—

"It was about 11.45 on Sunday night when the disaster occurred. It had been a beautifully clear spring night, but fog was just commencing to descend. There had been dancing and music on board, and many of the passengers were still on deck and in the saloon

"There was a sudden crash amidships, but no immediate commotion. The passengers were somewhat startled, but they did not at first realise the extent of the disaster. The officers of the ship reassured the passengers, but at that time they themselves did not know that anything serious had happened.

"It was fully half an hour before the full realisation of the effect of what had happened dawned upon both officers and passengers. The ship began to fill and to settle down by the head. The wireless operators began sending out signals of distress, and these were kept up for at least two hours.

"In fact, the wireless apparatus was not out of commission until just before the ship sank. When the vessel began to settle down we thought it advisable to begin lowering the lifeboats. The nearest ship was seventy miles away, and we knew it would be morning before any rescue vessels could arrive. As the liner began to settle down rapidly all the lifeboats were lowered from the starboard side.

"The men were only permitted to join their wives on the port side to say "Goodbye," as the order had been given that the women and children were to be placed in the boats. Even then no one seemed to realise that the situation was so serious. I heard Colonel Astor tell his wife that he would meet her in New York. He then exchanged an affectionate farewell with her.

"Major Butt was very calm. He gave orders and pacified the men who were inclined to be panicky. The last I saw of him he was standing against the rail looking into the water.

THE BAND PLAYING.

"All the lifeboats reached the water safely. As the boats were being lowered the orchestra were playing operatic selections and some of the latest popular melodies of Europe and America. It was only just before the liner made her final plunge that the character of the programme was changed, and then they struck up "Nearer, My God, to Thee."

"I should think we were in the lifeboats for about two hours when we saw the Titanic give a lurch upward and then disappear.—Exchange Telegraph Company.

ABOVE: Lady Duff Gordon, a leading fashion designer had been travelling to the States on business with her husband Cosmo. As the ship was sinking the couple got into lifeboat No. 1 designed for 40 people. However on setting sail there were only 12 occupants. This was questioned closely at the enquiry and it seemed that there were no other passengers around at the time. Questions were also asked about why the lifeboat did not turn back to collect more passengers but no conclusions were drawn.

OPPOSITE PAGE: Portrait of the survivor Mrs. J.J. Margaret Brown. She was championed by the press after assisting many people into the lifeboats before she was shepherded into lifeboat No. 6. There she took charge of the occupants, often taking a turn at rowing and challenging the decisions of Quartermaster Hichens. Later she became known as the 'Unsinkable Molly Brown' and was the subject of a musical and a subsequent film.

The men were only permitted to join their wives portside to say "Good-bye".

DISTINGUISHED PASSENGERS UNACCOUNTED FOR

MR. W. T. STEAD. - The famous English journalist and an extensive traveller. Was on his way to New York to speak at a convention in which President Taft was to take part. Mr. Stead was the founder and editor of the Review of Reviews and was formerly editor of the Pall Mall Gazette. A vigorous opponent of wars, he for many years engaged on a peace crusade in connection with which he visited the Czar and twice attended the Hague Conference.

MR. THOMAS ANDREWS. - One of the managing directors of Harland and Wolff. Son of Mr. Thomas Andrews, chairman of Belfast and County Down Railway.

MR. CHISHOLM. - Chief draughtsman of both the Olympic and the Titanic.

COLONEL JOHN JACOB ASTOR. - Multi-millionaire, soldier, and inventor, is a great-grandson of John Jacob Astor, the founder of the family in America. He was born in New York in 1864: has built some of New York's mammoth hotels - the Waldorf-Astoria, the Hotel St Regis, and the Hotel Knickerbocker. He published in 1894 "A Journey in Other Worlds." He gave a fully equipped battery of artillery to the United States when the war with Spain broke out, and he also served in the Army with distinction. Colonel Astor invented a pneumatic machine for the mending of roads, and a turbine engine.

He married at Philadelphia in 1891 Ava L. Willing, and has two children, William Vincent Astor and Ava Alice Muriel Astor. Last September Colonel Astor married Miss Madeleine Farce, a beautiful girl eighteen years of age. Colonel and Mrs. Astor left New York in the Olympic in January last for Paris as part of the honeymoon trip. From there they went to Egypt, and were returning home in the Titanic. Colonel Astor's body is reported to have been picked up. Mrs. Astor was among the rescued.

MR. ISADOR STRAUS. - Millionaire, was born in Bavaria in 1845. In 1854 he migrated to America, where he built up many great commercial interests. He was elected a member of Congress in 1893, and as an intimate friend of William L. Wilson was constantly consulted in the formation of the Wilson Tariff. He married in New York City in 1871, Ida Blun, and has six children.

MR. BENJAMIN GUGGENHEIM. - Millionaire, one of the famous family associated with Mr. Pierpont Morgan.

MR. HENRY B. HARRIS. - Former Mayor of Chelsea, much interested in art matters, and took a prominent part in discussions at the Mansion House regarding the King Edward memorial.

MAJOR ARCHIBALD BUTT. - Aide-de-Camp to President Taft. He was returning to Washington after visiting the Pope.

MR. JACQUES FUTRELLE. - A story-writer, author of "The Thinking Machine," "The Chase of the Golden Plate," and many detective stories.

MR. FRANCIS DAVIS MILNET. - Prominent American artist, war correspondent, and author. He has had an adventurous career serving n the Civil War as drummer and assistant surgeon, acting as correspondent of the New York Herald and the London Daily News in the Russo-Turkish war, and war correspondent for The Times in the Philippines expedition of 1898. Had the Legion of Honour of France decoration. Has a painting in the Tate Gallery, London, and a residence at Broadway, Worcestershire.

MR. WASHINGTON AUGUSTUS ROBBLING. - A millionaire. In conjunction with his father, built the Brooklyn Bridge and the Pittsburg and Cincinnati and Covington suspension bridges. He served in the Union Army as a private.

JONEHEER J. G. REUCHLIN. - Joint managing director of the Holland-America Line.

MR. GEORGE E. WIDENER. - American traction magnate and millionaire. Son of Mr. Peter A. Widener, of Philadelphia, who recently purchased the famous Rembrandt picture "The Mill" from Lord Lansdowne for £100,000. Mr. George Widener had a large number of works of art in the Titanic, including a piece of Sevres china purchased in London for a large sum.

There were no happier persons in the Titanic before disaster befell her than Mr. and Mrs. D. W. Marvin, a newly married American couple, aged nineteen and eighteen, who were returning to New York from a three weeks' honeymoon in England. Mrs. Marvin's name appears in the list of survivors, but her husband apparently has not yet been accounted for.

Mr. Marvin was the son of the head of one of the largest cinematograph organisations in America, and was being trained as an engineer. Mr. A. Hamburger, a director of

the Dover-street Studios, London, who knew Mr. H. M. Marvin intimately, said yesterday: "He was a splendid specimen of American youth - strong, athletic, and well-set-up. Mrs. Marvin is an extremely pretty and vivacious girl. They were both of them full of the joy of life and affection for each other, and when in England behaved just like two happy school children on a holiday. They spent most of their time sight-seeing and going to parties, dances, and the like. Everyone made much of them. The girl's parents are wealthy, and she had received £2,000 from her mother as a wedding present."

Among the survivors are Mr. Edward Beane and Mrs. Ethel Beane, second-class passengers, who were married at Norwich several days ago. Both are of Norwich parentage, and Mr. Beane, who has been engaged in the building trade in America, returned to England about three weeks ago to get married. Only a few days of the honeymoon had been spent at Norwich before they started for America.

CAPTAIN'S DEATH.

ON THE BRIDGE UNTIL THE END.

New York, Thursday Night.
Captain Smith was last seen on the bridge just before the ship sank, leaping into the sea only after the decks were awash.—Reuter.

New York, Thursday.
Mr. Lawrence Beesley, a young Londoner, a second-class passenger, who was taken off in a lifeboat said: "As we rowed away Captain Smith could be seen by the bright lights which still shone on the sinking ship, standing on the bridge, and he continued directing his men right up to the moment when the bridge became level with the water. He then calmly climbed over the rail and dropped into the water."—Exchange Telegraph Co.

The 'Millionaires' Captain

Edward John Smith, White Star Line's most senior commander, described his 40-plus years sailing the world's oceans as 'uneventful'. He oozed authority and inspired confidence, both in his employers and his crew. Second Officer Charles Lightoller said: 'He was a great favourite, and a man any officer would give his ears to sail under.' Passengers held him in similar regard, many seeking out Smith's ships for their intercontinental travels. He rubbed shoulders with some of the world's wealthiest individuals, titled aristocrats, the elite of Western society; Smith's 'millionaires' captain' tag was well merited.

Many of White Star's maiden voyages were entrusted to his capable hands, including the Olympic, his most recent ship, which he went on to captain on a number of occasions. The experience and seniority of a man who had been with White Star since 1880, its commodore since 1904, was reflected in his £1,250 salary, double that which most liner captains earned. At 62 he was ready to retire. After overseeing Titanic's maiden trip, he was signing off to spend more time with his wife and daughter in their imposing Southampton residence.

Smith's record hadn't been quite as uneventful as he maintained. In September 1911 he had been in charge of the Olympic when she was involved in a collision with HMS Hawke while leaving Southampton harbour. The smaller ship appeared to be sucked towards what was then the world's largest liner, an incident foreshadowing the near-miss involving Titanic and New York seven months later. On this occasion, however, both ships sustained serious damage, and White Star lost the subsequent suit.

Change of course ordered

At 9.00 pm on the night of April 14, 1912, Captain Smith was on the bridge discussing weather conditions with Lightoller. At least some of the ice reports had reached him, and just before 6.00 pm he had ordered a change of course, Titanic sailing around five miles further south than was normal for the time of year. Whether this was a precautionary move is unclear. Smith retired for the night at 9.20 pm, telling his Second Officer: 'If in the slightest degree doubtful, let me know.' By the time the captain was next on the bridge, Titanic had been struck her fatal blow.

Smith's cool assertiveness seem to have deserted him over the next two and a half hours. With the lifeboats made ready, Lightoller had to suggest to his captain that they ought to begin the evacuation procedure. Smith's own fate after 2.17 am, when he advised that it was 'every man for himself', is uncertain. He was seen on the bridge, one witness report referring to his 'benign, resigned countenance...like a solicitous father'. Another account had him washing up against one of the lifeboats and helping a child to safety but refusing to be hauled aboard, instead pushing off and disappearing from view.

Giving his life in the course of discharging his duty did not spare Smith from the forensic gaze of those investigating the disaster. He was criticised for handing one of the ice reports to J Bruce Ismay, an act that helped fuel suggestions that White Star's managing director had influenced navigational decisions. The US inquiry concluded that Smith was 'over-confident and careless'. Its British counterpart found him culpable in regard of Titanic's 'excessive speed', which was a contributory factor in the calamity.

Of almost 900 crew members, two-thirds had Southampton connections. Edward J. Smith was among the casualties that prompted one reporter to note: 'The town is as if widowed.'

ABOVE: The first class Georgian style reading and writing room on the port side of the ship. As men used the smoking room this was designed as a retreat for the female passengers. It featured white panelled walls and moulded ceilings with an electric clock on the hooded fireplace. Passengers were provided with the ship's own headed writing paper.

OPPOSITE: The Promenade Deck of the Olympic, the sister ship to the Titanic. The construction work on the ship began three months before the Titanic but the two ships were very similar in design. She had picked up the distress signal from the Titanic but was 100 miles away at the time and therefore unable to help. After the disaster the Olympic was rapidly equipped with additional collapsible lifeboats but was then called back into dock in October 1912 to amend her design and fit additional wooden lifeboats.

MR. ISMAY.

His Statement of What Actually Occured.

New York, Friday.

Mr. Bruce Ismay, on landing from the Carpathia, said: "In the present state of my affairs my feelings are too deep for expression. I can say, however, that the White Star Line officers and employés will do everything possible to alleviate the sufferings and sorrows of the relatives and friends of those who perished.

"The Titanic was the last word in ship-building. Every regulation prescribed by the British Board of Trade was completely complied with. The officers and crew were the most skilful in the British service.

"I understand that a Committee of the United States Senate has been appointed to investigate the cause of the accident. I welcome the most complete and exhaustive inquiry. The company has nothing to conceal. Any aid which I or my associates or the shipbuilders can render is at the service of the United States or the British Government. Further than this I prefer to say nothing.

"The Titanic, after striking the iceberg on Sunday night, remained above the water for two hours and 25 minutes. She then sank. Whether there were enough lifeboats on the Titanic to care for all her passengers I do not care to say."

Mr. Ismay was asked in which lifeboat in the order of their leaving the Titanic he made his escape. He replied: "I took the last lifeboat which pulled out from the Titanic."

"Were there any women or children on board when you left the Titanic?"

Mr. Ismay: "I am sure I cannot say."

Discussing the nature of the Titanic's injury, Mr. Ismay said the whole bilge was ripped out where the iceberg caught her. She struck the berg a blow on the starboard side. There was no explosion.

He was in bed asleep, and was awakened by the shock. It felt as if she were going up on something. The vessel seemed to climb upon a submerged part of the iceberg.

The reason the Titanic's watertight compartments did not save her was because all the plates along her starboard side were loosened and all the forward compartments on that side were flooded.

He said he sent a statement of the wreck to the White Star offices at New York on Monday.

Vice-President Franklin said this statement was not received until yesterday afternoon, and it was not given out then because the whole of the accident was known.—Exchange.

RESCUE WORK.

Some of the Titanic's Boats Not Half Full.

New York, Friday.

A passenger on board the Carpathia made the following statement:—"I was awakened at 12.30 in the morning by a commotion on the decks which seemed unusual. There was no excitement, however, as the ship was still moving. I paid but little attention to the disturbance and went to sleep again.

"About three o'clock I was again awakened, and I noticed that the Carpathia had stopped. I went up on to the deck and found that our vessel had changed her course.

"The lifeboats had been sighted and began to arrive one by one. There were sixteen of them in all.

"The transfer of the passengers was soon being carried out. It was a pitiable sight. Ropes were tied round the waists of the adults to help them in climbing up the rope ladders.

"The little children and babies were hoisted on to our deck in bags. Some of the boats were crowded, but a few were not half full. This I could not understand.

"Some of the people were in evening dress, while others were in their night clothes or wrapped in blankets. They were all hurried into the saloon at once for hot breakfast, of which they were in great need, as they had been in open boats for four or five hours in the most biting air I have ever experienced.

"There were husbands without their wives, wives without their husbands, parents without their children, and children without their parents, but there was no demonstration and not a sob was heard. They spoke scarcely a word and seemed to be stunned by the shock of their experiences.

"Immediately after breakfast was over Divine Service was held in the saloon.

"One of the women and three of the others taken from the lifeboats died soon after reaching our deck, and their bodies were lowered into the sea at five o'clock in the afternoon.

"The rescued had no clothing other than that they were wearing, and a relief committee was formed, our passengers contributing enough to meet their immediate needs.

"The survivors were so close to the sinking steamer that they feared that the lifeboats would be sucked down into the vortex.

"On our way back to New York we steamed along the edge of the icefield, which stretched as far as the eye could see. To the north there was no blue water to be seen at all. At one time I counted thirteen icebergs."—Reuter.

He was the sole survivor after the wave that swept the liner just before the final plunge. By great good fortune he managed to grasp the brass railing on the deck above.

"Were there women or children on board when you left the Titanic?" Mr Ismay: "I am sure I cannot say".

MAIN PICTURE: The exposed electrical panel room on the stern of the Titanic. Rusticles created by extrusions of iron produced by anaerobic bacteria, hang over the edges.

THE LAST SAVED.

Went Down With Titanic and Was Picked Up.

NEW YORK, Thursday (11.50 p.m.).

Colonel Archibald Gracie, an officer of the United States army, who was the last man saved, actually went down with the Titanic, but was picked up by a lifeboat.

He told a remarkable story of personal hardship, but emphatically denied the reports to the effect that there had been any panic on board. He praised in the highest terms the behaviour of both passengers and crew, and paid a high tribute to the heroism of the women passengers.

Colonel Gracie said:—"When Sunday evening came, we all noticed the increased cold, which gave plain warning that the ship was in close proximity to icebergs and an ice field. I am credibly informed that the officers had been advised by wireless of the presence of dangerous floes in the vicinity.

"The sea, however, was a smooth as glass, and the weather was clear, so that there seemed to be no occasion for fear. When the vessel struck the passengers were not alarmed, but joked over the matter.

"The few who appeared on deck had taken time to dress properly. There was not the slightest indication of panic."

The most thrilling portion of Colonel Gracie's narrative was that in which he told how he was driven to the topmost deck when the ship settled down. He was the sole survivor after the wave that swept the liner just before the final plunge.

By great good fortune he managed to grasp the brass railing on the deck above. He hung on with might and main. When the ship plunged he was forced to let go. He was swirled around and around for what seemed to be an interminable time.

Eventually he came to the surface unhurt and managed to seize a wooden grating that was floating near by. When he recovered his breath he discovered a large canvas and cork raft which had floated up. A man was struggling towards it from some wreckage to which he had clung.

"The two of us," Colonel Gracie continued, "then began the work of rescuing those who jumped into the sea and were floundering about in the water. When dawn broke there were thirty of us on the raft standing knee deep in water and afraid to move lest we should be overturned.

"The hours that elapsed before we were picked up by the Carpathia were the longest and most terrible I have ever spent."—Reuter's Special.

Survivors' Stories of the

NO SCENES OF PANIC ON BOARD.

THE CAPTAIN ON THE BRIDGE UNTIL THE END.

GRAPHIC NARRATIVES.

LAST MAN SAVED RELATES HOW HE WAS PICKED UP.

ONLY 705 PERSONS SAVED.

The Carpathia has reached New York, and to-day the silence hanging over the loss of the Titanic is broken.

All is not yet clear, but this one thing is certain. There was no panic on board, and the men went like heroes to their deaths.

The captain, according to the latest report, was on the bridge to the end. Earlier reports were that both Captain Smith and the chief engineer shot themselves after the berg had been struck.

An Exchange message from New York states that according to official figures which have been issued by the officers of the Cunard Line, only 705 of the persons aboard the Titanic at the time of the collision were saved.

Of this number 202 were first-class passengers, 115 second-class, and 178 third.

The remaining 210 saved were members of the crew.

Many survivors were picked up from the water.

and looking through the window had seen a huge iceberg go by close to the side of the boat. They thought that we had just grazed it with a glancing blow, and they had been to see if any damage had been done.

"None of us, of course, had any conception that she had been pierced below by part of a submerged iceberg.

"The game of cards was resumed, and without any thought of disaster I retired to my cabin to read until we started again. I never saw any of the players or the onlookers again.

"A little later, hearing people going upstairs, I went out again and found that everybody wanted to know why the engines had stopped. No doubt many of them had been awakened from their sleep by the sudden stopping of the vibration to which they had become accustomed during the four days we had been on board.

"Going up on the deck again, I saw that ther was an unmistakable list downwards from the stern to the bows, but knowing nothing of what had happened, I concluded that some of the front compartments had filled and weighed down.

ALL ON DECK.

"Again I went down to my cabin, where I put on some warmer clothing. As I dressed I heard the order shouted, 'All passengers on deck with lifebelts on.'

"We all walked up slowly with the lifebelts tied on over our clothing, but even then we presumed that this was merely a wise precaution the captain ...

Most of the ... see if this ... was, and s... call, 'Any ... "Lookin... saw boat N... It was hal... call was rep... saw none c... looked up ... deck, sir?' "'Then ... dropped an... boat as the... "As the ... ladies were ... crowd on B... old was pa... down we w... directions t... 'Aft,' 'Ste... we were so... "Here ... moment we ... experience ... the deck to ... "Immedi... exhaust of ... stream of w... from the sh... line. It wa... smart away ... swamping w...

NO ...

"We had ... petty officer ... charge, so ... 'Some one ... boat from t... one knew w... as we coul... sides, but fo... to move am... sixty or sev... "Down ... floated with ... the stream ... washing us ... sel, while t... back agains... "The res... that we wer... side, and ... which had fi... coming dow... ened to sub... "'Stop lo... and the crew ... feet above, ... tance to t... seventy fee... pulleys mus... those above... feet, ten fee... I reached u... the swingin... next drop w... heads. "Just b... stoker spra...

NO PANIC OR RUSH

NEW YORK, Thursday (11.45pm)

The following account of the disaster is given by Mr Beesley, of London:

"The voyage from Queenstown was quiet and successful. We had met with very fine weather. The sea was calm, and the wind was westerly to south-westerly the whole way. The temperature was very cold, particularly on the last day. In fact, after dinner on Sunday evening it was already too cold to be on deck at all.

"I had been in my berth about ten minutes when at about a quarter past ten, I felt a slight jar. Then soon afterwards there was a second shock, but it was not sufficiently large to cause any anxiety to anyone, however nervous they may have been. The engines, however, stopped immediately afterwards. At first, I thought that the ship had lost a propeller.

"I went up on deck in my dressing gown and I found only a few people there who had come up in the same way to inquire why we had stopped, but there was no sort of anxiety in the mind of anyone. We saw through the smoking room window that a game of cards was going on, and I went in to ask if they knew anything.

"They had noticed the jar a little more, and looking through the window had seen a huge iceberg go by close to the side of the boat. They thought that we had just grazed it with a glancing blow, and they had been to see if any damage had been done.

"None of us, of course, had any conception that she had been pierced below by part of a submerged iceberg.

"The game of cards was resumed, and without any thought of disaster I retired to my cabin to read until we started again. I never saw any of the players or onlookers again.

"A little later, hearing people upstairs I went out again and found that everybody wanted to know why the engines had stopped. No doubt many of them had been awakened from their sleep by the sudden stopping of the vibration to which they had become accustomed during the four days we had been on board.

Titanic Disaster.

LONDON PASSENGER TELLS FULL STORY

"Going up on the deck again, I saw that there was an unmistakable list downwards from the stern to the bows, but knowing nothing of what had happened, I concluded that some of the front compartments had filled and weighed down.

ALL ON DECK

"Again I went down to my cabin, where I put on some warmer clothing. As I dressed I heard the order shouted 'All passengers on deck with lifebelts on.'

"We all walked up slowly with the lifebelts tied on over our clothing, but even then we presumed this was merely a wise precaution the captain was taking, and that we should go in a short time to go to bed. There was a total absence of any panic or expression of alarm.

"I suppose this must be accounted for by the exceeding calmness of the night and the absence of any sign of accident. The ship was absolutely still, and except for the gentle tilt downwards, which I don't think one person in ten would have noticed at the time, there were no visible signs of the approaching disaster.

The sailors saw that they could do nothing but row from the sinking ship and so save, at any rate, some lives.

"She lay just as if waiting for the order to go on again when some trifling matter had been adjusted. But, in a few moments, we saw the covers being lifted from the boats and the crews allotted to them standing by and uncoiling the ropes which were to lower them. We then began to realise that it was a more serious matter than we had at first supposed.

"My first thought was to go down to get more clothing and some money, but seeing people pouring up the stairs, I decided that it was better to cause no confusion to people coming up by attempting to get to my cabin.

"Presently we heard the order, 'All men stand back away from the boats. All ladies retire to the next deck below,' which was the smoking room or B deck. The men all stood away and waited in absolute silence, some leaning against the end railings of the deck, others pacing slowly up and down.

"The boats were then swung out and lowered from A Deck. When they were level with B deck, where all the women were collected, the women got in quietly, with the exception of some, who refused to leave their husbands.

"In some cases they were torn from their husbands and pushed into boats, but in many instances they were allowed to remain, since there was no one to insist that they should go.

"Looking over the side, one saw the boats from aft already in the water slipping quietly away into the darkness.

"Presently the boats near me were lowered with much creaking as the new ropes slipped through the pulleys and blocks down the ninety feet which separated them from the water.

"An officer in uniform came up as one boat went down and shouted out 'When you're afloat, row round to the companion ladder and stand by with other boats for orders.'

'Aye aye sir,' came the reply, but I don't think any boat was able to obey the order, for when they were afloat and had their oars at work the condition of the rapidly settling liner was much more apparent. In common prudence the sailors saw that they could do nothing but row from the sinking ship and so save, at any rate, some lives.

"They, no doubt, anticipated that the suction from such an enormous vessel would be more than usually dangerous to the crowded boat, which was mostly filled with women.

"All this time there was no trace of any disorder. There was no panic or rush to the boats, and there were no scenes of women sobbing hysterically, such as one generally pictures happening at such times.

"Everyone seemed to realise so slowly that there was imminent danger that when it was realised that we might all be presently in the sea, with nothing but our lifebelts to support us until we were picked up by passing steamers, it was extraordinary how calm everyone was, how completely self-controlled we were as, one by one, the boats filled with women and children were lowered and rowed away into the night.

"Presently word went round among us that men were to be put in boats on the starboard side, I was on the port side.

"Most of the men walked across the deck to see if this was true. I remained where I was, and slowly afterwards I heard the call 'Any more ladies?'

When they were level with B deck, where all the women were collected, the women got in quietly, with the exception of some, who refused to leave their husbands.

"Looking over the side of the ship, I saw boat no. 13 swinging level with B deck. It was half full of women. Again the call was repeated 'Any more ladies?' I saw none coming. Then one of the crew looked up and said 'Any more ladies on your deck sir?' 'No,' I replied.

" 'Then you'd better jump.' he said. I dropped and fell into the bottom of the boat as they cried 'Lower away.'

"As the boat began to descend two ladies were pushed hurriedly through the crowd on B deck, and a baby ten months old was passed down after them. Then down we went, the crew shouting out directions to those lowering us. 'Level,' 'Aft,' 'Stern,' 'Both together!' until we were some ten feet away from the water.

"Here occurred the only anxious moment we had during the whole of our experience from the time of our leaving the deck to our reaching the Carpathia.

"Immediately below our boat was the exhaust of the condensers, and a huge stream of water was pouring all the time from the ship's side just below the waterline. It was plain that we ought to be smart away from it if we were to escape swamping when we touched the water.

DEATH OF THE TITANIC

"We had no officers on board, and no petty officer or member of the crew to take charge, so one of the stokers shouted, 'Some one find the pin which releases the boat from the ropes and pull it up.' No one knew where it was. We felt as well as we could on the floor and along the sides, but found nothing. It was difficult to move among so many people. We had sixty or seventy on board.

"Down we went, and presently we floated with our ropes still holding us, and washing us away from the side of the vessel, while the swell of the sea urged us back against the side again.

"The resultant of all these forces was that we were carried parallel to the ship's side, and directly under boat no. 14, which had filled rapidly with men and was coming down on us in a way that threatened to submerge our boat.

" 'Stop lowering 14,' our crew shouted, and then the crew of no. 14, now only twenty feet above, cried out the same. The distance to the top, however was some seventy feet, and the creaking of the pulleys must have deadened all sound to those above, for down she came – fifteen feet, ten feet, five feet, and a stoker and I reached up and touched the bottom of the swinging boat above our heads. The next drop would have brought her on our heads.

"Just before she dropped, another stoker sprang to the ropes with his knife open in his hand. 'One,' I heard him say, and then 'Two,' as the knife cut through the pulley rope.

"The next moment the exhaust stream carried us clear, while boat no. 14 dropped into the water, taking the space we had occupied a moment before. Our gunwales were almost touching. We drifted away easily, and when our oars were got out we headed directly away from the ship.

"The crew seemed to me to be mostly cooks. They sat in their white jackets, two to an oar, with a stoker at the tiller. There was a certain amount of shouting from one end of the boat to the other, and the discussion as to which way we should go was finally decided by our electing as captain the stoker who was steering, and by all agreeing to obey his orders. He set to work at once to get into touch with the other boats, calling upon them and getting as close to them as seemed wise, so that when search boats came in the morning to look for us there would be more chance that all would be rescued.

A CALM SEA

"It was now one o'clock in the morning. The starlight night was beautiful, but as there was no moon it was not very light. The sea was as calm as a pond. There was just a gentle heave as the boat dipped up and down in the swell. It was an ideal night, except for the bitter cold.

"In the distance the Titanic looked enormous. Her length and her great bulk were outlined in black against the starry sky. Every porthole and saloon was blazing with light. It was impossible to think that anything could be wrong with such a leviathan were it not for that ominous tilt downward in the bows, where the water was by now up to the lowest row of portholes.

"At about two o'clock, we observed her settling very rapidly with the bows and the bridge completely under water. She slowly tilted straight on end with the stern vertically upwards. As she did so the lights in the cabins and the saloons which had not flickered for a moment since we left, died out, flashed once more and then went out altogether.

"At the same time, the machinery roared down through the vessel with a groaning rattle that could have been heard for miles.

"It was the weirdest sound, surely, that could have been heard in the middle of the ocean. It was not yet quite the end. To our amazement she remained in that upright position for a time, which I estimate as five minutes.

"It was certainly for some minutes that we watched at least 150 feet of the Titanic towering up above the level of the sea, looming black against the sky. Then with a quiet, slanting dive she disappeared beneath the waters. Our eyes had looked for the last time on the gigantic vessel in which we set out from Southampton.

"Then there fell on our ears the most appalling noise that human being ever heard—the cries of hundreds of our fellow-beings struggling in the icy waters, crying for help with a cry that we knew would not be answered.

"We longed to return to pick up some of those who were swimming, but this would have meant the swamping of our boat and the loss of all of use"

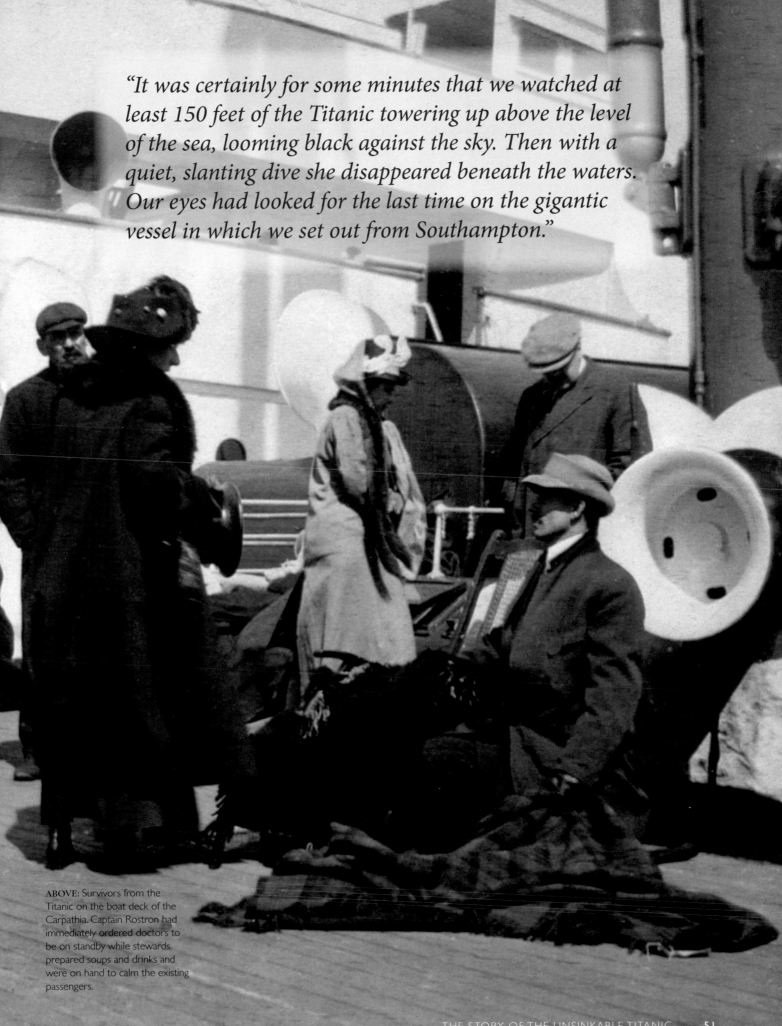

"It was certainly for some minutes that we watched at least 150 feet of the Titanic towering up above the level of the sea, looming black against the sky. Then with a quiet, slanting dive she disappeared beneath the waters. Our eyes had looked for the last time on the gigantic vessel in which we set out from Southampton."

ABOVE: Survivors from the Titanic on the boat deck of the Carpathia. Captain Rostron had immediately ordered doctors to be on standby while stewards prepared soups and drinks and were on hand to calm the existing passengers.

THE LANDING OF THE SURVIVORS.

Affecting Scenes of Joy and Sorrow,

THINLY CLAD WOMEN.

Men Kiss the Knees of Their Loved Ones.

NEW YORK, Friday.

The scenes in dock as the survivors landed were full of suppressed excitement.

Men were in hysterics, women fainting, children almost crushed in the arms of those welcoming them.

Men fell down to kiss the knees of their beloved ones, women shrieked and wept, and collapsed in the arms of their brothers and husbands.

The number of badly injured was not nearly so large as had been imagined.

The cases requiring hospital attention were few, but the strain of the trial of their lives had left unmistakable signs in the faces of the arrivals.

Some could barely talk, others could not refrain from shouting. What was a joyous occasion to some killed the last rays of hope in the breasts of others.

Many were the affecting scenes both of joy and sorrow.

The process of docking actually began shortly after nine o'clock in the evening. The disembarking of the survivors had practically concluded by half-past ten.

When most of the passengers had departed crowds remained about to get a glimpse of the rescuing steamer and to hear the harrowing stories which had been brought back by the ship.

DRAWN FACES.

Among the most affecting scenes at the landing was the sight of the women steerage survivors as they came down from the deck. Thinly clad and shivering, their eyes red with constant weeping. In their faces was the drawn, tense look of a desperate haunting fear.

They were taken care of at once by members of the numerous charitable organisations who were at hand.

Among these was a committee of Stock Exchange brokers, who went distributing gold, part of the 20,000 dol. subscription that had been made up in the past few days.

It was learned from the survivors that five, some said six, of the rescued died on board the Carpathia, and were buried at sea.

Three of these were sailors, the other two or three were passengers.

Exposure to the ice and the cold sea where the Titanic foundered had brought about their deaths, though everything possible was done for them.—Reuter.

J. Bruce Ismay

Ismay appeared shell-shocked as he holed himself up in isolation aboard Carpathia, trying to take in the enormity of what had happened. The press on both sides of the Atlantic – in particular the Hearst newspapers in America - turned their guns on White Star's managing director. There was no hiatus while official inquiries took their course; Ismay was damned by the very fact that he had survived when so many souls were lost. One piece of vituperative journalism suggested the White Star logo should be changed to 'yellow liver'. There was personal animosity between Hearst and Ismay, which went a long way to explaining the amount of opprobrium heaped upon White Star's senior executive.

The charges were serious enough to stir Ismay into publishing a rebuttal before testifying at the US inquiry. With regard to getting in the lifeboat he said: 'At that time there was not a woman on the boat deck, nor any passengers of any class, so far as we could see or hear.' Perhaps the most serious allegation was that he had interfered in the running of the ship, effectively pulling rank on Captain Smith. Ismay insisted he was aboard only as a passenger and observer, and wielded no executive power. Countering passenger testimonies that he had discussed the issue of making good time with Smith, Ismay said he gave Titanic's master no instruction to press on at 22 knots through the ice field in order to reach New York ahead of schedule, nor did he pressurise him into doing so. Captain Smith, of course, was unable to tender his opinion, but Carpathia's Captain Rostron assured the inquiry that he - Smith – would have ignored any such overtures had they been made.

ABOVE: Benjamin Guggenheim, the wealthy American, also went down with the ship. It later emerged he had boarded the ship with his mistress the French singer Madame Léontine Aubart. It was reported that after escorting Madame Aubert and her maid to the lifeboats he returned to the grand staircase with his secretary to drink brandy and smoke a cigar saying 'We've dressed our best and are prepared to go down like gentlemen'.

OPPOSITE: J. Bruce Ismay, the director of the White Star Line. His father Thomas had founded the company and Ismay took over as chairman after his death in 1899. Before the Titanic was built the company already had a dubious safety record with several ships and many lives lost.

Exonerated

Second Officer Charles Lightoller, the most senior surviving crew member, gave testimony that showed Ismay in a more favourable light. Far from labelling Ismay's survival story a piece of craven self-preservation, Lightoller said he 'kept repeating that he ought to have gone down with the ship because he found that women had gone down'.

Mr A Clement Edwards, MP, Counsel for the Dock Workers' Union at the British Inquiry, took a different view. He argued that because of his position Ismay should have done more than cast a cursory glance around the boat deck before entering the lifeboat. 'A managing director going on board a liner, commercially responsible for it and taking upon himself certain functions, had a special moral obligation and duty more than is possessed by one passenger to another passenger.' Lord Mersey, who headed the British Inquiry, thought moral duty beyond the purview of the investigation. He exonerated Ismay, saying it was perfectly reasonable for him to climb into a lifeboat after helping so many in their bid for safety. 'Had he not jumped in he would simply have added one more life, namely his own, to the number of those lost.'

J. Bruce Ismay was aloof and socially awkward. He had pared construction costs to a minimum, but they met existing Board of Trade regulations. Given that Captain Smith was a veteran with over 40 years seafaring experience – and on his last trip before retirement – it seems highly improbable that he would have bowed to undue influence. Ismay's survival was a different matter; a stick that many could, and did, beat him with. By June 1913 he had stepped down as White Star chairman and president of International Mercantile Marine. He died in 1937, aged 74.

RACKETS CHAMPION.

How Mr. Charles Williams Escaped From the Doomed Ship.

NEW YORK, Friday.

Mr. Charles Williams, the racket player, of Harrow, who was on his way to New York to defend his title of world's champion, said he left the squash court on the Titanic at 10.30.

He was in the smoking room when he first felt the shock. He rushed out and saw an iceberg which seemed to loom over a hundred feet above the deck. It broke up amidships and floated away.

Eventually he jumped from the boat deck on the starboard side into the sea, getting as far away from the steamer as possible.

He was nine hours in a small boat standing with the water up to his knees before he was picked up.—Reuter.

JUMPED LIKE SHEEP.

NEW YORK, Friday.

Mr. George Brayton, of California, related how he was standing beside Mr. Henry B. Harris when the latter bade his wife goodbye. Both started towards the side where the lifeboat was being lowered. Mr Harris was told of the rule that the women should leave first.

"Yes, I know," he replied," I will stay.

Shortly after the lifeboat left a man jumped overboard, and the other men followed. It was like sheep following their leader.

Shortly before the ship sank there was an explosion which made the ship tremble from stem to stern.

Mr. Brayton also said that he saw one of the stewards shoot a foreigner who tried to press past a number of women in order to gain a place in the lifeboats.—Reuter's Special.

IN A COLLAPSIBLE BOAT.

NEW YORK, Friday.

Mr. August Wennerstrom, of Sweden, spied a collapsible boat behind one of the smoke stacks as the vessel was sinking.

With three other men he managed to tear it from its lashings, and the four jumped overboard with it. The boat turned over four times, but each time they managed to right it.

While drifting about Mr. Wennerstrom said he saw at least two hundred men in the water who were drowned.—Reuter's Special.

TURNED OUT OF THE BOATS.

NEW YORK, Friday.

A thrilling story was told by Ellen Shine, a twenty-year-old girl from County Cork.

"Those who were able to get out of bed," said Miss Shine, rushed to the upper deck, where they were met by members of the crew, who endeavoured to keep them in the steerage quarters. The women, however, rushed past these men and finally reached the upper deck.

"When they were informed that the boat was sinking most of them fell on their knees and began to pray.

"I saw one of the lifeboats and made for it. In it there were already four men from the steerage, who refused to obey an officer who ordered them out. They were, however, finally turned out."—Reuter's Special.

LEAPS FROM DECKS

THE SPECTACLE THE SURVIVORS SAW FROM THE BOATS

All the best accounts vary with regard to the amount of disorder on the Titanic.

Of the many descriptions given most agree that the shock of striking, although ripping the great sides, did not greatly jar the entire vessel, for the blow was a glancing one.

The most distressing stories are those giving the experiences of passengers in the lifeboats. These tell not only of their own suffering : they give harrowing details of how they saw the great hull break in two and sink amid explosions.

It now appears that the after-part sank first and the sinking of the forward portion of the vessel followed.

As the groups of survivors witnessed this awful spectacle they plainly saw many of those whom they had just left behind leaping from the decks into the water.

OPPOSITE PAGE TOP: The forward staircase in the first class accommodation was the ship's crowning glory and featured ornate gilded balustrades and oak panelling. Above it rose an impressive wrought iron and glass dome with a clock on the upper landing with distinctive carvings depicting the figures of Glory and Honour. These led to the reception room then onto the dining saloon. From the staircases the passengers could reach their staterooms which provided every luxury. Silver plated lamps and satin counterpanes were provided with en-suite marble bathrooms.

OPPOSITE PAGE BELOW RIGHT: A portrait of the ship painted in the trademark White Star Line colours dominated an advertising poster for the Titanic and the Olympic. She was to attract a wide range of passengers from the very rich travelling in first class to immigrants of several different nationalities travelling in third class, hoping to start a new life in North America. In normal circumstances the ship would have carried its maximum capacity of 2436 passengers but the long running coal dispute had made travel uncertain and many deferred their plans. Eventually there were only 1317 passengers on board alongside the crew members.

LEFT: Lady Duff Gordon survived in a boat carrying just 12 people.

OPPOSITE PAGE BELOW LEFT: The Titanic boasted an indoor swimming pool located on the middle deck. Measuring 32 feet by 13 feet and tiled in blue and white, it was available only to first class passengers with special times set aside each day for female and male bathers. Adjacent to this was the Turkish and Electric Bath Establishment. Sauna rooms and Electric Turkish baths were available with masseurs on hand. A gymnasium and a full-size squash court complemented these facilities.

Miss Shine rushed to the upper deck where they were met by members of the crew, who endeavoured to keep them in the steerage quarters.

The 'mystery ship'

In the blackest moments aboard Titanic, when all hope appeared to be lost and the prospect of catastrophic loss of life loomed large, a ray of hope seemed to appear well inside the horizon. A ship was spotted some six miles away a fraction off Titanic's port bow. Fourth Officer Joseph Boxhall had the potential saviour under observation for a considerable time and fired off a number of distress rockets to alert her to their plight. Although attempts to contact the ship by Morse lights failed, Boxhall testified that the ship was, for a time, heading in Titanic's direction. Such was Captain Smith's confidence that here lay miraculous salvation that he ordered Lifeboat No. 8 to row towards the mystery neighbour.

Hopes were dashed almost as soon as they were raised. The ship turned about, as Boxhall said, 'until at last I only saw her stern light'. Lifeboat No. 8 had covered three or four miles by daybreak, but made no headway in reaching the ship. By the time Carpathia arrived on the scene, the mystery vessel was nowhere in sight.

The subsequent inquiries assumed the ship Boxhall spotted was the Californian, which only served to fix the Leyland liner and her captain as the villain of the piece. To muddy the waters further, Californian also sighted an unidentified ship sometime before 11 pm. Stanley Lord, Californian's master, said it was around the same size as his own vessel – 6,200 tons – and definitely not Titanic. Rockets were observed, but these were not interpreted as distress signals. Attempts to contact the ship failed and it eventually sailed away.

The position of the Californian relative to the Titanic has been estimated at anything from 8 to 21 miles. What is certain – and may exculpate Lord – is that the Californian was stationary from 10.20 pm until 6.00 am. That doesn't tally with Boxhall's account of a ship that headed in Titanic's direction before turning tail – in short, a ship clearly under way.

The 'mystery ship' remains a nautical enigma. The 1912 inquiries overlooked ill-fitting pieces of the puzzle, and Stanley Lord carried the stigma of the Titanic disaster to his grave in 1962.

MR. ISMAY'S TELEGRAM

The managers of the White Star Line at Liverpool have received the following telegram from New York:—

Press here to-day comment most favourably on the behaviour of the officers and crew of the Titanic under extraordinary and trying circumstances, and we are satisfied that the discipline was everything that we could desire.—ISMAY.

OFFICERS ISOLATED.

NEW YORK, Friday.

The officers and sailors saved from the Titanic are being kept practically isolated on board the Red Star liner Lapland.—Reuter's Special.

CREW TO RETURN AT ONCE.

NEW YORK, Friday (7.30 p.m.).

Arrangements have been made for 182 men and 20 women survivors of the Titanic's crew to sail for England tomorrow on board the Lapland.—Reuter.

THE LAST OF MR. STEAD.

NEW YORK, Friday, 7.30 p.m.

Some of the newspapers print a brief account of the death of Mr. W. T. Stead, whom some of the survivors think they saw on a raft with Colonel Astor after the Titanic had sunk.

Other witnesses say they saw Colonel Astor, with Major Butt, President Taft's aide-de-camp, on the bridge as the ship took her final plunge. If this is correct it is probable that both Mr. Stead and Colonel Astor, when they found themselves in the sea, swam to an overturned raft in a final effort to escape.

At any rate, the two men who were taken to be Mr. Stead and Colonel Astor finally succumbed to cold and exposure, released their hold on the raft, and disappeared into the sea.—Reuter.

OPPOSITE PAGE: Another of Browne's photographs shows a view of Titanic's bridge and one of her lifeboats. At the enquiry held after the disaster it was revealed that the regulation lifeboat drill had failed to take place on the Sunday morning.; both passengers and crew members were unfamiliar with the ship's layout, routines and the equipment.

LEFT: The first class dining saloon measured over 100 feet in length and was designed with Jacobean style alcoves and leaded windows. It was able to seat 554 diners who were greeted by flowers, silver and cut crystal. Eleven course dinners were served with wine and included delicacies such as caviar, lobster and champagne.

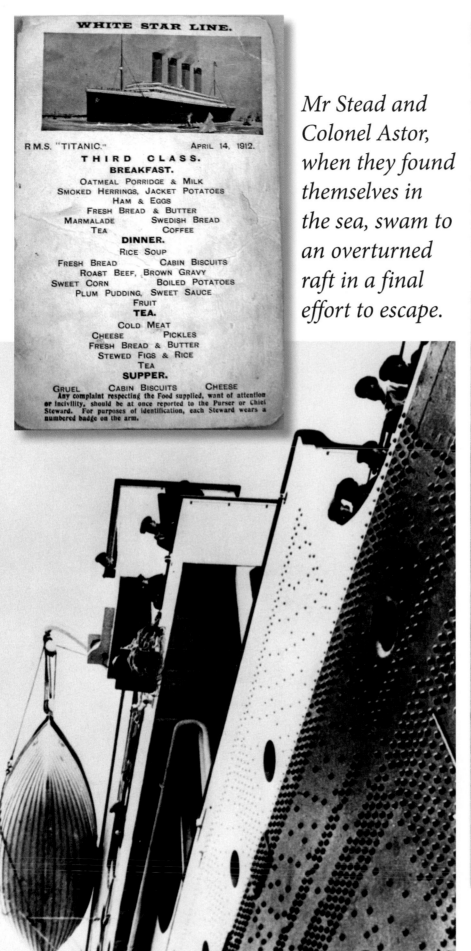

WHITE STAR LINE.

R.M.S. "TITANIC."   APRIL 14, 1912.

THIRD CLASS.

BREAKFAST.
OATMEAL PORRIDGE & MILK
SMOKED HERRINGS, JACKET POTATOES
HAM & EGGS
FRESH BREAD & BUTTER
MARMALADE   SWEDISH BREAD
TEA   COFFEE

DINNER.
RICE SOUP
FRESH BREAD   CABIN BISCUITS
ROAST BEEF, BROWN GRAVY
SWEET CORN   BOILED POTATOES
PLUM PUDDING, SWEET SAUCE
FRUIT

TEA.
COLD MEAT
CHEESE   PICKLES
FRESH BREAD & BUTTER
STEWED FIGS & RICE
TEA

SUPPER.
GRUEL   CABIN BISCUITS   CHEESE
Any complaint respecting the Food supplied, want of attention
or incivility, should be at once reported to the Purser or Chief
Steward. For purposes of identification, each Steward wears a
numbered badge on the arm.

Mr Stead and Colonel Astor, when they found themselves in the sea, swam to an overturned raft in a final effort to escape.

HUGE DEMAND FOR BOATS.

CHANGES IN LINERS.

COLLAPSIBLES FOR THE OLYMPIC.

MR. ISMAY'S ORDER.

Whatever the Board of Trade may do, the disaster to the Titanic is causing several of the leading passenger lines to make an immediate increase in the number of boats their vessels carry. In some cases they have already decided to supply sufficient boats for every person on board.

A Reuter telegram from New York, dated Saturday, stated: "Mr. Ismay announced that he has given instructions to all lines under the control of the International Mercantile Marine Company to equip all steamers with sufficient lifeboats and rafts to carry all the passengers and crew without regard to the regulations prescribed by the Government of any nation."

The International Mercantile Marine Company comprises the White Star, American, Red Star, Atlantic Transport, Leyland, and Dominion Lines. It has 126 ships, with a gross tonnage of 1,136,082.

Our special correspondent in Southampton telegraphs: "I have made a tour of the Olympic, sister ship to the Titanic. I counted sixteen lifeboats and four rafts, but the White Star Line are evidently determined to take no more risks, for moored alongside were lighters containing ten collapsible boats, while many others were lying on the quay. Altogether, I learned, forty additional collapsible boats will be carried by the Olympic when she sails for New York on Wednesday."

Mr. Hugh A. Allan, chairman of the Allan Steamship Line, in an interview with a representative of *The Daily Mail*, said: "We are arranging to put eight more boats in the Tunisian immediately. As soon as we can obtain them additional boats will be supplied to all the ships of the line, sufficient to carry every passenger and every member of the crew wherever there is enough deck space to hold the craft. In my opinion, the disaster will lead to the supply of two wireless operators for every liner crossing the Atlantic. At present only the biggest ships carry two operators. And an operator, like everybody else, must sleep sometimes."

The Welin Davit and Engineering Company inform us that as an immediate consequence of the calamity they have sent away a deck plan for an important Transatlantic vessel making provision for 44 boats. Before the disaster the vessel would probably have been fitted with only 20 or 24 boats.

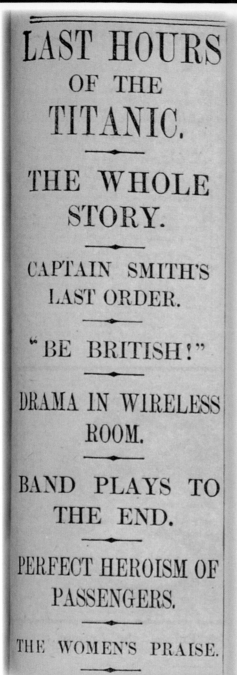

LAST HOURS
OF THE
TITANIC.

THE WHOLE
STORY.

CAPTAIN SMITH'S
LAST ORDER.

" BE BRITISH ! "

DRAMA IN WIRELESS
ROOM.

BAND PLAYS TO
THE END.

PERFECT HEROISM OF
PASSENGERS.

THE WOMEN'S PRAISE.

The secret of the greatest catastrophe in the annals of seafaring was disclosed in the series of special editions of *The Daily Mail* published late yesterday morning. We now know in what wise the Titanic met her doom.

It is a thrilling, heroic, yet tragic and terrible story, worthy to take its place in maritime history with the matchless conduct of the British soldier in the Birkenhead and of the British Bluejacket in the Victoria—a story of death confronted with firmness—of unselfish love, of devotion to duty such as will ever render glorious the name of the wireless telegraphist Phillips.

The Titanic was steaming at 21 knots, somewhat less than full speed, on Sunday night, in clear weather and under a starlit sky. The temperature was low, indicating the proximity of ice. Most of the passengers had gone below for the night, but a card party or two were playing in the smoke-room.

Suddenly, at 11.40pm, the ship struck the ice, not violently, but with a gentle glancing blow. Incredible as it sounds, the concussion was scarcely felt by hundreds of the 2,340 people on board.

Yet the blow had been fatal. With a dreadful sound of rending metal the bottom plating of the Titanic was ripped off from her stem to the centre of the mammoth hull. She stopped her engines, cleared the ice with the way still on her, and lay to.

The boats were swung out and orders were issued to all below to come on deck. The men were commanded to stand aside and make way for the women. Then followed eternal partings, filled with all the anguish of death, as the peril was realised. Some wives refused to leave their husbands; others were hurried weeping into boats. There was no confusion or disorder. Perfect discipline was maintained by the officers and men. Among the passengers Major Butt, Colonel J. J. Astor, Mr. Stead, Mr. Howard Case and the American novelist Mr. Jacques Futrelle were conspicuous for their fine conduct, assisting the women and children into boats. All remained to perish.

Three Italians who disobeyed the rule of the sea, "women and children first," were shot down.

Meanwhile Phillips, the wireless operator, was calmly and coolly sending out the cry for help over the cold dark sea. He continued, "sending... sending" in the graphic words of Mr Bride, the assistant telegraphist, with entire disregard of self. His messages, transmitted with precision, were read by half a dozen ships, which turned their heads towards the scene of disaster. He continued at his post of duty even after the captain told him that there was no more to be done, and gave the order, "Every man for himself."

While the boats were filling, the Titanic's band mustered on deck and continued

ABOVE: (left to right) Crew members William Murdoch, Henry Wilde, Joseph Boxhall and Captain Edward Smith. Murdoch, the first officer, was in command of the Titanic at the time of the collision and was in charge of the lifeboats on the starboard side. He went down with the ship.

playing up to the very end, and from the boats as they rowed off, its strains could be heard. As the ship went down at 2.20am on Monday morning, it struck up an American recessional, and with that ringing in their ears the 1,635 living beings who died in the Titanic went down.

Captain Smith was on the bridge immediately after the disaster. He remained at his post throughout, issuing orders with perfect composure and taking every measure for the safety of those committed to his care. After the boats had cleared the ship he gave a brief order to the multitude on board:

"Men, you have done your full duty. You can do no more. It's every man for himself."

As the ship sank lower in the water, as the tilt of the boat increased, as the moment of death approached, Captain Smith took his megaphone and shouted, "Be British" the electrical word, the "Nelson touch" which raises the weakest of men above himself. And still there was perfect order in that dying ship.

The wireless weakened, the list grew, Phillips was still "sending... sending" details to the Carpathia of where the Titanic lay. The last messages flickered out. His work was done. It remained for him and his companion Mr Bride to take their chance outside the wireless cabin.

From afar, the boats witnessed the last stupendous scene. The bows of the Titanic sank in the sea. Her stern rose in the air, rose steadily, till it was upright. The whole vessel took a plunge and disappeared. In the thrilling words of Mr Beesley, a former science master at Dulwich College (as told to Reuter):

As the ship sank lower in the water, as the tilt of the boat increased, as the moment of death approached, Captain Smith took his megaphone and shouted, "Be British".

"Then there fell on our ears the most appalling noise that human being ever heard—the cries of hundreds of our fellow beings struggling in the icy waters, crying for help with a cry that we knew could not be answered".

To answer this last despairing appeal meant death to the women and children in the boats, and for that reason the survivors had to close their ears and steel their hearts to the tragedy enacted in their sight and hearing.

At the final moment, Captain Smith climbed down from the bridge and committed himself to the water. A boat offered aid , but he refused it at the price of risk to others and chose for himself the lot of death, British to the last.

In the ship a great number of men struggled for a raft which floated among the wreckage and escaped being drawn down by the swirl when the Titanic sank. Some thirty-five men gained the raft. Colonel Gracie, of the United States Army, tells a moving story which will ever redound to the glory of man. When the full complement that the raft would bear had been reached other men in the water forbore to fight for a place upon it, and, shouting their blessings and their farewell, threw up their hands and went down.

All ranks and all stations responsible for the work of the ship were true to their duty from first to last. It is this fact which crowns that scene of agony with such imperishable glory.

The sufferings of the women and children in the boats were heartrending. The cold was bitter; there was no food; they lay huddled together; waiting through that fearful night for the Samaritan ship Carpathia to arrive, with the memory of the scenes through which they had passed and the immense personal bereavement which many of them had suffered harrowing their souls.

The official figures of saved are now 705 and of the dead 1,635.

Of the survivors, no fewer than 85 were yesterday in various New York Hospitals suffering from the terrible shock they had undergone.

WOMEN AND HEROES
Story of the Man at the Wheel
From Our Own Correspondent, New York, Friday

The outstanding feature of practically all the narratives of the great tragedy of the Atlantic is the testimony they bear to the unflinching heroism of passengers and crew alike.

Nothing impressed me more in the performance of my sad duty last evening when gathering the facts of this incredible disaster from the bereaved and distracted survivors than the admiration expressed by the women for the men who sacrificed their lives in order that the women might escape. "We think," one woman exclaimed with a sob, "that the men did too much for us. More of them ought to have got into boats."

There are only a few exceptions to the unvarying tales of heroism, and the exceptions are due to the excitement at the last moments in the steerage, which forced the officers to shoot three Italians, and to the frenzy which apparently seized some of the stokers, who, it is alleged, try to seize the boats.

The bearers of every name familiar to the world, Mr. Stead, Major Butt, Colonel Astor, Mr. Isidor Straus and others comported themselves according to the highest standards of chivalry and self sacrifice. Mr. Stead and Colonel Astor, according to one witness, were last seen clinging to a piece of wreckage from which, when their limbs were frozen, they slipped to death.

Smiling and lifting his hat while his feet were immersed in the water creeping over the deck, Major Butt's last recorded act was to assist a lady into a boat and bid her farewell. Colonel Astor, says Miss Hilda Slater, assisted his young wife into a boat and took, by invitation, the last seat, which, however, he relinquished when he saw a woman hurrying up.

"Ladies must go first," the millionaire observed, and then lit a cigarette and leaned over the rail. He shouted to his wife "Goodbye, dearie, I'll join you later."

Even more heroic, if possible, was the behaviour of the great merchant Mr Isidor Straus, who when urged to save himself exclaimed, "Not as long as a single woman remains aboard." Sailors tried to force Mrs Straus into a boat but she clung to her husband and said, "I'll stay where you are. We've lived for forty years together, and will not part now in old age." She died in his arms as the giant ship plunged to the depths.

Apart from the heroism displayed, the most conspicuous feature of the disaster seems to have been the invincible confidence of everyone aboard of the floating qualities of the Titanic. When told that she had collided with an iceberg, their attitude

CAPTAIN SMITH.

HOW HE WENT DOWN WITH HIS SHIP.

"BE BRITISH!"

The reports circulated in New York immediately after the Carpathia's arrival that Captain E. J. Smith, the Titanic's commander, committed suicide on the bridge were baseless slanders on a brave man dead. Our New York correspondent's prompt information enabled us to suppress the story almost as soon as it was published.

The fuller reports available to-day combine to show that the captain was on the bridge at the time of or immediately after the slight shock caused by the collision with the iceberg. He took all steps humanly possible to minimise the consequences.

His first act was to send for the carpenters to sound the ship and report the extent of the damage. While they were doing so he told the wireless operators to prepare to send out the call for help. Ten minutes later he knew the ship was sinking and ordered the call to be sent.

At the same moment the captain's order was being shouted through the ship for all passengers to put on lifebelts and come on deck. The boats were lowered under the captain's orders, and the women and children saved. When all the boats had gone Captain Smith still stood on the bridge. On this point all the narratives are clear.

"Captain Smith's unparalleled self-sacrifice and heroism," says one account, "are commended by high and low. Before he was washed off the bridge he called through his megaphone 'Be British' to the mass on the decks below. Later he was seen helping those struggling in the water, refusing an opportunity to save himself. Other officers followed this noble example. The bravery of the whole ship's company is a matter to record."

The captain went down with his ship, though the actual manner of his drowning can only be judged from the confused accounts of the survivors. One of these says that as the Titanic began to plunge the captain leapt from the bridge and was seen no more; another that a wave swept him from the bridge into the icy water; and a third that an effort was made to drag him into a lifeboat, but that he cried, "Let me go!" and jerked himself free and went down.

seemed to say, "So much the worse for the iceberg."

When the vessel struck, relates Colonel Gracie, the passengers were so little alarmed that they joked, and some of them facetiously picked up fragments of ice which had fallen on the deck and offered them to friends as mementos of the occasion.

Many, after the initial shock, retired to their cabins, where death apparently overtook them in their sleep. "You're a fool if you jump," are the last recorded words of Colonel Astor to Mr Barber, who urged him to get clear of the ship. "The Titanic can't sink."

ABOVE: Commander J.J Boxhall pictured in 1957 when he was appointed technical adviser on the film *A Night to Remember* which portrayed the sinking of the Titanic. He was the fourth officer on the ship and was responsible for calculating the position of the ship for the distress signal. He was put in charge of lifeboat No. 2 and was able to alert the Carpathia with a green flare when he spotted her on the horizon.

UNFILLED BOATS

In the smoking saloon several men resumed a game of cards which the rasping of the iceberg on the sides of the liner interrupted. They were never seen again.

Others for a long time after the collision were seen calmly promenading the decks, undecided whether it was necessary to take refuge in one of the boats. In many instances the officers were obliged to exert their persuasive powers to the utmost to induce ladies to leave the vessel, telling them that it was advisable to lighten the damaged liner, and that as soon as the mischief was ascertained and repaired they might return. This accounts in large measure for the fact that several boats left the Titanic half filled and carrying male passengers.

The first lifeboat to leave is said to have contained only thirteen persons, although its capacity was fifty. "The fact is," Mrs Edgar Myer, of New York, declared, "We were not made to realise the seriousness of the situation and accepted so completely the statement that there was no danger that many people got into the boats as though it were an unnecessary nuisance. The big vessel seemed so much safer."

"The people," said another lady, "filled the boats in any order just as though they expected to get out again, and were doing it only because they were obliged to by the management. The work of lowering the boats was done in a haphazard way, and the crew appeared not to have had enough practice in manipulating them."

All the time the band kept up its cheerful performance of "ragtime" music, which only changed to more solemn strains in the last despairing heroic moments.

There is no shadow of doubt, apparently, that, despite repeated warnings of icebergs, the Titanic was steaming at 21 knots when she met her doom. This is testified to by Colonel Gracie and by numbers of seamen and passengers, who state that in the first-class saloons the conservation all day was occupied with the record they were understood to be making.

THE MAN AT THE WHEEL

What happened immediately after the collision occurred is told by Robert Hitchens, one of the surviving quartermasters of the Titanic and a native of Southampton, where he has a wife and two children. Hitchens was on duty at the wheel, and his story is as follows:

"I went on duty at eight o'clock on Sunday night and stood by the man at the wheel until ten. At ten o'clock I took the wheel for two hours. On the bridge from ten o'clock were First Officer Murdock, Fourth Officer Boxhall, and Sixth Officer Moody. In the crow's nest were Fleet and another man, whose name is unknown.

"Second Officer Lightoller, who was on watch while I stood by carrying messages and the like from 8 to 10, sent me soon after 8 to tell the carpenter to look out for the fresh water supply, as it might be in danger of freezing at the temperature, which was then 31 deg. He gave the crow's nest a strict order to look out for small icebergs.

"Second Officer Lightoller was relieved by First Officer Murdock at 10. I took the wheel then.

"At 11.40 three gongs were sounded from the crow's nest, the signal for something right ahead. At the same time one of the men in the nest telephoned to the bridge that there was a large iceberg right ahead.

"As officer Murdock's hand was on the lever to stop the engines the crash came.

"He stopped the engines and then immediately by another lever closed the watertight doors. The skipper, Captain Smith, came from the chart room on to the bridge. His first words were, 'Close the emergency doors.'

" 'They are already closed, sir' Mr Murdock replied. 'Send to the carpenter and tell him to sound the ship,' was the skipper's next order. The message was sent to the carpenter, but the carpenter never came up to report. He was probably the first man to lose his life.

"The skipper looked at the commutator, which shows what direction the ship is listing. He saw she carried a five-degrees list to starboard. The ship was then rapidly settling forward and all the steam sirens were blowing.

"By the skipper's orders given in the next few minutes the engines were put to work at pumping out the ship, and distress signals were sent by the Marconi wireless. Rockets were sent up from the bridge by Quartermaster Rowe, and all hands were ordered on deck.

"Lifebelts were served out to the crew, and every passenger and the stewards and other hands helped the sailors in getting the boats out.

"The order, 'Women and children first,' was given and enforced.

"I was at the wheel until 12.25am. It was my duty to stay there until relieved, and I was not relieved by anyone else but simply sent away.

"Second Officer Lightoller ordered me away. He told me to take charge of a certain boat and load it with women. I did so. There were thirty-two ladies, a sailor, and myself in the boat when it was lowered some time after one o'clock. I can't be sure of the time.

"The Titanic had 16 lifeboats and 2 collapsible boats.

ABANDONED RAFT

"All of them got away loaded, except that one of the collapsibles did not open properly and was used as a raft. Forty sailors and stewards who were floating in the water got on this raft later, had to abandon the raft, and were picked up by different boats. Some others were floating about on chairs when picked up.

"Every boat, so far as I saw, was full when lowered, and every boat that set out reached the Carpathia. A green light in one of the boats helped to keep us together, but there were other lights. One was an electric flashlight that a gentleman carried in his pocket.

"Our boat was 400 yards away when the ship went down. The suction near by must have been terrific, but we only rocked somewhat.

G. Whiteman, of Palmyra, New Jersey, the Titanic's barber, believes that the machinery was in some way so damaged by the crash that the front water-tight compartments failed to close tightly, although the rear ones were secure.

Whiteman's manner of escape was unique. He was blown off the deck by the second of two explosions in the boilers, and was in the water for more than two hours before he was picked up by a raft. The explosions,

Whiteman said, were caused by the rushing in of the water on the boilers.

"A bundle of deck chairs roped together was blown off the deck with me, and struck my back, injuring my spine, but it served as a temporary raft."

"The crew and passengers," Whiteman added, "had faith in the bulkhead system to save the ship. We were lowering the Berthon collapsible boat, but all were confident that the ship would get through until she took a terrible dip forward, and the water rushed up and swept over the deck into the engine rooms. The bow went clean down. I caught the pile of chairs as I was washed up against the rail. Then came the explosions which blew me fifteen feet.

"After the water had filled the forward compartments the ones at the stern could not save her. They did delay the ship's going down, and but for them hardly anyone could have got away. The water was too cold for me to swim. I was hardly more than a 100 feet away when the ship went down. The suction was not what one would expect and only rocked the water around me. I was picked up after two hours. I have done with the sea!"

The narrative of the greatest coherence by the survivors is that of Mr. Robert W. Daniel, of Philadelphia.

Not until two minutes before the Titanic went down did he leap from her rail, clad only in a bathrobe. For an hour he swam through the icy water naked, the robe having drifted off. He was picked up by a lifeboat frozen and semi-conscious. When he revived he was in the steerage of the Carpathia, where he lay between two sailors with both feet frozen.

Mr. Daniel is a Philadelphia banker and went to London on business in August. He was in the Carlton Hotel at the time of the fire there.

The Titanic was running along at twenty knots, he said, as he rested after being assisted from the Carpathia by two stewards. The night was clear and the stars shining brilliantly.

Danger was far from our thoughts, even when we entered the icefield. I was in my room when the shock came, and it did not seem great.

I ran on deck. A huge iceberg was floating by. It was at least 150 feet in the air and towered far above the Titanic. Beneath I heard it tearing into the sides of the vessel. From stern to stern the Titanic was ripped. We had not struck bow on but diagonally.

The ship pounded along the ice, her side being torn to shreds and the air compartments and bulkheads being pierced or smashed as the steel plates were ripped, the ship was doomed at once.

No one knew it, however. That was the real tragedy. There was no panic. People rushed on deck, of course, all in their nightclothes, but they were calm.

The officers went among the passengers assuring them that nothing was wrong and that the ship was unsinkable. They said it over and over again, and they repeated it— "unsinkable!" My friends and I myself even then thought the Titanic was as unsinkable as a railway station.

The iceberg swept astern like a mistwraith. On and on we went, our momentum carrying us forward. Not until we were a mile from the scene of the shock did the Titanic come to a stop. The decks were coated with snowy splinters of ice.

THE LAST SCENES

Assured that the accident would mean nothing more than a short delay I returned to my room. Half an hour later the alarm was sounded, voices crying through the ship: "All hands on deck. Adjust life-preservers."

This and the sound of hurrying feet roused me from bed. Throwing on a bathrobe I hurried on deck. Still nothing appeared to be wrong. The sea was perfectly calm and the Titanic lay motionless.

Men and women were on the decks apparently unexcited. There was absolutely no panic even then, but the crew had begun to swing out the lifeboats, and rafts were being lowered. I stood watching, unafraid, like the majority of others, because of my conviction that the Titanic could not go down.

I learned later that there was a conflict of orders given. When the boats were filled on the starboard side husbands were ordered to enter the smaller craft with their wives on the port side. The husbands were then driven back, the order being, "Women and children first." That explains why so many men survived.

In many instances within the range of my vision wives refused point-blank to leave their husbands. I saw members of the crew literally pull the women from the arms of the men and throw them over the side into the boats.

Mrs Isidor Straus clung to her husband, and none could force her from his side.

Not until the last five minutes did the awful realisation come that the end was at hand. The lights became dim and went out, but we could see. Slowly, ever so slowly, the surface of the water seemed to come up toward us. So gradual was it that even after I had adjusted the lifejacket about my body it seemed a dream.

Deck after deck was submerged. There was no lurching or grinding or crunching. The Titanic simply settled.

I was far up on one of the top decks

when I jumped. About me were many others in the water. My bathrobe floated away and it was very cold. I struck out at once. I turned my head, and my first glance took in the people swarming on the Titanic's deck. Hundreds were standing there helpless to ward off approaching death.

I saw Captain Smith on the bridge. My eyes seemingly clung to him. The deck from which I had leaped was immersed. The water had risen slowly, and was now to the floor of the bridge. Then it was to Captain Smith's waist. I saw him no more. He died a hero.

The bows of the Titanic were far beneath the surface, and to me only the four monster funnels and the two masts were now visible.

It was all over in an instant. The Titanic's stern rose completely out of the water and went up thirty, forty, sixty feet into the air. Then, with her body slanting at an angle of 45 deg., slowly the Titanic slipped out of sight.

GRIEF AND JOY.

SOUTHAMPTON'S MIXED EMOTIONS.

FROM OUR SPECIAL CORRESPONDENT.

SOUTHAMPTON, Friday.

Joy and sorrow met in the crowd which saw the last list of the survivors of the Titanic posted up outside the White Star Line offices here early this morning. Name after name was recognised and joyfully shouted from one to another, and name after name was sought and found missing. Smiles and tears, shouts and sobs. Here a woman fainting with the weight of despair; there a woman in hysterics with the shock of sudden joy.

Well-dressed women, poverty-stained women, old women, and young girls rubbed shoulders in the craving for names. It was a painful contrast between warm joy and grey despair; fate juggling with the masks of grief and laughter. Soon the happy ones went away, and there were left only those who could not believe in the finality of the posted lists and those who were left in a maddening state of uncertainty owing to the absence of initials to the firemen's names. For instance, there were 5 Olivers, 3 Blakes, 2 Cunninghams, 3 Moores, and 2 Barretts on the boat, and of the 1 or 2 saved none could say who was who.

FRANTIC WITH SUSPENSE.

The wives of these and other men of the same name were frantic with suspense, and throughout the day they were appealing for further information. "Is it my Jack or is it her George?" was the pathetic request uttered again and again by a woman who wore widow's weeds. Many names were duplicated and others wrongly spelt.

Now that the mayor is administering the distress fund destitution is vanishing from the stricken quarters. Well-known South-ampton women are visiting and relieving the cases I mentioned yesterday, but there still remain bedridden women who cannot get to the town hall, and unless they are sought out they will starve amid plenty. This afternoon I met Sister Frances Mag-dalen in a tramway-car on her way to an isolated case. She had just come away from a woman whose baby was two hours old. "Many of these women are lying help-less," she said, "and unless neighbours bring us information they will be left to lie in their poverty." There is another class of women who are in danger of starving; the women who do not live with their hus-bands, but whose men have gone down in the Titanic. These women will not go to the town hall for relief, but there are chil-dren to be considered.

The Mayor of Southampton's fund is growing every hour. This evening the total was well over £6,000. One woman who had received relief promptly returned the money to the mayor when she found her husband's name among the survivors.

The National Union of Ships' Stewards, Butchers, and Bakers to-night decided to start a fund for the distressed relatives of the members through the Titanic disaster, and instructed the Southampton secretary to grant meantime £2 per member to meet immediate needs.

The US Inquiry

Even as Carpathia was steaming towards New York with Titanic's survivors, America was making ready to learn the truth about why the world's greatest ship had foundered with so many of its citizens on board. Speculation was rife. The Hearst newspapers in particular were having a field day. There were chaotic scenes outside New York's White Star office. More heat than light was being generated, something Senator William Alden Smith decided to address as head of a government-level inquiry.

Smith knew he had to strike while the iron was hot, both to find answers while the episode was fresh in the mind, and also to circumvent any jurisdictional issues that might arise if the foreign contingent – including Bruce Ismay and the crew – were allowed to repatriate immediately, as had been their intention.

The proceedings began at the Waldorf-Astoria hotel on Friday 19 April, a mere four days after Titanic went to the bottom of the Atlantic Ocean. It sat for 18 days and heard testimony from over 80 witnesses.

Bruce Ismay, the first witness called, insisted Titanic was 'the latest thing in the art of shipbuilding; absolutely no money was spared in her construction'. On the issue of lifeboat provision, Ismay clung to the line that statutory requirements were met. Senator Smith said the fanfare and acclamation that greeted Titanic's launch masked insufficient testing of machinery and safety equipment. 'When the crisis came,' he said, 'a state of absolute unpreparedness stupefied both passengers and crew.'

BELOW: Stern Railings from the ship. The first main discovery made by the team of scientists was that the ship had split in half with the bow and the stern lying 600metres apart and both facing in opposite directions.

OPPOSITE PAGE: The first photograph of the Titanic's life boats on the side of the Carpathia as it entered the Cunard Line Pier in New York. She initially sailed to Pier 59 to drop off the lifeboats as property of the White Star Line before sailing onto Pier 54 for passengers to disembark.

THE HEROIC BAND.

The orchestra who played on the decks as the vessel was sinking were: W. Hartley, bandmaster, Surreyside, West Park-street, Dewsbury; J. Hume, 42, George-street, Dumfries; P. C. Taylor, 9, Fentiman-road, Clapham, London; J. W. Woodward, The Firs, Windmill-road, Headington, Oxon; R. Bricoux, 5, Place du Lion d'Or, Lille, France; F. Clarke, 22, Tunstall-street, Smithdown-road, Liver-pool; G. Krius, 10, Villa-road, Brixton, London; W. T. Brailey, 71, Lancaster-road, Ladbroke-grove, London.

PARTING OF WIVES AND HUSBANDS

THROWN INTO THE BOATS

WOMEN'S PRAYERS

Many pathetic severances of wives and husbands—the former to live, the latter to die—added special sadness to the work of launching the Titanic's lifeboats, and there were instances in which wives refused to accept this safety through separation. The passage to each lifeboat for the women and children was superintended by a ship's guard.

Mr Isidor Straus supporting his wife on the way to the lifeboat, was held back by the inexorable guard. An officer strove to help her to a seat of safety (says Reuter), but she brushed away his arm and clung to her husband crying "I will not go without you." Another woman took her place. Her form, clinging to her husband's, became part of the picture impressed indelibly on many minds. Neither, so far as anyone knows, reached a place of safety.

COLONEL AND MRS ASTOR

Mrs J. J. Astor said that she had no very definite idea as to how her husband, Colonel Astor, whom she married only last year, met his death. She recalled that in the confusion, as she was about to be put into one of the boats, he was standing at her side. Her impression was that the boat she left in had room for at least fifteen more persons.

From other narratives it appears that Colonel Astor devoted all his energies to saving his wife, who was in delicate health. He helped to get her into the boat, and as she took her place he requested the permission of the second officer to go with her for her own protection. "No, sir," replied the officer, "no men shall go in the boat until the women are all off."

Colonel Astor inquired the number of the boat and then helped to clear the other boats and to reassure frightened and nervous women.

Mr. George D. Widener, who had been in Captain Smith's company for a few minutes after the crash, was another whose wife was parted from him and lowered a moment later to the calm surface of the sea.

Mr. Jacques Futrelle said adieu to his wife and steadfastly refused to accept a chance to enter a lifeboat. How he went to his death is told by Mrs Futrelle : "Jacques is dead, but he died like a hero, that I know. Three or four times after the crash I rushed up to him and clasped him in my arms, begging him to get into one of the lifeboats. 'For God's sake, go,' he screamed, and tried to push me towards the lifeboat. I could see how he suffered. 'It's your last chance, go,' he pleaded. Then one of the ship's officers forced me into a lifeboat and I gave up all hope that he could be saved."

"REMEMBER OUR CHILD"

Mrs. Edgar J. Meyer of New York, said that she and her husband ran to the lifeboats. She pleaded with him to be allowed to remain with him. He threw her into the lifeboat, reminding her of their nine year-old child at home. There were about seventy of us widows on board the Carpathia.

Mr. George Brayton, of California, related that he was standing beside Mr. Henry B. Harris when the latter bade his wife good-bye. Both started towards the side where the lifeboat was being lowered. Mr. Harris was told of the rule that women should leave first, "Yes, I know," he replied, "I will stay."

Mrs W. D. Marvin, of New York, who was on her honeymoon trip, was almost prostrated when she learned on reaching New York that her husband had not been picked up by some other boat. "As I was put into the boat," she said, "he cried to me: 'It's all right, little girl you go: I will stay.' As our boat shoved off he threw me a kiss."

Mrs Esther Hart and her five year-old daughter, going from London to a farm in Winnipeg, were saved. Her husband, she said, had a place in the lifeboat, but gave it up to a woman. "He kissed me and the little girl good-bye and said he would see us in New York. He expected to be saved by another ship."

THE WIRELESS OPERATOR.

LAST WORDS OF THE CAPTAIN.

"MEN, YOU HAVE DONE YOUR DUTY."

BAND GOES DOWN STILL PLAYING.

A HERO'S STORY.

This statement was dictated by Mr. Harold Bride, the surviving Marconi operator of the Titanic, in the wireless cabin of the Carpathia a few minutes after the steamship touched the pier:

"In the first place the public should not blame anybody because more wireless messages about the disaster to the Titanic did not reach the shore from the Carpathia.

I positively refused to send Press despatches, because the bulk of the personal messages was so large. The wireless operators on board the cruiser Chester sent to meet us got all they asked for.

When I was dragged aboard the Carpathia I went into hospital. I stayed there ten hours. Then somebody brought word that the Carpathia's wireless operator was "getting queer" from work.

They asked me if I could go up and help. I could not walk, as both my feet were broken or something, I do not know what. I

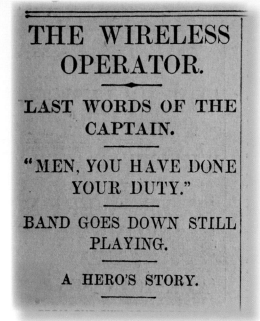

Mr. HAROLD BRIDE.

went up, with somebody helping me. I took the key, and I never left the wireless cabin after that. Our meals were brought us, and we kept the wireless working all the time. Sometimes I did so: There was a bed in the wireless cabin, and sometimes I could sit on it and rest my feet while sending.

I joined the Titanic at Belfast. I did not have much to do aboard her, except to relieve Phillips, the first operator, from midnight until some time in the morning. On the night of the accident I was not "sending" but was asleep. There were three rooms in the wireless cabin. One was the sleeping room, one the dynamo room, and the other the operating room.

I took off my clothes and went to sleep in bed. I was conscious of waking up and hearing Phillips sending to Cape Race. I read what he sent; it was traffic matter. I remembered how tired he was, and got out of bed without my clothes on to relieve him.

I did not even feel a shock. I hardly know anything had happened. I was standing by Phillips telling him to go to bed when the captain put his head in the cabin.

"We've struck an iceberg," he said, "and I'm having an inspection made to tell what it's done to us. You'd better get ready to send out a call for assistance; but don't send it until I tell you."

THE CALL FOR HELP

The captain went away, but in ten minutes, I estimate, he came back. We could hear terrible confusion outside, but there was not the least thing to indicate that there was any trouble. The wireless was working perfectly.

"Send a call for assistance," ordered the captain, barely putting his head in the door.

"What call should I send?" Phillips asked.

"The regulation international call for help, just that." Then the captain was gone.

Phillips began to send the "C.Q.D." [the old signal now replaced by "S.O.S."]. He flashed away at it. We joked while he did so. All of us made light of the disaster. We joked that way while he flashed signals for about five minutes. Then the captain came back.

"What are you sending?" he asked. "C.Q.D.," Phillips replied.

The humour of the situation appealed to me. I cut in with a little remark that made us all laugh, including the captain. "Send S.O.S." I said, "it's the new call. It may be your last chance." Phillips, with a laugh, changed the signal to "S.O.S."

The captain told us we had been struck amidships or just back of amidships. It was ten minutes, Phillips told me, after he had noticed a slight jolt. That was the only signal to us that a collision had occurred.

In the next few minutes we picked up the first steamship, the Frankfurt. We gave

"I looked out. The boat deck was awash. Phillips clung on ... sending ... sending. He clung on for about ten minutes, or maybe fifteen minutes, after the captain released him. The water was then coming into our cabin while he worked."

her our position, and said we had struck an iceberg and needed assistance. The Frankfurt's operator went away to tell his captain. When he came back we told him we were sinking by the head. By that time we could observe a distinct list forward.

CARPATHIA'S ANSWER

The Carpathia answered our signal. We told her our position and said we were sinking by the head. The operator went to tell his captain, and five minutes after returned and told us the Carpathia was putting about and heading for us. Our captain had left us at this time, and Phillips said to me: "Run and tell him what the Carpathia has answered." I did so, and went through an awful mass of people to his cabin. The decks were full of scrambling men and women. I saw no fighting, but I heard talk of it.

I came back and heard Phillips giving the Carpathia fuller directions. Phillips told me to put on my clothes. Until that moment I had forgotten I was not dressed.

I went to my cabin and dressed. I brought an overcoat to Phillips; it was very cold, and I slipped the coat upon him while he worked.

Every few minutes Phillips would send me to the captain with little messages, merely telling how the Carpathia was coming our way, and giving her speed. I noticed as I came back from one trip that they were putting off the women and children in lifeboats.

I noticed that the list forward was increasing. Phillips told me the wireless was growing weaker, and the captain came and informed us that our engine-rooms were taking in water, and that the dynamos might not last much longer. We sent those facts to the Carpathia.

I went out on deck and looked around. The water was close up to the boat deck. There was a great scramble aft, and how poor Phillips worked through it I don't know.

He was a brave man. I learned to love him that night, for I suddenly felt for him a great reverence, seeing him standing there sticking to his work while everybody else was raging about. I will never forget the work of Phillips in the last awful fifteen minutes.

THE HERO PHILLIPS

I thought it was about time to look about to see if there was anything detached that would float. I remembered that every member of the crew had a special lifebelt and ought to know where it was. I remembered that mine was under the bunk, and went and got it. Then I thought how cold the water was, and I put my boots and an extra jacket on.

I saw Phillips standing out there still sending away, giving the Carpathia details just how we were doing.

We picked up the Olympic and told her we were sinking by the head.

"We're about all down." As Phillips was sending that message I strapped his lifebelt to his back. I had already put on his overcoat, and I wondered if I could get him into his boots. He suggested with a sort of laugh that I should look out and see if all the people were off in the boats or if any boats were left, or how things were.

I saw a collapsible boat near the funnel, and went over to it. Twelve men were trying to boost it down to the boat deck. They were having an awful time. It was the last boat left. I looked at it longingly for a few minutes, then I gave them a hand. Over she went, and they all started to scramble in.

I walked back to Phillips and said: "The last

Mr. PHILLIPS. [Stedman.

From aft came the tunes of the band. There was a ragtime tune, I don't know what, and then there was 'Autumn'.

raft is gone." Then came the captain's voice:

Men, you have done your full duty. You can do no more. Abandon your cabin now. It's every man for himself. You look out for yourselves. I release you - that's the way of it at this kind of time, every man for himself.

I looked out. The boat deck was awash. Phillips clung on ... sending ... sending. He clung on for about ten minutes, or maybe fifteen minutes, after the captain released him. The water was then coming into our cabin while he worked.

Something happened now that I hate to tell about. I was back in my room getting Phillips' money for him. As I looked out of the door I saw a stoker or somebody from below decks leaning over Phillips from behind. Phillips was too busy to notice what the man was doing. He was slipping the lifebelt off Phillips' back.

A COWARD'S DEATH

He was a big man, too, and as you can see I am very small. I don't know what it was I got hold of. I remembered in a flash the way Phillips had clung on; how I had to fix that lifebelt in place because he was too busy to do it.

I knew that the man from below decks had his own lifebelt and should have known where to get it. I suddenly felt a passion not to let that man die a decent sailor's death. I wished he might have stretched a rope or walked the plank. I did my duty ... I hope I finished him; I don't know. We left him on the cabin floor of the wireless room, and he wasn't moving.

From aft came the tunes of the band. There was a ragtime tune, I don't know what, and then there was "Autumn" (used as a recessional in America).

Phillips ran aft, and that was the last I saw of him. I went to the place where I had seen a collapsible boat on the boat deck. A large wave came awash of the deck and carried the boat off.

I had hold of an oarlock. I went off with it, and the next I knew I was in the boat. But that wasn't all. I was in the boat, and the boat was upside down, I under it.

I remember realising that I was wet through, and that whatever happened I must breathe. I knew I had to fight for it, and did. How I got out from under the boat I don't know, but I felt a breath of air at last.

There were men all around me, hundreds of them. The sea was dotted with them, all

depending upon their lifebelts. I felt simply that I had to get away from the ship.

She was a beautiful sight then. Smoke sparks were rushing out of her funnel. There must have been an explosion, but we had heard none. We only saw a big stream of sparks.

The ship was gradually turning on her nose, just as a duck does that goes down for a dive. I had only one thing on mind, to get away from the suction.

The band was still playing. I guess all of them went down. They were playing "Autumn."

Then I swam with all my might. I suppose I was 150 feet away when the Titanic, on her nose, with her after-quarter sticking straight up in the air, began to settle slowly. When at last the waves washed over her rudder there was not the least bit of suction that I could feel.

"Then I swam with all my might. I suppose I was 150 feet away when the Titanic, on her nose, with her after-quarter sticking straight up in the air, began to settle slowly."

I forgot to mention that besides the Olympic and Carpathia we spoke to some German boat - I don't know which - and told them how we were. We also spoke to the Baltic. I remembered those things as I began to figure what ships would be coming towards us.

I felt after a little while like sinking. I was very cold. I saw a boat of some kind near me, and put all my strength into the effort to swim to it.

It was hard work; and I was all but done when a hand reached out from the boat and pulled me aboard. It was our same collapsible boat, and the same crowd was in it.

There was just room for me to roll on the edge, and I lay there, not caring what happened. Somebody sat on my legs, causing

> *"The crew, for self-preservation, had to refuse to permit any others to climb on board. This was the most pathetic and horrible scene of all. The piteous cries of those around us ring in my ears, and I will remember them to my dying day."*

Captain E. J. SMITH, of the Titanic.

me pain, and I hadn't the heart left to ask the man to move. It was a terrible sight. All around men were swimming and sinking. I lay where I was, letting the man wrench my feet out of shape. Others came near, but nobody gave them a hand.

The boat already had more men than it would hold, and it was sinking. At first the larger waves splashed over my clothing. Then they began to splash over my head, and I had to breathe when I could.

Some splendid people saved us. They had a right-side-up boat, full to capacity, yet they came up to us and loaded us all into it.

I saw some lights off in the distance, and knew that a steamship was coming to our aid. I didn't care what happened, and just lay and gasped when I could. I felt great pain in my feet.

At last the Carpathia was alongside, and the people were being taken up by a rope ladder. Our boat drew near, and one by one the men were taken off.

One man was dead. I passed him. He was Phillips. He had died on a raft from exposure and cold.

He had been "all in" from work before the wreck came. He stood his ground until the crisis had passed and then had collapsed, I suppose. But I hardly thought that then; I didn't think much about anything.

I tried the rope ladder. My feet pained terribly, but I got to the top and felt hands reaching out to me. The next I knew a woman was leaning over me in the cabin, and I felt her hand waving back my hair and rubbing my face. There was somebody at my feet, and I felt the warmth of a jolt of liquor. Somebody got me under the arms; then I was hustled down below to hospital.

That was early in the day, and I suppose I lay in the hospital until nearly night. They told me, as I said, that the Carpathia's wireless man was getting queer, and asked if I would help. After that I never was out of the wireless room. I knew it soothed the hurt, and it felt like a tie to the world of friends at home.

I was still sending my personal messages, and there were maybe 100 left. I would like to send them all, because I could rest easier if I knew that all these messages had gone to friends waiting for them.

The parents of Harold Bride, who reside at Shortlands, Bromley (Kent), received this cable from New York: "Safe. Two pounds Mayor's Fund - Harold."

ON THE RAFT
PRAYERS OF LIVING, BLESSING OF DYING

NEW YORK, Friday.

Of all the adventures in the disaster that of Colonel Gracie, of the United States Army, who jumped from the topmost deck when the ship sank and was sucked down with her, is most extraordinary.

"After sinking with the ship," he said, "it appeared to me as if I was propelled by some great force through the water. This might have been occasioned by explosions under the water, and I remembered stories of people being boiled to death.

"Innumerable thoughts flashed through my brain. I thought of those at home as if my spirit might go to them to say 'Goodbye.' Again and again I prayed although I felt sure the end had come. I knew that once I inhaled the water would suffocate me. When I got under water I struck out with all my strength for the surface. I got to the air again after a time which seemed to be unending. There was nothing in sight save the ocean dotted with ice and strewn with large masses of wreckage. Dying men and women all about me were groaning and crying piteously.

"The second officer and Mr. J. B. Thayer jun., who were swimming near me, told me that just before my head appeared above the water one of the Titanic's funnels separated and fell apart near me, scattering the bodies in the water. I saw wreckage everywhere, and all that came within reach I clung to."

Colonel Gracie relates how at last by moving from one piece of wreckage to another he reached the raft. "Soon the raft became so full that it seemed as if she would sink if more came on board her.

"The crew, for self-preservation, had to refuse to permit any others to climb on board. This was the most pathetic and horrible scene of all. The piteous cries of those around us ring in my ears, and I will remember them to my dying day.

"'Hold on to what you have, old boy,' we shouted to each man who tried to get on board. 'One more of you would sink us all.'

"Many of those whom we refused to save answered as they went to their death 'Good luck! God bless you!'

"All the time we were buoyed up by hope of rescue. We saw lights in all directions. Particularly frequent were some green lights which, as we learned later, were rockets fired in the air by one of the Titanic's boats. So we passed the night with the waves washing over and burying the raft deep in water.

"We prayed through all the weary night. Men who seemed long ago to have forgotten how to address their Creator recalled the prayers of their childhood and murmured them over and over again. Together we said the Lord's Prayer again and again. - Reuter's Special.

COLLAPSIBLE BOATS FOR THE OLYMPIC.

A barge-load of collapsible boats at Southampton ready to be placed on board the Olympic for her next voyage.

LADY DUFF-GORDON

NEW YORK, Friday.

Lady Duff-Gordon, who left in one of the last boats, said that panic had begun to seize some of the remaining passengers by the time her boat was lowered. Everyone seemed to be rushing for that boat.

"A few men who crowded in were turned back at the point of Captain Smith's revolver, and several of them were felled before order was restored.

"I recall being pushed towards one of the boats and being helped in. Just as we were about to clear the ship a man made a rush to get aboard our lifeboat.

"He was shot and apparently killed instantly. His body fell in the boat at our feet. No one made any effort to move him, and his body remained in the boat until we were picked up. I saw bodies in the water in all directions. The poor souls could not live long in the terribly cold water." - Reuter's

BELOW: Rescued passengers aboard the Carpathia. Although several men were saved, the majority of them were women due to the policy of 'women and children first'. Aboard the Carpathia a service of thanksgiving was held for the survivors and also a funeral service for those who had died.

INCIDENTS.

"I WENT ON DICTATING."

Mr. Robert E. Daniel, a young cotton broker, of Philadelphia, said: "I was in my cabin dictating to the typist when the ship struck the berg. The officers who survived told me afterwards the Titanic slipped up on the iceberg and tore her bottom out. No one seemed to be alarmed at first. I went on dictating until somebody knocked at my door and cried out that the ship was sinking. There was no panic." Mr. Daniel leaped overboard (says Reuter) and was picked up by one of the boats.

SAD HOMECOMING.

There was an impressive scene at Montreal Railway Station yesterday when Mrs. Hays, whose husband, the president of the Grand Trunk Railway, was one of the drowned, and Mrs. Davidson, whose husband was also drowned, arrived by special train. The bell of the locomotive was tolled, and the station flag was at half-mast. Every head was uncovered as Mrs. Hays and Mrs. Davidson stepped from the train.

HALF-FULL BOATS.

A passenger in the Carpathia said: "Ropes were tied round the waists of the adult survivors to help them in climbing up the rope ladders from the boats to the Carpathia. The little children and babies were hoisted on to our deck in bags. Some of the boats were crowded, but a few were not half full."

MEETING WITH LOVED ONES.

When the survivors landed there were affecting scenes at the dock. Men were in hysterics and fell down to kiss the knees of beloved ones; women shrieked and wept and collapsed in the arms of husbands and brothers; children were almost crushed in the arms of those welcoming them.

A LUCKY DELAY

"I recall being pushed towards one of the boats and being helped in. Just as we were about to clear the ship a man made a rush to get aboard our lifeboat."

Help the Titanic's Widows and Orphans.

OUR INSTANT DUTY.

STRICKEN HOMES OF SAILOR HEROES.

SEND NOW!

MANSION HOUSE TOTAL £61,000.

THE "E.N." FUND.

APPEAL FOR GREAT WEEK END EFFORT.

The stories of the last hours of the Titanic have been told and retold in many forms, and very little is to be added to the graphic and thrilling narratives which crowded the pages of The Evening News last night.

From the dark horror and sadness of it all there emerge a beacon-light of calm unselfishness and heroism in the face of death. Many of those stories will take their place among the imperishable records of our maritime history. Little further remains to be said on this point; in fact, as a Reuter's Agency message from New York says, the stories of the closing scenes on the Titanic, multiplying on every hand, are largely repetitious.

So we turn from the history of this great sea tragedy to emphasise what is now an insistent and sacred duty.

Helping the Fund at the Mansion House.

At the request of the Lord Mayor of London, The Evening News has opened a subscription list, which we have headed with one hundred guineas, in connection with the Mansion House Fund.

The response has been a generous one, but we would ask for more. The shadow of starvation must be kept from those who have lost their dear ones. We appeal with confidence to the sympathy of those who may picture to themselves the positions of the widows and the fatherless.

Let this week-end bring to the stricken homes the immediate prospect of relief, and remember above all that "he gives twice who gives quickly."

The third "Evening News" list of

WHERE TO SEND THE MONEY.

"THE EVENING NEWS," (Titanic Fund), Carmelite House, London, E.C.

How were the passengers selected to fill the boats?—By sex. Who determined who should go?—I did. The stewardesses turned back.

its a woman of great personal beauty and attractiveness.

"Nearer, my God, to Thee" is known wherever the English language is spoken; it has been translated into every language and dialect where missionaries work, is sung and known by the natives of Nigeria and Uganda as much as it is by English and Americans.

No other hymn has so attracted musicians. Sir Arthur Sullivan, Dr. J. B. Dykes, and Dr. L. Mason, among others, have written tunes for it. Altogether there are eight well-known tunes, the best known on this side of the Atlantic being that by Dr. J. B. Dykes, whose "Horbury," set to "Hymns Ancient and Modern," was published in The Evening News yesterday.

The favourite tune in America, and one which has been arranged for orchestra, is that by Dr. L. Mason and named "Bethany." This is played by bands, the

Our Titanic Number

CONGRATULATIONS AND AN APOLOGY.

Yesterday the sale of The Evening News was remarkable even in its record of huge sales.

And to-day the conductors of the paper are listening to a chorus of congratulations—and a storm of complaints.

The complaints come, not from the people who read The Evening News, but from those who couldn't get it to read.

To take the praise first; it is acknowledged on all sides that yesterday's Evening News contained by far the most coherent, logical, and accurate account of the dreadful fate of the Titanic. In newspaper phrase the "whole story was covered," and covered completely.

Take the 5.30 edition: the front page contains, in the space of a column, an eloquent summary of the events of the wreck; the most salient and moving incidents being set out clearly with all the aid of typographical resource.

Then follows an account of the memorial service at St. Paul's Cathedral, a description of the scene outside, illustrated by a photograph. So much for the outer page.

THE OPERATOR'S VIVID STORY

Page 4 contains the story told by the Marconi operator, the narrative of Mr. Laurence Beesley, a photograph of the Titanic leaving Queenstown, and a poem by C. E. B., appealing for help for the widows and orphans of the drowned heroes.

The chief feature on Page 5 is "The Titanic's Swan-Song"; the words and music of the hymn, "Nearer, my God, to Thee." With this is a portrait of the leader of the Titanic orchestra, with a brief account of his career.

Then seven columns of letterpress describe various aspects and incidents of the wreck; taking the narrative down to the landing of the survivors at New York.

And, finally, on Page 6, a leading article sums up the whole situation, and draws the moral of the terrible history.

Nothing was left out; but to ensure this complete survey of the wreck of the Titanic it was necessary that The Evening News should be a well-staged paper.

And the cause of the congratulations which the conductors of the journal have

HEROIC GIRL.

Life Sacrificed to Save a Wife.

WOMEN AT THE OARS.

How Mr. Stead is Thought to Have Been Lost.

A story of a woman's heroism told by an American magistrate named Cornell, whose wife and two sisters were among the rescued, is reproduced by the New York correspondent of the *Standard*.

" Miss Edith Evans, aged twenty-five, the niece of Mrs. Cornell, and my wife's sister, Mrs. Brown," he said, " were assigned the same boat.

" When they were about to be lowered it was found that it contained one more passenger than its capacity.

" The question arose: who should leave? Miss Evans left the boat, saying that Mrs. Brown had children at home, while she was unmarried. She said she would take her chance with another boat, but that chance never came."

Widow's Tribute to her Husband.

When the Titanic was sinking Mr. Jacques Futrelle said adieu to his wife and steadfastly refused to accept a chance to enter a lifeboat. How he went to his death is told by Mrs. Futrelle: " Jacques is dead, but he died like a hero, that I know. Three or four times after the crash I rushed up to him and clasped him in my arms, begging him to get into one of the lifeboats. 'For God's sake, go,' he screamed, and tried to push me towards the lifeboat. I could see how he suffered. 'It's your last chance, go,' he pleaded. Then one of the ship's officers forced me into a lifeboat and I gave up all hope that he could be saved."

" Think of Your Mother."

There is a picture of Major Butt, the President's Chief Military Aide-de-Camp, standing revolver in hand keeping back some of the panic-stricken emigrants so that the women and children might seek safety. There is young Marvin, the husband of a few weeks, forcing his bride into a boat. She refused to go unless he accompanied her. " Think of your mother," was his final appeal as he gently compelled her to leave him.—*Morning Post* correspondent.

"The Titanic, which was illuminated from stem to stern, was perfectly stationary, like some fantastic piece of stage scenery. For three hours cries of anguish were heard like some vast choir singing a death song."

ABOVE LEFT: Having rescued all passengers, the crew from the Carpathia haul one of the wooden lifeboats aboard ship.

OPPOSITE PAGE: The White Star Line logo on a silver object salvaged from the wreck.

PLACE IN A BOAT GIVEN UP

Colonel Astor, says Miss Hilda Slater, assisted his young wife into a boat and took, by invitation, the last seat, which, however, he relinquished when he saw a woman hurrying up. "Ladies must go first," the millionaire observed, and then lit a cigarette and leaned over the rail. He shouted to his wife : "Good-bye, dearie, I'll join you later."

SAD PROCESSION

I was going out of the door adjusting my life preserver, says another passenger, when my room steward happened along, cool and calm, and assisted me in buckling it. Poor little chap, he was a good man, but I believe he was drowned. Then I walked along the passage way and saw other people filing out of their cabins. It was a solemn procession, absolutely orderly. Quiet, too, except for an occasional woman's low sob, and now and then a little cry of "Oh, oh, oh!" from some woman.

"LIKE A DEATH SONG"

The following description is given of the last spectacle :

"When our boat had rowed about half a mile from the vessel the spectacle was fairylike. The Titanic, which was illuminated from stern to stern, was perfectly stationary, like some fantastic piece of stage scenery. The night was clear and the sea perfectly smooth. Presently the gigantic ship began to sink by the bows. . . . Suddenly the lights went out and an immense clamour filled the air in one supreme cry for help. . . For three hours cries of anguish were heard like some vast choir singing a death song. At moments the cries of terror were lulled, but the next instant they were renewed in still keener accents of despair."

SACRIFICED HIS LIFE

Bound for a little farm in Winnipeg, Canada, Mrs. Esther Hart and her five year old daughter landed from the Carpathia having left her husband behind on the Titanic. Her husband, she said, sold all his property in London to buy a farm at Winnipeg. He had a place in the lifeboat but gave it up to a woman. "He kissed me and the little girl goodbye and said he would see us in New York. He expected to be saved by another ship, but I am afraid he won't come now."

SHIP OF MOURNING
OLYMPIC'S SAD HOME-COMING AT PLYMOUTH

Today the Olympic arrived, with all her flags at half mast. It was a terrible home-coming.

If ever there was a ship of mourning it was the Olympic.

Passengers, officers and crew alike were affected. It was a startling contrast to the arrival of a month ago, when she was captained and manned by many of those who died heroically at their posts on the Titanic.

Many had lost relatives, brothers or fathers, in the Titanic, whilst there was scarcely a man who has not been deprived of a friend or shipmate of many years.

Sad-hearted Captain Haddock was indignant today when he heard of the false stories which have been attributed to him. Forcibly he denied having sent off any messages to the effect that the Titanic was being towed to Halifax by the Virginian, and that all passenger were safe.

He characterised it as a flagrant invention, and repudiated all knowledge of it.

The Olympic heard the Titanic's call for aid about twenty minutes after the mishap occurred. It came through the Celtic, and never at any time did Captain Haddock hear direct from Captain Smith.

BEAT THE BEST PACE

Five hundred miles separated the giant liners, and, utilising every pound of steam, the Olympic was pressed forward at a pace that she has never before steamed—between twenty-four and twenty-five knots.

Hours passed, and it was heard that the race had been in vain, as the Carpathia announced that she had the survivors on board, and that the Titanic had disappeared.

A committee was formed under the chairmanship of Mr. Albert Wiggin, a new York bank president, with Mr. Edmund Jackson, of Liverpool, as secretary, the other members being Lord Ashburton, the Earl of Leitrim, Mr. Casimir-Perier, Monsignor Robert Hugh Benson, Mr. Francis L. Hine, Mr. E. Marshall Fox, and the Hon. Cyril Ward.

The result of the effort was a collection of nearly fifteen hundred pounds for the Titanic Relief Fund.

Among the victims was Mr. W. H. Parr, an electrical engineer on the Titanic, who had only been married fifteen months, and leaves a wife and baby girl, twelve weeks old.

NEW YORK ENQUIRY.
The Man Who Decided Who Should Stay.

The full report of the investigation of the Senate Committee in New York into the loss of the Titanic is available to-day, and throws much new light on the last scenes.

Mr. Ismay's evidence has already been reported. When the committee asked him the circumstances under which he entered the lifeboat he replied in a whisper (according to the Exchange Telegraph Company) : "One lifeboat was being filled." Asked if there were any women left aboard the Titanic, he answered, "There were none, and no more passengers on deck. As the boat was being lowered I got into it. I wore slippers, pyjamas, suit, clothes, and overcoat."

Captain Rostron, of the Carpathia, who followed, declared (the Central News says) that the Titanic was on the course which was the proved one for this time of the year.

A Reuter's special message gives the important evidence of Mr. Lightoller, the second officer of the ship, in full. He said he was in the sea with a lifebelt on an hour and a half.

"Where were you," he was asked, "when the Titanic sank?".

"In the officers' quarters," he replied.

Were all the lifeboats gone?—All but one. Mr. Murdock (the first officer) was managing the tackle of it, and trying to launch it.

When you saw Mr. Ismay twenty minutes after the collision were other passengers near him?—I did not see anyone in particular, but there might have been.

The witness said that although ice had been reported he was not anxious about it.

You did not post an additional look-out? —No.

Mr. Lightoller added that Mr. Murdock relieved him at ten o'clock on Sunday evening. The weather was calm and clear, and the stars on the horizon were observable. After the crash witness found Mr. Murdock and Captain Smith on the bridge. He last saw Captain Smith walking the bridge.

What was the last order of Captain Smith?—"Put the women and children into the boats and lower away."

The witness added that when the Titanic sank he clambered into a flat collapsible boat, on to which later thirty other persons clambered.

Among these was the first Marconi operator (Phillips) who perished of cold. Several others also died of exposure.

Did any others try to get on board?—We took all we could.

Were not others in the water?—Not near, but half a mile off.

Episodes of the Wreck.

THE DISASTER IN DETAILS.

Without Fathers.

In a single school in Southampton there are 125 children whose fathers have all perished in the wreck of the Titanic.

Mr. Ismay's Plight.

Mr. Bruce Ismay was a pitiable sight when rescued. He wore a pair of slippers, a suit of pyjamas, and an overcoat, and was without a hat.

The Cause of the Horror.

It appears from other narratives that the crash against the iceberg which was sighted a quarter of a mile away came almost simultaneous with the click of the levers operated from the bridge which stopped the engines and closed the bulkheads.

Lord Pirrie's Nephew Lost.

Mr. Thomas Andrews, managing director of Messrs. Harland and Wolff, and a nephew of Lord Pirrie lost his life. The Titanic officers say he was heroic up to his death, thinking only of the safety of others.

Cowardly Chinese.

Six Chinese, hidden beneath the seats of the Titanic's lifeboats, are among the survivors. They were not detected until the boats had been taken on board the Carpathia. Two of their companions, who were also in hiding, were crushed to death by the weight of other passengers sitting above them.

The Percentage of Women.

Mr. Jowett will ask the President of the Board of Trade to-morrow what percentage of first, second, and third class passengers respectively compared with the number of passengers carried were saved, the percentages of women passengers of each class who were saved, and the percentage of men.

Family Wiped Out.

One of the many tragedies was the loss of the parents of four girls and three boys who were placed together in one of the lifeboats. Two of these children, whose names could not be ascertained, were removed to hospital on their arrival in New York. One of them is suffering from scarlet-fever and the other from meningitis.

Twenty Widows.

MR. ISMAY'S VERSION.

Ruthless Cross-examination by a Senator.

Mr. Ismay's testimony before the Senate Committee of Inquiry is far the most important contribution to the history of the wreck (says the *Times* correspondent). Mr. Ismay said that he was asleep when the Titanic struck, and could not therefore tell how fast she was going. The Titanic, however, had not been pushed to her limit during the voyage. She was capable of 80 revolutions, but never exceeded 75, which he thought tantamount to 21 knots.

In answer to a question why the Titanic was on the northern route, Mr. Ismay replied, "We were on the southern route —the extreme southern route."

Asked to tell the circumstances in which he left the Titanic, Mr. Ismay said that a boat was lowered in which most of the passengers were women, and that when the officers in charge called for more women there was no response, and as there were no passengers on deck he took a place in the boat. He declared that apparently there were no other passengers in that part of the vessel.

Asked how long he had remained in the ship after the collision, he said, when pressed for an answer, that he thought he remained about an hour or an hour and a quarter, or perhaps longer. Soon after the collision he visited the bridge, where he found Captain Smith had already arrived.

"I did not see any women waiting when I entered the lifeboat, nor were any about at that time."

Senator Smith asked, "Were all the women and children on the Titanic saved?"

Mr. Ismay flushed at the question, and replied in a low tone, "I fear not."

GRIPPED BY A GLACIER.

Manchester Man Tells the Story.

LEAVING THE SHIP.

No Thought of Real Disaster.

LAST MOMENTS ON THE TITANIC.

(Received "via Commercial Cables.")

Mr. Adolphe Saalfeld, a Manchester merchant residing in Victoria Park, who is one of the survivors of the Titanic, last night sent the following exclusive cable to the "Sunday Chronicle":—

It was Sunday night, the time 11-45, and I was, with other passengers, in the smoking room of the Titanic, when all of us became aware of a slight jar. A tremor passed through the vast steamer, prompting in our minds the

Mr. ADOLPHE SAALFELD.

notion that some breakage of a trivial character had taken place in the machinery.

Then the throb of the engine died down and ceased, and, stepping out of the verandah of the café, we caught sight of the iceberg looming up out of the cold, starlit night.

Most of the passengers were in bed when the impact took place, and even five minutes later a strange stillness brooded over the steamer, emphasised by the unaccustomed quietude in the engine room.

All that was then visible of the effect of the collision on the vessel was a slight list, and, after surveying the scene for a while, we went down, only to meet many of the passengers coming on deck with lifebelts.

This was the first intimation I had that anything specially serious had happened, and on hearing of the general order I made for my cabin and slipped on a lifebelt, overcoat, and cap.

Reaching the deck again I saw the boats being lowered, though even then so far away from anyone's mind was the thought of catastrophe that there was a marked reluctance of the passengers to leave the ship.

A few men and women going into a boat, I followed, and we were safely lowered into the sea, and, pushing off, rowed some distance to avoid what then seemed the remote risk of suction in the event of the Titanic actually sinking.

No such contingency was seriously entertained by any of us at this stage, and we all expected to go back after the damage had been patched up, which did not present itself to us as an insuperable job.

But as we drifted away from her, we saw the Titanic slowly sinking lower and lower into the deep, until suddenly her lights went out, and some of my companions in the boat declared that they saw the great steamer disappear.

We were then two miles away from her, but over the waste of waters could be plainly heard the pitiful cries of the doomed men and women as they were engulfed in the turbulent sea.

Not one of my companions among the survivors knew how many lifeboats the Titanic carried, but as about 2½ hours elapsed before she sank, and the sea was calm, it should not have been difficult to save every soul on board had there been sufficient boats.

Dawn broke bitterly cold, the sea became choppy, and we were all relieved soon to see the lights of an approaching steamer, and to hear shortly afterwards the fog-horn of the Carpathia, which we reached in about an hour and a half.

Captain, officers, and crew did everything possible to make us comfortable, and on those of us who were sick or injured they lavished the tenderest care.

The scene from the deck of the Carpathia, to one crossing the Atlantic for the first time, suggested the regions of the Pole. Icebergs reared up out of the sea and broken fields of ice stretched for miles around us.

Soon, however, we got out of the danger zone, and, with more or less of bad weather throughout the voyage, storms and fog, we safely landed in New York.

> *"Dawn broke bitterly cold, the sea became choppy, and we were all relieved soon to sea the lights of an approaching steamer, and to hear the fog-horn of the Carpathia."*

ABOVE: The bow of the ship was found embedded in the ocean floor and was largely intact but the stern section was less well preserved. Scientists believed that this section had sunk with a large volume of air trapped inside. The difference between the internal and external pressure then caused an implosion with further damage caused when the stern hit the sea bed.

RUNNING AT FULL SPEED
AMONG THE ICE

The White Star Line telegraphed to
Liverpool from New York the following
report of the disaster:-

"Titanic followed strictly southermost
track westbound, changing course at corner
47 meridian 42 latitude, thence south 86deg.,
west true.

"All officers' watch perished except fourth,
Boxhall, who was working observations in
chartroom and making rounds.

"Night perfectly clear, starlight, no wind,
sea calm. Had encountered no ice previously.
Proceeding with vigilant lookouts, full
speed, but reduced consumption probably
21 to 22 knots.

"Engineers all perished. 11.45pm, April 14,
ship sighted low-lying berg directly ahead.
First officer starboarded helm, reversed
full speed, closed all compartments. Struck
berg bluff starboard bow, slight jar, but
grinding sound, evidently opening several
compartments starboard side. Boats cleared,
filled with women and children, lowered
and sent off under responsible persons.

"Ship sank, bow first, 2.20 am., all boats
away except one collapsible. Discipline
perfect. Carpathia rescued survivors 4am."

FINDING OF BODIES

The White Star Company announces that
the steamer Rehia notified the cableship
Mackay-Bennett, sent to collect the bodies of
the dead, that she had found floating bodies
on the scene of the wreck of the Titanic.

The Mackay-Bennett arrived there
yesterday and began operations this
morning—Reuter.

MEMORIAL SERVICES

Memorial services were held yesterday at
churches of all denominations throughout
the country. The most frequent hymn sung
was "Nearer, my God, to Thee." Moving
scenes were witnessed, in some cases, men
and women breaking down with grief for
lost relatives and friends. Tributes were paid
by the preachers to the heroes of the Titanic.

Orders were issued that divine service
on board warships in home ports yesterday
were also to be a memorial service for those
who lost their lives in the foundering of the
Titanic. During the service flags in the ships
were half-masted.

ABOVE LEFT: China collected from the Titanic.
Debris from the ship had been scattered over an
area a mile square. In 1994 ownership of these
artefacts was deemed to belong to RMS Titanic
Inc. and since then over 6,000 pieces have been
removed from the site and displayed in various
locations including the National Maritime Museum
in Greenwich, London.

OPPOSITE PAGE: One of the crowded Titanic
lifeboats is hoisted aboard the rescue ship
Carpathia. Tests in March had demonstrated
that each lifeboat could hold 70 people but it
was revealed that many had been launched with
considerably fewer on board. This was mainly due
to loading women and children only, limiting the
number of men and the passengers' inability to
find their way through the enormous ship to the
Boat Deck.

"The lights were burning until a few minutes before the ship took her final plunge. This proves that the officers and men below remained at their posts when they must have known that death awaited them any minute."

"Indifference to danger"

As the US inquiry progressed, Smith charged his namesake with maintaining excessive speed in the face of repeated ice warnings. 'Skilful seamanship', the Senator declared, 'finds little difficulty in avoiding these obstacles'. Because Titanic was presented as the ultimate in shipbuilding, she was considered above the precautions lesser ships might take. This hubristic attitude bred laxity and over-confidence, leading Captain Smith to exhibit 'indifference to danger'. There may have been no directive from Ismay to plough on through the ice field, but the Inquiry concluded that his and Thomas Andrews' presence probably affected Smith's judgment on the matter.

Failure to provide the crow's nest lookouts with binoculars was another contributory factor. Would glasses have made a difference, Fred Fleet was asked. 'We could have seen it a bit sooner…Enough to get out of the way,' came the reply.

A WOMAN'S SACRIFICE.

Much has been said of the heroism of the men who died in the Titanic, but the survivors say there were conspicuous instances of bravery among the women. Miss Evans, of New York, gave up her place in a lifeboat in order that her aunt might be saved. She declared that as she was unmarried while her aunt was married and had children, her aunt's life was more important. Miss Evans died.

"There was one woman in my boat as was a woman," said a seaman from Southampton. "She was the Countess of Rothes. There were thirty-five of us in the boat, mostly women. I saw the way she was carrying herself and the quiet, determined manner in which she spoke, and I knew she was more of a man than most aboard, so I put her in command at the tiller. There was another woman in the boat who helped, and was every minute rowing. It was she who suggested we should sing, and we sang as we rowed, starting with "Pull for the shore." We were still singing when we saw the lights of the Carpathia, and then we stopped singing and prayed."

Mrs. J. J. Brown, wife of a Denver mine-owner, said: "It was all so formal that it was difficult for anyone to realise it was a tragedy. Men and women stood in little groups and talked and laughed. I was looking down at the boats being filled when two men seized me, threw me into a boat, with the words, 'You're going too.' I owe my life to them. I can still see the men up on deck tucking in the women and bowing and smiling. It was a strange sight. It all seemed like a drama being enacted for our entertainment. It did not seem real."

"Men would say, 'After you,' as they made some woman comfortable and stepped back. I afterwards heard someone say that men went downstairs into the restaurant, and many of them smoked for a while. After we reached the water we watched the ship. We could hear the band, and every light was shining.

"It did not seem long before there was a great sweep of the water. A great wave rose once and then fell, and we knew the Titanic had gone. I saw no dead people. To me there was hardly one tragic or harrowing element near me. We were in a boat, we were safe, we were at work. I was simply hypnotised."

A certificate that he is honourably alive is exhibited by an officer of the Queen's Own Rifles of Toronto. The certificate runs:

Major Arthur Peuchen was ordered into the boat by me owing to the fact that I required a seaman, which he proved to be, as well as a brave man.—C. W. LIGHTOLLER, second officer, late steamship Titanic.

To the same category belongs a message brought to the Guggenheim family by a rescued steward. It runs:

From Benjamin Guggenheim. Tell my wife I drowned. I've tried to do my duty.

The steward narrated that Mr. Guggenheim assisted the officers in getting the women into the boats. "I woke him and his secretary," said the steward, whose name is Etches, "and I dressed them in heavy sweaters. An hour after I found them working in dress suits. 'What's this for?' I asked. 'We've dressed up in our best,' replied Mr. Guggenheim, 'and are prepared to go down like gentlemen.' Then he gave me the message to his wife."

Captain Lord's failure

The American Inquiry paid little heed to Captain Lord's assertion that Californian was 19 miles from Titanic. It favoured the testimony of those crewmen who described a ship half that distance away, a ship firing rockets that should have prompted urgent action. In his summation, Smith said: 'The failure of Captain Lord to arouse the wireless operator on his ship, who could have easily ascertained the name of the vessel in distress and reached her in time to avert loss of life, places a tremendous responsibility upon this officer from which it will be very difficult for him to escape.' The report said that Lord 'deluded himself' in believing the ship he saw was not Titanic but a third vessel on the scene. Senator Smith thus waved away the 'mystery ship' theory.

Miss Evans, of New York, gave up her place in a lifeboat in order that her aunt might be saved. She declared that while her aunt was married and had children, her aunt's life was more important. Miss Evans died.

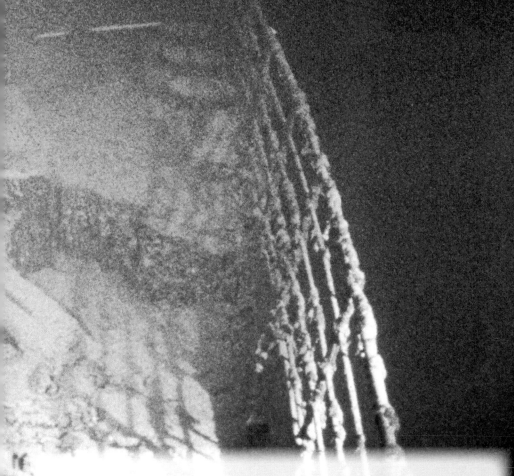

PROCEEDING TO WASHINGTON

The Senate Committee departed today for Washington, where tomorrow it will continue its investigation of the Titanic disaster. Some fifteen members of the Titanic's crew are proceeding simultaneously to Washington under the custody of the serjeant-at-arms in order that they may be at hand when evidence is required.

The chairman of the Committee, Senator Smith, announces that every survivor whose testimony can possibly be of value in elucidating the facts will be summoned in due course to Washington. He adds that he is "by no means through with Mr. Ismay." and intends to "question him at much greater length in Washington than I have been able to do here."

The course of the investigation so far has led to a general demand not only for the equipment of every liner with an adequate supply of lifeboats but for the standardisation of wireless apparatus and for governmental supervision of marine operators, such as exists in England and other countries. Amateur wireless operators must be rigidly controlled, and any violations by them of the regulations to be made must be treated as a criminal offence. This is the conclusion universally expressed.

Other points to which the legislators of the United States are directing attention are the training of sailors employed in great ocean steamships and the manner in which the ships are offered. It is argued that there are far too few officers on board big ships. In this respect the steamship companies, it is held, make it felt that they have not moved with the times. They employ for vessels of 20,000 or 40,000 tons no more officers than they did in the old days in small steamships.

In the Foreign Relations Committee of the Senate yesterday a resolution was passed calling upon the President to negotiate treaties with Great Britain, France, Germany, and other maritime Governments having for their object the standardisation of safety appliances and equipment. While the resolution was being debated, energetic protests were lodged by Senators McCullum and Lodge against the virulent denunciations of Mr. Bruce Ismay which marked the proceedings of the Senate.

Yesterday, Mr. McCullum said, one of the survivors of the lost ship, on flimsy reports, had been tried, condemned and executed in the Senate of the United States. "I wish to register a protest against this action and against the condemnation and denunciation of any survivors or surviving officers and seamen without the fullest consideration. When the feeling of the civilised world is that it desires a victim on which to vent its wrath, then of all times should we be deliberate."

CHIEF STEWARD'S STORY.

Among the statements made public to-day is one from Mr. Thomas Whiteley, first saloon steward, and now in St. Vincent's Hospital. Whiteley says he was saved by a boat that contained the two men who were in the crow's nest at the time of the collision. One of them, according to Whiteley, said, "No wonder Murdock (the first officer) shot himself." They were both very indignant, saying that their warnings had been ignored.

"I heard one of them say," Whiteley states, "that at 11.15 p.m. he reported to the first officer, Mr. Murdock, on the bridge, that he fancied he saw an iceberg. Twice after that, he said, he warned Mr. Murdock that an iceberg was ahead."

After the collision, according to the testimony of Mr. A. A. Dick, a survivor, Mr. Thomas Andrews, one of the designers of the Titanic, announced his intention of going below to investigate. "We begged him not to go, but he insisted, saying that he knew the ship as no one else did and might be able to allay the fears of the passengers.

"When he came back we hung on his words. They were these: 'There is no cause for any excitement. All of you get what you can in the way of clothes and come on deck as soon as you can. She is torn to bits below but will not sink if the after bulkheads hold. She has been ripped by an underlying peak of ice, and it has torn many of the forward plates from the bolts.'

"It seemed impossible to us that this could be true, and many in the crowd smiled, thinking that this was merely a little extra knowledge which Mr. Andrews thought fit to impart."

While detailed accounts are given of the last moments of Colonel Astor, Mr. Guggenheim, and others, few people seem to have observed Mr. Stead. He was seen walking the deck after the catastrophe, and discussed with one of the passengers the size of the iceberg that caused the damage. He said that it must have been over a hundred feet above the deck.

Two days before the famous journalist sat until midnight telling ghost stories.

Mr. Stead was last seen by Mr. R. L. Brekwith, just before the Titanic sank, pacing the decks unmoved. He was in evening dress. Another passenger believes, but cannot say positively, that Mr. Stead found refuge with Colonel Astor on a piece of wreckage, and that both men were forced to loosen their hold by the intense cold.

WRECKED GIRL'S WEDDING

TITANIC'S BANDMASTER

Mr. Wallace Hartley, the bandmaster of the Titanic, who played "Nearer, my God to Thee" as the ship was sinking, was, as the *Evening News* has already stated, a very popular figure in Yorkshire musical circles.

Last night a number of his friends conducted a little memorial service at one of the cafés in the town in which his orchestra had formerly played.

A number of members of Mr Hartley's former bands were present, and one of the most impressive items of the evening was a rendering of "Nearer, my God, to Thee," which was one of his favourite hymns.

A memorial tablet is to be fixed in a public place in the town, and an "In Memoriam" concert is being arranged for the purpose of raising the necessary funds. Mr. Hartley was to have been married this summer.

IN DEFENCE

Praise for Mr. Bruce Ismay from a First Class Passenger

PHILADELPHIA, Monday

Mr. Willian E. Carter, of Philadelphia says:-
"The statements made concerning Mr .Ismay's conduct are an injustice to him. While the lifeboats were moving away Mr. Ismay rowed with myself and two seamen until we sighted the Carpathia."

Mr. Carter says there were about forty women and children in the boat from the steerage.

"Mr. Ismay and myself and several officers walked up and down the deck crying 'Are there anymore women?' We called for several minutes, and there was no answer, and the officers said we could get into the

THE WARNING MESSAGE.

Handed by the Captain to Mr. Bruce Ismay on Sunday.

NEW YORK, Monday.

Mr. Ismay says that when he boarded the Titanic he intended to return by it. During the voyage he was simply a passenger, and was not consulted by the commander about the ship's speed, her navigation, or her conduct at sea.

He saw Captain Smith only casually. It was unqualifiedly false to say that he wished the Titanic to make a record or to increase her speed in order to get out of the ice zone.

The only information that ice had been sighted was a message from the Baltic, which Captain Smith handed to him without comment on the deck on Sunday afternoon. He read it casually, and put it in his pocket.

He says that at 7.10 on Sunday evening Captain Smith requested him to return the message for the purpose of posting it for the information of the officers.

"If," adds Mr. Ismay, "that information had aroused any apprehension in my mind, which it did not, I should not have ventured to make any suggestion to a commander of Captain Smith's experience. The navigation of the ship rested solely with him."—Reuter's Special

boat if we acted as seamen. They gave us this preference because we were first-class passengers.

"Mr. Ismay called again, and getting no reply, we embarked, took the oars and rowed about a mile off.

"When the Titanic sank Mr. Ismay did not turn to look. Instead, he was quietly pulling his oar. I desire to correct what has been said about him. He was perfectly cool and collected, and aided greatly in keeping the steerage women quiet.

"I can only say that Mr. Ismay entered the boat only after he saw that there were no more women on deck."—Reuter's Special Service.

CREW'S EVIDENCE

Mr Crooks Secures Adjournment of the House

Sir H. Dalzeil asked what steps were being taken to secure the attendance of every officer and member of the crew of the Titanic at the inquiry.

Mr. Buxton said the court would have power to call all the evidence they thought advisable.

Sir H. Dalzeil: Has the Board of Trade asked the White Star Company to see that all men were available for the purposes of the inquiry?

Mr. Buxton said he had no power to subpoena the crew, but as soon as the court was appointed they would have full powers to call for the attendance of any witness.

Sir H. Dalzeil: Will the right hon. gentleman request that the men should be kept in this country until their evidence is given?

Mr. Buxton again urged that the court would have full powers in the matter.

Mr. W. Crooks: Have we not the same power to compel their attendance as the Americans? (Hear, hear)

Subsequently Mr Buxton said he intended to communicate officially with the White Star Line, who courted the fullest enquiry.

Mr. Crooks, in view of the "unsatisfactory replies" given by the President of the Board of Trade, asked leave to move the adjournment of the House. On the Speaker calling for the necessary support, over forty members in all parts of the House stood up, and the question will come on at 8.15 this evening.

BELOW: The arrival of the Carpathia with rescued passengers. She finally sailed into New York's harbour at 8.00am on Thursday morning. Nearly 30,000 people had crammed into Pier 54 and at 9.00am the gangplank was lowered. First class passengers were allowed to disembark first.

> "When the Titanic sank Mr Ismay did not turn to look. Instead, he was quietly pulling his oar."

TOP: Titanic survivors huddled together after leaving the Carpathia. News of the disaster had spread very quickly. Vice-President of White Star Line Phillip A.S Franklin had been telephoned by a reporter at 1.40am in the morning who had discovered the details of the ship's radio distress call.

ABOVE: The anxious relatives and friends who gathered on the piers were also joined by further onlookers waiting for the Carpathia's arrival. Marconi was allowed on board with a New York Times reporter and obtained an exclusive interview with Harold Bride, one of the Titanic's radio operators.

THE OPERATOR.

Strain Which is Borne by the Man in Charge of Wireless.

Attention, says *The Times*, has naturally been drawn to the usefulness of the wireless operator at sea and his heroic devotion to duty, but the public have barely got an idea of the long, unintermittent strain involved by his position at ordinary times and in an ordinary ship.

Such a ship, the Carpathia, for example, carries only one operator. This means that he is always on duty.

There may be certain times publicly announced when passengers may hand in their messages for transmission. At other times "the office is closed," but the officer's ears, never.

Messages may be arriving at any moment, perhaps trivial, perhaps overwhelmingly vital. Unceasing vigilance is the price of others' safety.

The young man must get some sleep. And here it should be said that the exact position of his sleeping quarters is not as important as some have imagined.

It seems to have been thought that a message which passes unheard in the operator's absence would necessarily be heard if he was near. With the slow speed apparatus formerly used that was so.

THE PRESENT SYSTEM.

Under the present improved system the signals are only heard through a receiver, which the operator keeps pressed against his ear.

As a matter of fact, the operator nearly always sleeps in the instrument room, and it is pretty clear that this was the custom on board the Carpathia, as one message refers to a sleeping berth in the wireless apartment.

The officer must be content to take his sleep in instalments, like a doctor or a night porter; only they are called when they are wanted, and he has to call himself.

Occasionally an operator schools himself to sleeping with the receiver headdress on. Then every signal caught by the receiver strikes his ear, but he sleeps through them all—all but the one his ear is trained to expect, the call for his own ship, or that dreadful call on the universe for help, "S.O.S."

Then he wakes—and acts. It will be undestood that the wireless operator "hears" many calls which do not concern him. He hears as though he heard them not, just as a telegraphist, say, at Birmingham hears and ignores many calls sent from London to Liverpool, till his mind springs to "attention" at the sound of the Birmingham call.

The normal wireless operator, in a ship where he is single-handed, goes to sleep in the normal state, but gets himself into the habit of waking at more or less frequent intervals and putting the receiver to his ear in case he may be wanted.

Mr. and Mrs. Phillips, of Farncombe, Godalming, parents of the Titanic's chief Marconi operator, Mr. Jack Phillips, have received telegrams and letters from all parts of the United Kingdom, expressing admiration of his heroism and sympathy with his parents.

Mr. Phillips says that, while the death of his son is a great blow, he and his wife find some consolation in the fact that he died trying to save others and in the widespread sympathy which has been extended to them.

THE TALKING SHIPS.

WHAT PASSED BETWEEN THEM AFTER THE COLLISION.

Captain Gambell, of the Allan liner Virginian, which landed her passengers from Halifax yesterday, told our Liverpool correspondent the story of the rush of the great liners to the assistance of the Titanic.

"I left Halifax (Nova Scotia) at 8.51 p.m. on April 13 and came south of Sable Island," said Captain Gambell. "At 12.40 a.m. (ship's time) on April 15 I received the following message by wireless from Cape Race: 'Titanic struck iceberg. Wants immediate assistance. Her position, 41.16 N., 50.14 W.'

"I at once altered my course to go to her assistance, 178 miles south, and I advised Cape Race and Messrs. H. and A. Allan, of Montreal, of the fact. At 1.20 a.m. I got a further message from Cape Race which read: 'Titanic reports ship sinking, putting women and children into boats. Olympic making all speed towards Titanic, but much farther off than Virginian.'

"At 1.57 a.m. ship's time (5.27 a.m. Greenwich mean time) the Titanic's signals ceased abruptly as if the power had been suddenly cut off. At 3.45 a.m. I was in touch by wireless with the Russian steamer Birma and gave her the Titanic's position. She was then 55 miles from the Titanic and going to her assistance.

"At 4.45 a.m. I was in communication with the Californian, of the Leyland Line. He was 17 miles north of the Titanic and had not heard anything official of the disaster. I marconied him as follows: 'Titanic struck iceberg, wants assistance urgently. Ship sinking, passengers in boats.'

"Shortly after this I was in communication with the Carpathia, the Frankfurt, and the Baltic, all going to the Titanic. At 6.10 a.m. I marconied the Californian: 'Kindly let me know position of affairs when you get to Titanic.' He at once replied: 'Can now see Carpathia taking passengers on board from small boats. Titanic foundered about 2 a.m.'

"At 10 a.m. I received the following message from the Carpathia:—'Turn back. Everything O.K. We have 800 on board. Return to your northern track.'

"At the same time the Carpathia sent the following message to the Baltic:—'Am leaving here with all on board, about 800, chiefly third class, and a lot of stewards. Proceed on your voyage to Liverpool. We are proceeding to Halifax or New York under full steam.'

"I then altered my course to the eastward and proceeded on my voyage. In addition to the above messages, I learned from messages passing between the Carpathia and the Olympic that all the Titanic's boats had been accounted for, and that a careful search had been made for survivors among the wreckage and ice floes. I later learned that the Californian was going to remain in the vicinity for some time, and that the Carpathia had left for New York with the survivors on board. I am quite sure the captain of the Carpathia would not have advised me to continue my voyage if I could have been of the slightest use."

The British Inquiry

The British Wreck Commissioner's Inquiry, presided over by Lord Mersey, sat from 2 May–3 July 1912. Over the course of 36 days, some 25,000 questions were asked of 96 witnesses, whose number included Sir Ernest Shackleton and Guglielmo Marconi as well as surviving crew members, the most senior of whom was Second Officer Lightoller. Apart from J Bruce Ismay, the only passengers to appear were Sir Cosmo and Lady Duff Gordon, who faced particular charges that they could and should have done more from their fortunate position of occupying a two-thirds empty lifeboat. The Inquiry itself was attacked for its failure to hear evidence from any passenger from the lower decks.

With the aid of a 20-foot model of the ship and a plan measuring 33 feet by 5 feet, Lord Mersey and his team began sifting through thousands of pieces of evidence. Lightoller was a key witness, answering over 1,500 questions. It was put to him that Titanic's speed, around 21.5 knots, was 'utter recklessness' in the prevailing conditions. Lightoller countered that it was some way short of the speed she could have attained, adding that her rate of progress was commonplace even with ice in the vicinity. If Captain Smith was reckless, he said, then 'recklessness applies to practically every commander and every ship crossing the Atlantic Ocean'.

LEFT: A lifeboat windlass on the Boat Deck.

GOVERNMENT INQUIRY
ACTION BY BOARD OF TRADE
LORD MERSEY & SPECIAL COMMISSION

The President of the Board of Trade announced in the House of Commons last night that a wide and searching inquiry is to be conducted into the loss of the Titanic by a special Wreck Commission, of which Lord Mersey (better known as Mr. Justice Bigham) will be president.

The inquiry will include in its scope the questions of responsibility for the disaster, lifeboat accommodation, inaccurate telegrams, insurance and control of wireless. If the Commission's powers are insufficient, Mr. Buxton will ask Parliament for further powers.

The chief points of the statement were:

The Commission will be instituted immediately and sit as long as may be necessary.

Lord Mersey (ex-President of the Admiralty Division of the High Court) will preside and have expert assessors.

Poor witnesses will be maintained during the inquiry.

One hundred survivors are arriving by the Lapland next Monday, and summonses for witnesses among them will be issued by the Board of Trade.

The White Star Company has given an undertaking that every member of the crew who may be required shall give evidence before the Commission.

The Consul-General at New York is to collect evidence from passengers not returning to this country.

Lord Mersey is a former member for Liverpool, an ex-president of the Railway and Canal Commission, and a member of the South Africa Committee which was appointed to inquire into the origin and history of the Jameson Raid.

At length she was forced into a lifeboat, but sprang up crying that she preferred to die with her husband.

ABOVE: Lolo and Momon, the two French 'orphans' rescued from the ship on the last lifeboat to leave. Initially looked after by a fellow American passenger Miss Margaret Hayes, it later transpired their real names were Edmond and Michel Navratil. Their Slovakian father had separated from their mother and had absconded with them hoping to start a new life in the States. Newspapers after the disaster carried the story of the children until their photo was recognised by their mother Marcelle (centre) and she was finally reunited with them a month later.

OPPOSITE PAGE: Edward and Gerda Lindell both lost their lives during the disaster but a month later a gold ring was found in one of the

FROM OUR OWN CORRESPONDENT.

NEW YORK, Monday.

I called to-day on the two French boy babies from the Titanic, whose identity the Consul-General of France is vainly trying to establish. I found them under the shadow of a giant azalea playing with two brand new toy tin ships, quite unconscious of the incongruous character of the toys which apparently awakened in them no memory of the tragedy through which they passed.

The elder boy seems about four years old and the younger three. Both children have unusually beautiful chestnut-brown hair which curls in loose ringlets. Their eyes are dark and their faces, of a cherubic plumpness, wear the expression of mingled melancholy and mischief so characteristic of the children of the Latin races.

Miss Hayes, who has temporarily adopted them, denied the stories that the little waifs were saved in the same boat as herself and clung naturally to her as protectress. The smaller boy was tossed into one of the lifeboats without a stitch of clothing, and the elder child had only a shirt when he was taken on board the Carpathia. Miss Hayes took charge of the children at the request of the committee formed by the lady survivors of the Titanic.

The French Consul-General does not think the name of either of the children is Louis. "It seems to me more likely," he said, "that as they answer 'Oui, oui,' to everything, one of them was falsely understood to say his name was Louis."

It is believed that the children came on board with a Mr. Hoffman at Cherbourg.

Another orphan whose fate is exciting sympathy is the seven months Allison child who was brought on board the Carpathia by his aunt, Miss Sadie Daniels. Mr. Hudson J. Allison was a wealthy Montreal merchant, whose wife belonged to a prominent Milwaukee family. The couple had two children, the infant who is saved and a daughter, Lorraine Ellen, aged two and a half. After the Titanic struck the nurse took the infant and tried to find the mother, who was on deck. The mother returned to her cabin to find the infant gone, and she only recovered him after an agonised search. At length she was forced into a lifeboat, but sprang up crying that she preferred to die with her husband.

Mrs. Allison placed the infant in the arms of her sister and turned back to lift her little daughter in also, but the boat was full. Mrs. Allison went back to the Titanic, and Ellen held the hands of her father and mother as the Titanic went down. The infant is the only survivor of the family.

lifeboats. Tests revealed a Swedish inscription with the couple's names inscribed inside. It was later revealed that both had jumped from the ship. Edward had managed to get into a lifeboat but died before the rescue. His wife's hand was clung to by a Swedish survivor until he could no longer hold it and she slipped under the water.

"WOMEN FIRST"

FROM LADY ABERCONWAY

Sir,—In the sorrow which all hearts must feel for the sad disaster that fell upon the Titanic there is yet a glow of pride at the thought of men who stood aside to face a terrible death while the lifeboats pulled away saving the women and the children. I know not the origin of "this fine tradition of the sea," for surely there is no other instance in any of the serious affairs of life where the interests of women are preferred to those of men. Possibly this practice of saving women first from wrecks arose in the days when coasting steamers were the common mode of transit, and when women by custom and lack of opportunity rarely learnt the art of swimming. Then it might be rightly considered that men had a better chance of saving their lives unaided. Moreover, women passengers were in olden time but few in number.

In great disasters nowadays on the high seas, however, there is often no such great difference in the chances of rescue as between men and women, and in the case of the Titanic certain death awaited those brave men who waited and saw boatloads of women draw away, and stayed behind to die. Noble as was their devotion, it is in my opinion a sacrifice which ought not to be demanded of the male sex nor accepted by the female. The lives of children should come certainly first, but for themselves an equal chance of life is all that women in danger should ask or take from men. For what reason should a woman's life be accorded the more valuable? Women are not so highly favoured by law and social custom as men are : the adventures and businesses in which women can engage are more limited by convention ; under present conditions a woman's chance of happiness in life is not so great. Men stand in the full sunshine of a world arranged for their own interests, and throw their shadow over the lives of women, which are often harder, less free, more suffering than those of men. Thus life is of less value to a woman. Why, then, in shipwreck should it be considered first? Possibly because a woman has risked her life for every man born upon the earth. For this service, however, we disdain to take payment. Our gift is free.

Since the world began women have known how to die bravely: indeed, self sacrifice carried to excess is even a demerit of our sex. Which of us would value our life bought at the sacrifice of a husband or a son? Both are more precious than our own.

I understand that all officers in ships have standing orders in case of danger to save the women and children first. Observe that this traditional custom is now carried out

without the direct consent of the individual men who are thereby doomed to die, or of any wish expressed by women, who no doubt are almost equally deprived of choice. In darkness and confusion women are hurried into some boat—are told, no doubt, that all passengers will eventually be saved.

Officials separate even the bridegroom from his bride when both would choose rather to live or die together.

"The parting of the husband and the wife is like the cleaving of a heart: one half will flutter there, one here."

Few women would congratulate the bereaved wives and mothers speeding to safety landwards in the Carpathia; rather would most of us choose to lie with our dear ones deep in the cold dark waters than buy our miserable lives at such a cost. The pain of death is quickly over, and the dead have peace. To the survivors the thought of those left to perish would be a life-long agony.

The officers themselves are naturally last to leave the ship. Why should it be given to them to choose which of the passengers, men or women, should be sacrificed? All have an equal right to every chance of safety. Let the rule be to save the children first. Then save all passengers by lot, when time allows, without distinction of sex, husband and wife sharing an equal lot. Only those who voluntarily refuse to draw a chance of safety should be allowed the crown of heroism in death. Among all others strict justice should be done and equal chances given.

I beg women to urge this view upon all. Never let it be said that men can undo women in self-sacrifice and high devotion. In loss at sea we claim our right to die for those we love, or share their doom, as the lot falls.

Laura Aberconway. 43, Belgrave Square.

Help was only from 17 to 19 miles distant from the Titanic when she struck the iceberg and foundered.

That is what we learn by a Reuter telegram to-day.

In this message Mr. Lord, captain of the liner Californian, states that if he had known of the plight of the Titanic all the passengers might have been saved.

He, however, had steamed into an immense icefield on Sunday night and had stopped his engines.

"Our wireless apparatus was not working," he adds, " so that we did not learn of the Titanic's distress until the morning."

More remarkable evidence is being given in the United States Senate Committee's inquiry into the loss of the Titanic.

Mr. Pitman, the third officer, said that when the Titanic sank he heard moans and cries from those in the water for an hour, and he ordered his men to pull towards the wreck so that they might rescue a few more, but the passengers objected, and he allowed the boat to drift aimlessly, though it could have carried twenty more persons.

The witness could throw no light on the evidence of the fourth officer given on Monday as to a ship which, he said, he saw within about five miles of the Titanic as she was sinking.

All Mr. Pitman saw was a white light on the horizon which might have been a star.

Evidence was also given by the look-out man, who stated that he had no glasses, and if he had been supplied with them he would have seen the ice in time to avoid the danger.

The Mansion House Fund for the relief of the sufferers by the disaster last night amounted to £115,000.

MR. ISMAY'S STATEMENT.

"NAVIGATION RESTED SOLELY WITH CAPTAIN SMITH."

NEW YORK, Monday.

Mr. Ismay says that when he appeared before the Senate Committee he supposed it was the purpose of the inquiry to ascertain the cause of the sinking of the Titanic and determine whether legislation was required to prevent similar disasters. He did not suppose his personal conduct was the subject of inquiry, though he was ready to tell everything he did on the Sunday night.

"I don't think," he says, "that it requires me to be silent in face of the untrue statements of some newspapers." When he boarded the Titanic he intended to return by it. He was simply a passenger, and was not consulted about the ship's speed, navigation, or conduct at sea. He saw Captain Smith only casually.

It was unqualifiedly false to say that he wished the Titanic to make a record or to increase her speed in order to get out of the ice zone. The only information that ice had been sighted was a message from the Baltic, which Captain Smith handed to him without comment on deck on Sunday afternoon. He read it casually and put it in his pocket. At 7,10 on Sunday evening Captain Smith requested him to return the message for the purpose of posting it for the information of officers.

"If," adds Mr. Ismay, "the information had aroused any apprehension in my mind, which it did not, I should not have ventured to make any suggestion to a commander of Captain Smith's experience. The navigation of the ship rested solely with him."

Mr. Ismay says he was asleep when the crash came. He went on deck, asked about the damage, returned to his state room, dressed, returned to the boat deck, and helped clear the boats. When all the wooden boats to starboard had been lowered he assisted in getting out the collapsibles to starboard, and all the women were helped into them.

"NO WOMAN ON DECK."

"As they were going over the side Mr. Carter, a passenger, and myself got in. At that time there wasn't a woman on the boat deck, nor any passenger of any class so far as I could see or hear. The boat contained between thirty-five and forty persons, I should think, mostly women, with perhaps four or five men. Afterwards we discovered four Chinamen concealed at the bottom. When we reached the water I helped to row, pushing my oar from me as I sat. This is the explanation as to why my back was towards the sinking steamer.

"The messages I sent from the Carpathia were completely misunderstood. When they were despatched I had no idea that an inquiry was contemplated, and I did not know it until the arrival of the Carpathia. The reason I sent the messages was that I wished to have the crew returned to their homes for their own benefit at the earliest moment.

"When the Titanic was built I hoped she would be a vessel that could not be destroyed at sea. The accident has proved the futility of that hope. The present legal requirements are inadequate and must be changed. But whether they are changed or not this awful experience has taught steamship owners that too much reliance has been placed on watertight compartments and wireless telegraphy, and that they must equip every vessel with lifeboats and rafts sufficient to provide for every soul on board and sufficient men to handle them."

UNKNOWN STEAMER.

Fourth Officer's Story of a Boat He Said He Saw.

In his evidence Mr. Boxall, the fourth officer of the Titanic, said that under the weather conditions experienced at the time of the collision the lifeboats were supposed to carry 65 persons.

Under the regulations of the Board of Trade, in addition to oars, there were boats, water-dippers, bread, bailers, a mast, sail, lights, and a supply of oil in the boats. All these supplies were in the boats when the Titanic left Belfast. He could not say whether they were in the vessel when she left Southampton.

Questioned by the chairman, Mr. Boxall testified to the good habits and sobriety of the officers. He himself went on watch on Sunday night at eight o'clock. The officers were at their customary posts. He was relieved at ten o'clock by Mr. Murdock, who remained on the bridge until the accident occurred.

The sixth officer, Mr. Moody, was also on the bridge. The quartermaster was in the crow's nest.

He did not know of the proximity of icebergs.

THE COLLISION.

The witness said he was just approaching the bridge when the collision occurred, but he could not see what had happened.

The senior officer said, "We've struck an iceberg." There was just a little ice on the lower deck. There was a sharp report when the crash came, but he could see no iceberg. It was a glancing blow with only a slight impact, so slight that he did not think it serious.

Going immediately on the bridge he found Messrs. Murdock, Moody, and Captain Smith. The captain asked what was the trouble.

Mr. Murdock informed him that the vessel had struck an iceberg, adding that he had borne to starboard and reversed engines to full speed astern after ordering the watertight doors to be closed.

"We all walked to the end of the bridge," he continued, "to look at the iceberg, which we could see only dimly. It was lying low in the water, and was about as high as the lower rail, or about thirty feet out of the water.

"I had great difficulty in seeing it, as it was dark grey in colour. Then I went down to the steerage quarters, and inspected all the decks near the spot where the ship had struck."

What did you find?—I found no traces of any damage. I went directly to the bridge and reported accordingly.

What did the captain do?—He ordered me to send the carpenter to sound ship, but I found the carpenter coming up with the announcement that the ship was taking water. Then I went below to the mail room, where I found the mail sacks

"It was a glancing blow with only a slight impact, so light that he didn't think it was serious."

Grievous error

The British Inquiry found that while Captain Smith might have taken prudent action to avert the tragedy, such wisdom came only with the benefit of hindsight. Had Titanic's master reduced speed or plotted a more southerly course, she might have made untroubled progress. The change in course that was made just before 6 pm - taking Titanic a few miles further south than would normally have been the case – was considered nugatory; Smith would have had to take his ship much further south if the intention was to steer clear of ice hazards. But in the actions he did take, Smith was adhering to a template he and other commanders had laid down over many years in similar circumstances. No catastrophe had yet befallen anyone following such a precedent, therefore it was believed – wrongly – to be safe. No grounds were found to substantiate the claim that Smith had yielded to pressure from Ismay with regard to maintaining speed and making good time. In short, Captain Smith erred with grievous consequences, but no blame could be laid at his door as the actions he took were in accordance with common practice. While that exculpated Smith from a charge of negligence, anyone repeating his mistakes would be open to such a charge.

TUESDAY, APRIL 23, 1912

THE TITANIC COURT OF INQUIRY.

The public will receive with satisfaction the announcement made by Mr. Buxton last night that the special court of inquiry to investigate the circumstances of the Titanic disaster is to have Lord Mersey as its President. Lord Mersey has a wide experience in maritime affairs as the former President of the Admiralty Court, and the tribunal, whose proceedings he will direct, will be invested with the widest possible powers. It will have authority to require the attendance of any witness and to make searching investigation into all the questions that have arisen. Among these the inaction of the Board of Trade must inevitably be scrutinised. The country has still to learn why it was that this Department, charged with a duty so important and so grave, neglected that duty and failed to remodel its regulations determining the provision of boats in passenger steamers so as to keep pace with the rapid advance of these vessels in size. Between 1894 and 1912 the tonnage of steamers quadrupled. But the number of the boats required remained always the same.

The want of boats was the cause of the fearful tragedy in the Titanic whereby 1,635 human beings lost their lives. Men conversant with seafaring matters may contend that even if boat accommodation is provided for every person on board one of the modern monster ships, the chances are that with a list or the damage caused by a collision it will be impossible to get the people into the boats and to launch them; and that, if launched, they will never live in a wild sea. This may be true —in certain cases. But in the case of the Titanic the boats carried were launched; the people were got on board them; the sea was calm; and every boat that reached the water lived. It was a sufficiency of boats that was wanting, and the insufficiency of boats must be ascribed to the negligence of the Board of Trade. No excuse, no special pleading, can get over this grim fact. Yet even now, though many of the great shipping companies have taken action, the Board of Trade remains inert. The first and immediate lesson of the loss of the Titanic is that every soul on board the passenger ship must be given at least a chance of life; and that in every ship boat accommodation must be provided for all on board.

The question of speed at sea is only second in importance. The Cunard Company, whose instructions to captains we summarise in another column, expressly urges its officers to place safety above speed. But, notwithstanding these orders, there is a general belief that captains are expected to bring their ships into harbour to the scheduled time. The man who must be supreme must be the officer whose business is navigation—the man who in catastrophe pays the penalty with the sacrifice of his life. The coming inquiry may provide a satisfactory explanation of the fact that the Titanic maintained a high speed before she struck the berg, though ice had been reported in her course. Fair-minded men will be slow to pronounce hastily, and no doubt these enormous ships are difficult to manœuvre at low speed. This is a point to which the court will unquestionably direct its attention. Till the facts have been ascertained judgment must be reserved.

TITANIC EVIDENCE.

THIRD OFFICER'S STATEMENTS.

20 VACANT PLACES IN HIS LIFEBOAT.

PLIGHT OF THE DROWNING.

TWO MYSTERIES.

UNKNOWN SHIP AND ICE WARNINGS.

Further extraordinary evidence was given at Washington yesterday before the Senate Committee investigating the loss of the Titanic.

The statement of the fourth officer that an unknown ship close to the sinking Titanic failed to answer distress signals was generally borne out.

The third officer, Mr Pittman, related that as he sat in the lifeboat which he commanded he heard rising from the sea after the Titanic had gone down "one long continuous moan". there was room for twenty more people in the lifeboat, but he was prevailed upon by his passengers not to attempt to save any of the drowning.

Fleet, the look-out man in the crow's nest, stated that he asked for glasses for his work and was refused them. He said that if he had had them he would have seen the iceberg in time to avoid the collision.

THIRD OFFICER
THE ICE WARNINGS TO THE TITANIC
WASHINGTON, Tuesday
When the investigation into the loss of the Titanic was resumed today at 10.15, it was announced that Mr J B Boxhall, the fourth officer of the vessel, was ill. Mr H J Pittman, the third officer was called.

Senator Smith began by asking Mr Pittman if he were present during the trial tests of the Titanic.—Yes. I was on the bridge most of the time. The tests consisted of steaming in circles and performing evolutions.

Were there any trials of speed?—No, I believe that we have no such tests in the White Star.

Only sixteen men participated in the Southampton drill?—Yes.

Was there any fire drill in the Titanic after she left Southampton?—No.

Did you hear anything about a wireless message mentioning ice?—Yes, I did. It was either on Saturday night or Sunday morning, when Mr Boxhall put it on the chart.

Did you talk to the captain?—It was not my place to talk to the captain.

Did you see any ice on Sunday?—No, I didn't. The fact that the temperature was lower would not indicate the presence of ice. Virtually the only way to discover the proximity of icebergs is to see them.

Senator Smith sought to make the witness admit that there were other indications than this and finally asked: Then you are convinced that there is no other way of telling?—There is no other way. Science may hold that there are numerous ways, but they have never been demonstrated.

You say that the fourth officer reported ice on Saturday night and marked it on the chart with a cross. Was this mark on or near the ship's course?—As near as I recollect it was north of our course.

Did you have any ice on Monday?—Yes, when I was in the lifeboat going to the Carpathia. I saw several icebergs, maybe half a dozen of them.

Were those bergs high above the water?—About 150ft. above the water.

How many of these were really large icebergs?—Really, I could not say.

Senator Smith questioned the witness

as to his whereabouts on the night of the collision. "From 6 to 8 on that evening," he replied "I was on the bridge, after which I went to my berth."

Did you hear anything about a warning by the Californian that ice was in the vicinity?—No.

You heard nothing whatever from the second officer, Mr Lightoller, or the captain when you were on the bridge that night?—No. The Titanic had been keeping a special look out for ice on Sunday. This was done because the captain had been warned that ice was near.

Who warned him?—I don't know.

Who told you he had been warned? Were you told before the disaster or afterwards?—I cannot remember who told me. I think it was after the wreck.

> *"Officer Murdoch told me to get into the boat and row around to the after gangway. I thought that was the thing to do because I expected to bring all the passengers back to the ship again."*

Can you tell what speed the ship was making on Sunday evening?—About 21½ knots.

Were you trying to reach 24 knots?—No, because we did not have coal for it.

Asked again about the iceberg warnings, Mr Pittman said: "I did hear about Mr Lightoller's warning to Mr Murdock about ice. While in the ship we talked about it ourselves. On Sunday night Mr Lightoller remarked that we would be in the vicinity of ice about the time of his watch."

Continuing, the witness said: "I left my cabin at about 11.50 on Sunday night just after the collision. There was the smallest impact. I was half asleep and half awake, and wondered sleepily where we were anchoring. I walked on the deck for three or four minutes, and then I returned and lighted my pipe and dressed leisurely, for it was near the time for my watch.

"Just as I finished dressing Mr Boxhall came up. I asked him what was the matter. He said that we had struck an iceberg.

Moody asked him if he'd seen the iceberg. He said that he hadn't, but added there was ice on the deck. To satisfy myself I went forward. I saw the ice and then walked back.

"I saw a flock of fireman coming up. I asked them what was the matter, and they said, 'There's water in the hatch.' I looked down and saw the water flowing over the hatch. Then I went up on the deck. I met a man in a dressing gown, who said, 'Hurry. There's no time for fooling.' Then I went to the boats."

Did you know who that man was?—Not then. I do now.

Who was it?—Mr Ismay. Later he told me to get the women and children into the boats. I lowered one, and then Mr Ismay came to the boat and helped me. I put in quite a number of women and a few men, and then I called for more women, but there were none to be seen. Then I stepped back on the ship again. The officer Murdock told me to get into the boat and row around to the after gangway. I thought that was the

thing to do because I expected to bring all the passengers back to the ship again.

"Just before the boat pulled away Murdock leaned over and shook hands with me and said 'Goodbye. Good luck, old man.' I pulled away intending to remain near the ship in case a wind should spring up."

There were five members of the crew in the lifeboat commanded by him and forty passengers. His boat did not have lights, although the regulations of the Board of Trade required that they should be carried. Of the women, he said: "They behaved splendidly. All of them wanted to help in the rowing to keep themselves warm. The boats were some distance from the Titanic when she went down."

How did she sink?—She settled by the head. Then, suddenly, she got on end and dived right straight down.

Did you hear any explosions?—Yes, four, they sounded like big guns in the distance.

What were these explosions?—I think they were the bulkheads.

As the ship went down, what did you observe on the after deck? Did you see people?—Oh, no. I wasn't close enough for that.

When did you last see Captain Smith?—When I went to the bridge. I asked him if I should fill No. 5 boat with women.

What did he say?—"Carry on."

When you shook hands with Murdock did you expect to see him again?—Certainly.

Do you think he expected to see you again?—Apparently not, but I expected fully to be back on the ship in a few hours.

CRIES FROM THE WATER.

Did you hear any cries of distress?—Oh, yes.

What, crying and shouting? Was it in the water?—Yes, from the water. I heard no cries of distress before the ship went down. The cries were probably several hundred yards away. Then I told my men to get out the oars and pull towards the wreck so that we might be able to save a few more. They demurred, saying that it would be a mad idea. It was not the crew who demurred, but the passengers.

Even the women did not urge him to go back. He yielded to the importunities of the

passengers and let the boat drift aimlessly.

"Describe the scenes," said the chairman.

"Don't, sir, I would rather not."

Senator Smith pressed him. Mr Pittman gave harrowing details of the last scene, the relating of which evidently caused him great pain.

He was asked if the screams were intermittent or spasmodic.—It was one long, continuous moan. The moans and cries continued for an hour.

He did not go to the rescue.

He appeared acutely sensitive with regard to Senator Smith's question as to why he drifted while people were drowning. He admitted that his load of 40 persons did not tax the capacity of his boat, which, he said would have carried 60 at a tight fit. He had transferred women and a child from his boat to boat no. 7.

Then you think that boat no. 7 could have held more people?—Yes.

Both these boats could have held more people then?—Yes.

Why were not more taken?—There were no more women about when my boat was lowered. I can't say about no. 7

Were there any men around?—There may have been.

"ALL CRIES HAD CEASED."

Why weren't they taken then?—I thought I had enough when my boat was lowered. I can't say about the others. I think that some boats had as many as 60 in them when they reached the Carpathia.

Senator Smith called attention to Mr Lightoller's evidence that the capsized collapsible boat had 35 persons in it, and asked: If that boat could keep afloat with 35 men when capsized wouldn't you think that the regular lifeboats could hold 60?—Yes, but there would be no room to move.

"When I saw the light of the Carpathia I slipped the rope that held our two boats together and pulled for it. This was about 4 o'clock. All moans and cries had ceased."

Did you see any bodies in the water?—No, at no time.

OPPOSITE PAGE: Commander Charles Lightoller was the ship's second officer and was off duty at the time of the collision. He was tasked with supervising the lifeboats on the port side of the ship. When collapsible lifeboat B was washed into the sea, he dived into the water and took charge of organising about 30 people onto the upturned boat and helped them keep it upright until they were rescued.

ABOVE LEFT: Henry Wilde was appointed Chief Officer just before the ship set sail. He was also off duty when the Titanic collided with the iceberg. He initially assisted with lowering the lifeboats on the port side and then moved to the starboard side. Wilde was last seen trying to launch the collapsible lifeboats.

He appeared acutely sensitive with regard to Senator Smith's question as to why he drifted while people were drowning. He admitted that his load of 40 persons did not tax the capacity of his boat, which, he said would have carried 60 at a tight fit.

While you were lying on your oars, did you see any lights of any kind apart from those of the Carpathia and the other lifeboats?

Yes. We saw a light on the horizon. A white light.

Was it on the track of the Titanic?—Yes, but we did not follow it. It might have been one of our own boats.

The witness did not see any Morse signals on the Titanic, but twelve or more rockets were fired.

Senator Smith, seeking to verify Mr Boxhall's evidence yesterday regarding the strange ship that failed to give aid, asked Pittman about the point. He knew nothing of his own knowledge as to the presence of the ship, but he had heard later that one did pass.

Did you fix the time when the Titanic sank?—I took out my watch when she sank and said, "It's 2.20," and the passengers around me heard.

Did you when aboard the Titanic hear anything about the proximity of the Frankfurt or any other ship?—No.

Mr Pittman said that there was a watertight door lever on the bridge. He did not know really whether the doors were closed or not, but the doors would have been no use in any case, because the iceberg had torn out the side of the ship. If the vessel had struck the berg head on she would be afloat today.

Mr Burton interrogated him about the white light he had seen from the lifeboat. The witness said that it appeared to him like a fixed light. It might have been a star. He did not see any red side light. He "supposed" the Titanic was going at top speed when she crashed into the iceberg. They had the exact position of the iceberg, he continued. It was some distance from the Titanic's course. The information came in a marconigram from "some ship." When the collision occurred the Titanic was going at the greatest speed attained during the trip.

If the Titanic had carried searchlights do you believe that these might have revealed the proximity of the icebergs?—I think so, possibly.

Do you know of any reason why the speed of the Titanic was not reduced after the warning about ice?—No. It is customary to reduce speed.

He was asked if the steam whistle or siren was used to detect the presence of ice by means of an echo?—No. I wouldn't have any faith in such a test.

Did you ever hear anything about a boat known as the Hellig Olav?—No.

The Olav docked in New York on April 17 and is reported to have encountered an iceberg near the spot where the Titanic sank. It has been suggested that the Olav

may have been the "mystery ship" whose lights were seen by Mr Boxhall, the fourth officer.—Reuter's Special.

THE LOOK-OUT MAN
NO GLASSES TO WATCH FOR
THE ICE WITH.

Frederick Fleet, twenty-five, sailor and the look-out man, said he had Sailor Leigh in the crow's nest with him.

Did you see any ice?—Yes. At seven bells (11.30 pm) I reported a black mass ahead.

What did you do when you saw the iceberg?—I sounded three bells and then telephoned to the bridge. I got prompt response to my ring, and the report was not delayed.

Was it five minutes or an hour before the collision that you saw the iceberg?—I don't know.

If you had had glasses could you have seen the iceberg sooner?—We could have seen it a bit sooner.

How much sooner?—Enough to get out of the way.

Were you and Leigh disappointed that you had no glasses?—Yes.

Did the officers on the bridge have glasses?—Yes.

Fleet then told of the launching of the lifeboat No. 5 of which he and Quartermaster Hichens took charge until they were picked up by the Carpathia. "We had three male passengers and about twenty five women. We had orders to pull for a light off the Titanic port bow, but we could not get to her. At one time she was abreast of us but she slipped by."

Were there other lights ahead when you were in the crow's nest?—No. We didn't see

> ## "After you gave the telephone signal was the ship stopped?"— "No, she did not stop until after she struck the iceberg, but she started to go to port after I telephoned."

After you gave the telephone signal was the ship stopped?—No, she did not stop until after she struck the iceberg, but she started to go to port after I telephoned.

Did the collision alarm you?—No. I thought it was a narrow shave.

Did you have glasses?—No.

Isn't it customary for look-outs to use glasses in their work?—Yes, but they did not give us any in the Titanic. We asked for them at Southampton, but they said there were none for us.

Whom did you ask?—Mr Lightoller (the second officer).

the light off the port bow until after we were in the lifeboat.

"THIS BOAT CAN'T SINK"
Major Arthur Peuchen of Toronto, said: "We were all pleased with the trip until the crash. After a few minutes following the collision I went to my friends and said that it was not serious.

"Fifteen minutes later I met Mr Charles M Hayes, of the Grand Trunk Railway. I asked him, 'Have you seen the ice? and I took him up and showed him it. Then I noticed that the ship was listing, and I said to Mr Hays,

"We heard a whistle. It was the signal to us to come back to the ship. We didn't want to go, because the quartermaster said that it was our lives against theirs."

'She's listing. She should not do that.' He said, 'Oh, I don't know. This boat can't sink.' He had a good deal of confidence, and said, 'It does not matter what we've struck, she is good for eight or ten hours.' I went back to the cabin deck where I met men and women coming up.

"The boats were being prepared for lowering on the port side. Women came forward one by one accompanied by their husbands. They would only allow women to pass, and the men had to stand back. The second officer stood there, and that was the order enforced. No men passengers got into the boat.

"I was surprised that the sailors were not at their posts as they should have been. I've seen fire drills and the action of the sailors did not impress me. They seemed to be short of sailors round the lifeboats where I was.

"When I came on deck first it seemed to me that about 100 stokers came up and crowded the deck. One of the officers, a splendid man, drove these men right off the deck like sheep. When we got to the next boat a quartermaster and a sailor were put in, and the boat was then filled with women.

"We called out for more women. Some would not leave their husbands. The second boat was lowered, and, as it was going down, the second officer said, 'I can't manage this boat with only one seaman.' I was standing by and said, 'Can I be of any assistance? I'm a yachtsman.' He replied, 'Yes, I would rather have you than a sailor.' I got hold of a rope and lowered myself into the boat.

"We got the rudder in and I took an oar with a sailor. We were told to row away as fast as we could to get clear of the suction."

PROTEST OF THE WAVES

We heard a whistle. It was the signal to us to come back to the ship. We didn't want to go, because the quartermaster said that it was our lives against theirs. There was an instantaneous protest from the married women, who wanted to return.

What did you do?—I said nothing. The quartermaster ordered us to resume rowing from the Titanic, which we did. The quartermaster imagined that he saw a light away from the vessel, and insisted on rowing towards it.

The final disappearance of the Titanic was followed by the rumbling sound of two explosions, and then by dreadful cries, which grew fainter and fainter. The women in the lifeboats rowed and were most plucky. Miss E A Norton, of Acton-lane, London, was one of them.

Probably the failure to sound the general alarm after the collision accounted for the non-appearance of many of the women on the decks in time to take the lifeboats. There were no more women about when the two lifeboats which he helped to launch were got off. He wondered why more men were not taken. No one could live in the icy water more than an hour.

He was of opinion that if the look-outs had had glasses the ship might have been saved.

OPPOSITE PAGE: Lord Pirrie, the Chairman of Harland and Wolff (left) and Ismay making a final inspection of the Titanic as it stood on the slipway on May 31, 1911. Pirrie was due to have sailed on the maiden voyage but had pulled out due to illness.

BELOW: Survivors from the Titanic on board lifeboat No. 6 with Quartermaster Hichens standing at the stern.

LIFEBOATS IN LINERS.

To the Editor of *The Daily Mail.*

Sir,—As we are now to have an inquiry into the boat question in liners, I think it is only right to draw your attention to one point which would seem to have escaped notice so far.

In the case of a davit that carries more than one boat the experience gained is that when the first boat is lowered the falls jam and it is most difficult to round up the blocks to hook on the second boat. What should be done is that in each boat there should be one spare set of blocks and fall coiled down forward and one aft. The pin in the davit head should be of a metal that would not rust and should be taken out quite easily, so that directly the first boat was lowered you would shackle on your second block and lower away the boat quite irrespective of your first block and tackle.

I think most nautical men will agree that it would be far quicker and easier to shackle on a fresh block than to round up the block that had already been used, as the block would most probably have canted over and the fall would be kinked, making it quite a difficult job to get ready for the second boat. I have consulted very carefully with a nautical friend of mine who has had vast experience with boats and boat lowering, and he quite agrees with me in this matter.

With regard to collapsible boats, these should be kept each side of the ship, and a small derrick should be kept rigged so that they could be put over quickly without interfering with the working of the ordinary boats from the davits. These collapsible boats have absolutely no weight, and a very small derrick would do this work quite well.

In conclusion, my opinion of the Board of Trade regulations is that not only are they out of date, but that their inspectors should be seamen, not men picked after a scientific examination, but picked on account of their experience absolutely in boat work, and these inspectorships should be kept open to men serving as chief officers in the large liners. WILFRED DULCKEN.

19, Swan-street, Minories, E.C.

THE BRAVERY OF THE TITANIC ENGINEERS.

To the Editor of *The Daily Mail.*

Sir,—There are many accounts of heroism among both passengers and ship's company, but no single mention of the engineer officers.

Not a man of the engineer staff has been saved, but we know that the pumps were running (water from discharge nearly swamping a lifeboat) and that the lights burned until just before the end.

This means that these men were at their posts and met their deaths, not upon the deck under God's open sky and with a fighting chance, but down in pump-room, dynamo-room, or stokehold, boxed up in steel compartments, where they found it their duty to be.

As in the Victoria so in the Titanic these men died under circumstances that would shake the fortitude of the normally courageous.

As Kipling puts it in "A Fleet in Being," their "bill was presented to them down there, under steel decks, to be peeled, boiled, blinded, or flayed."

And we do not find one of them in the boats nor hear of the presence of any of them upon the deck.

The Victoria's engineers were mentioned in the House; surely these men deserve some special mention, some special honour.

Dilton House, Rugby. H. F. L. HEMMINGS.

"WOMEN FIRST!"

To the Editor of *The Daily Mail.*

Sir,—Your correspondent Lady Aberconway writes from the calm shelter of her study table her views on "Women First." Whether she would still have maintained these views had she been on board the Titanic one may be permitted to doubt.

However, had such been the case she could have avoided the slightest chance of rescue first by locking herself in one of the dressing-rooms until the last boat had left the ship; no one would have had time to look for her.

As a seasoned traveller, it gives me much pleasure to point out to any member of my sex who may some day find herself liable to be rescued from a sinking ship this easy method of asserting her views as to the rights of women to drown and of men to be saved.

That any crumb of comfort which can be found by the poor widows, mothers, and orphans of the brave dead should be taken from them by the expression of such views at such a time as those contained in the letter you publish is my reason for holding them up to ridicule.

FRANCES M. GATTY.
Benarth Hall, Conway, North Wales.

To the Editor of *The Daily Mail.*

Sir,—The rule that women and children should first be saved seems to have involved in the Titanic that men should not be saved at all.

There are those, in consequence, who contend that the requirements of the absent wife and child should be considered by the husband and father upon whom they depend before those of the casual woman in distress.

CHARLES ED. JERNINGHAM.
14, Pelham-crescent, Thurloe-square, S.W.

To the Editor of *The Daily Mail.*

Sir,—It was with great satisfaction that I read the letter from Lady Aberconway in *The Daily Mail.* I am very glad indeed that the question has been raised by a woman of standing and intellectual ability, and I have much pleasure in supporting Lady Aberconway's claim for equal treatment of men and women in such a case as the wreck of the Titanic.

It is a false and foolish idea that women prefer and must be given life at any price, and equally foolish and cruel to force women to live against their will under circumstances which may make life worthless to them, and to force men to give up their lives, however valuable to themselves and others.

As a woman Suffragist, I claim the right equally with men to be regarded as a citizen of the Empire. I have made six voyages of over 7,000 miles each, besides short voyages between India and Burma, and I shall certainly claim the right to be treated as a man in case of shipwreck on my next voyage.

I thank Lady Aberconway for expressing so ably my views and feelings on this subject, which is in the minds of all. And I feel sure that all women Suffragists and all devoted wives and loving mothers of sons—if not all women the world over—will support this view, and desire this equal right to die bravely, the right to save a man's life and to share a man's death.

ALICE MARY DAWSON.
68, Wymering-mansions, W.

CAPT. SMITH'S £1,250.

EXCEPTIONAL SALARY.

The salaries paid to the captains and other officers employed by the great Atlantic shipping lines are furnished by our Liverpool correspondent. Captain Smith, the commander of the Titanic, received £1,250 a year, but his salary was exceptionally large.

The following is a table of the salaries paid by some of the leading lines:—

WHITE STAR.
Captains ....£350 to £1,000 per annum.
Chief officers ....£14 to £20 per month.
Second officers ....£9 to £12 per month.
Third officers ....£9 per month.
Fourth officers ....£8 10s. per month.

CUNARD LINE.
Captains ....£275 to £650 a year.
Chief officers ....£16 to £22 per month.
Second officers ....£11 to £12 per month.
Fourth officers ....£8 per month.

P. AND O.
Captains ....£400 to £900 per year.
Chief officers ....£14 to £20 per month.
Second officers ......£10 to £13 per month.
Third officers ....£9 per month.
Fourth officers ....£7 per month.

CAPTAIN SMITH'S INSURANCE.

The White Star Line's insurance and pension scheme applies to the senior members of the different departments on board ship. According to a table furnished by the company the payment due to the widow of Captain Smith is £1,168.

Any man on the ship's articles, whether officer or ordinary member of the crew, whose total earnings do not reach £250 will come under the scope of the Workmen's Compensation Act.

M.P.s AND TITANIC INQUIRY.

TREATMENT OF BRITISH WITNESSES.

FOREIGN OFFICE VIEW.

Mr. Munro Ferguson asked in the House of Commons yesterday what were the grounds on which an inquiry was being held into the loss of the Titanic in America, what was the status of the court holding the inquiry, and what was the precedent for a foreign inquiry into the loss of a British ship?

Mr. Acland (for the Foreign Office): I am not aware of the precise grounds on which the inquiry is being held. I understand the object to be to determine the responsibility for the wreck. Sections 101-2-3-4 of the revised statutes of the United States give power to a committee of either the Senate or the House of Representatives to summon witnesses and to administer oaths, and any person refusing to answer is guilty of a misdemeanour. It would seem, however, that the witnesses appeared voluntarily and had not been subpœnaed. So far as I am aware there has been hitherto no case of a foreign inquiry into the wreck of a British vessel on the high seas.

Mr. Munro Ferguson: What will happen if witnesses required for the British inquiry are detained in America? Have any instructions been sent to the British Ambassador at Washington?

Mr. Acland: With regard to the first question, I feel sure we may trust to the usual good sense of the American Senate and people in not desiring to detain persons whose attendance may be required by the statutory court of inquiry in this country. As to the second question, no definite instructions have yet to my knowledge been sent to our Ambassador.

Mr. Lee asked whether instructions would not be sent to the Ambassador at Washington to give such protection as was within his power to the British subjects summoned before the American Committee, who apparently have no one to defend their rights at present.

Mr. Acland: If the circumstances arose in which protection was desired instructions would be sent, but we hope that that case may not arise.

COMPULSORY WIRELESS.

Mr. Buxton, in reply to several questions, said the subject of wireless telegraphy was being considered by the court of inquiry. Compulsory installations would of course be under discussion. There would be no avoidable delay in issuing revised regulations with regard to life-saving appliances, but to insist upon one particular form of safeguard might be actually to incur new risks. It would not be necessary to wait for the verdict of the court of inquiry before issuing the revised regulations, but there were important points on which he could not take action until the inquiry had made some progress.

The number of women and children who perished in the wreck, he added, was 156.

Mr. Samuel said he had called for reports of all wireless messages sent from ships and wireless stations. Calls for distress from ships had priority over all other messages.

Mr. Churchill informed Major Archer Shee that the lifeboat accommodation provided in all military troopships was in excess of the number of troops and crew carried.

British Inquiry Recommendations

Lord Mersey's report, delivered July 30, 1912, included 24 recommendations to promote the safety of vessels and persons at sea, applicable to 'foreign-going passenger and emigrant steamships'. A committee was established to look into the practicality of extending the use of double-skinned hulls above the waterline. Titanic had only a double bottom. The committee also examined the design of watertight bulkheads. Titanic's bulkheads had been lowered to accommodate Ismay's vision for the glass-domed Grand Staircase, which swept majestically down over five levels, from the boat deck to the first-class accommodation, Turkish bath and swimming pool on E deck. Never again should the height of the bulkheads be governed by such grand designs.

Lifeboat provision ought to be based on the number of persons, not tonnage. Lifeboats should be manned by competent crewmen, with drills more frequent than was currently the case. The Mersey Report also recommended that a round-the-clock wireless telegraphy system be instituted, and that when ice was in the vicinity, ships should proceed 'at a moderate speed' in the hours of darkness, or alternatively, plot a course 'well clear of the danger zone'. The risk of collisions with icebergs was further reduced with the introduction in 1913 of the International Ice Patrol, under the aegis of the US Coast Guard.

Mersey also highlighted an existing regulation on the matter of vessels going to the aid of those in distress 'when possible to do so', clearly a shot across the bows of the Californian and her beleaguered captain Stanley Lord.

Just beyond were the bodies of a dozen more all in life-preservers and locked together as if they had died in the struggle for life.

OCEAN GRAVEYARD
WOMEN'S BODIES SEEN AMONG THE ICE

NEW YORK, Wednesday.
The German steamer Bremen on arrival to-day reported that she had sighted a hundred bodies from the Titanic. Mrs. Johanna Stunke, a cabin passenger, said: "We saw one woman in a nightdress with a baby clasped closely to her breast. Several of the women passengers screamed at the sight and left the rail in a fainting condition. There was another woman fully dressed with her arms tightly clutching the body of a shaggy dog. (It will be remembered that some of the survivors stated that one lady preferred to perish in the Titanic rather than leave her Pomeranian dog behind.)

"We noticed the bodies of three men in a group clinging to a steamer chair, and just beyond were the bodies of a dozen more all in life-preservers and locked together as if they had died in the struggle for life. We could see white life-preservers dotting the sea all the way to the iceberg." - Reuter's Special.

IN DISGUISE
MAN WHO SAYS HE DRESSED HIMSELF AS A SAILOR

Mme. Cardeza, whose husband and mother-in-law were among the survivors of the Titanic disaster, will go to New York today in order to accompany her husband on the homeward voyage.

She has received a letter from her husband, in which he states that he bribed two sailors to give him sailor's clothing.

He and his secretary, dressed in these clothes with his mother and her companion, succeeded in gaining the lifeboat as they were supposed to be sailors.—Central News.

RESPONSIBILITY OF THE BOARD OF TRADE

Sir,—Putting aside for the moment, and until reliable evidence is forthcoming on the points, the vital question of the speed at which the Titanic was moving when she struck the iceberg, the glaring fact stands out with ghastly prominence that this was one of the rare occasions on which, had there been sufficient boat accommodation, probably a very large proportion of the lives on board would have been saved, for the night, though dark, was a calm one.

Who is responsible for this excessive loss of life? The answer seems unquestionably to be "The Board of Trade." Mr. Buxton admits the responsibility and further admits that practically no steps have been taken to keep pace with the gigantic increase of modern ships in size-tonnage and carrying capacity. The result of this criminal negligence is a disaster involving a record loss of life in an accident at sea.

Mr. Carlisle and Mr. Wehlin in their letters dispose of the flimsy arguments against carrying more boats—the difficulty of lowering them without swamping is, of course, quite another question, and in rough weather (which does not apply in the case of the Titanic) must always be a serious factor, but in any case, I should fancy, a sufficiency of boats is more important than ridiculous private lounges for millionaires.

I do not entirely absolve the company from blame, though they seem to have exceeded the wickedly inadequate provisions of the Board of Trade regulations; but I do say this, that apathy and negligence, even undue dilatoriness on questions of such vital importance, is criminal, and if, as appears to be the case, the Board of Trade are responsible for the framing of safety regulations to guide the owners of British seagoing vessels, the authorities of that department should be brought to book at once in unmistakable and practical fashion.

Ernest Goldschmidt
Queen Anne's Mansions, S.W.

SHOTS ON TITANIC.
Steward's Story of the Fate of Two Passengers.

PEALS FOR THE DEAD.

Those survivors of the Titanic's crew who arrived at Plymouth yesterday on the liner Lapland and did not journey to Southampton will reach the latter port to-day.

Mr. Fitzpatrick, one of the stewards who were rescued from the Titanic, stated in an interview with an Exchange representative, that on Sunday, April 14, as he was serving the lunch in the engineers' mess, the chief steward, who had been an old seafaring man, said that he knew ice was in the vicinity of the ship by the smell of the air.

"We retired to our cabin," he continued, "which was situated on deck above the engine-room, and were settling down to sleep when we were aroused by a sudden lurch of the vessel.

"After a few minutes the engines were stopped. I inquired the reason for this sudden stoppage of the engines, and after being informed that the ship had struck an iceberg and that she was not seriously injured I settled myself to sleep again.

"I was awakened by a fireman. I went on deck, and the the ship was listing to port. As one of the lifeboats was being filled with women and children a foreigner tried to jump on the boat.

"The officer told him to go on deck. He refused, and the officer fired and the man fell dead on deck. The crowd of foreigners who were hanging around the lifeboat cowed back when they found one o ftheir countrymen dead.

"The lifeboat was lowered, and the officer kept on firing his revolver till he was level with the water.

"I saw a similar instance occur on the port side. A passenger tried to claim a seat in one of the boats. The officer told him to leave at once, and as he hesitated a revolver shot was fired and he dropped dead in the water.

"As the liner was dipping I jumped overboard in the icy water, and struck out with every effort I could in order to escape the suction.

"I was picked up by a lifeboat and afterwards taken on board the Carpathia."

OPPOSITE PAGE: English boy scouts collecting for the disaster fund. All around the country donations poured in to assist the bereaved families. Some parts of Britain fared worse than others. 724 crew members came from the Southampton area and only 175 survived. A report in the Hampshire Chronicle calculated that virtually every street in the Chapel district lost at least one resident.

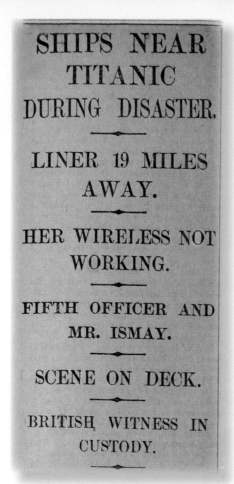

SHIPS NEAR TITANIC DURING DISASTER.

LINER 19 MILES AWAY.

HER WIRELESS NOT WORKING.

FIFTH OFFICER AND MR. ISMAY.

SCENE ON DECK.

BRITISH WITNESS IN CUSTODY.

The further the investigation of the loss of the Titanic proceeds the more extraordinary are the facts revealed.

The captain of the Leyland liner Californian now states that his vessel was only seventeen to nineteen miles distant from the Titanic when the latter struck the iceberg. The Californian steamed into the ice-field at 10.30pm on the Sunday (less than two hours before the Titanic struck), and then stopped her engines and waited for daylight.

The wireless apparatus was not working, as it was apparently run by the main engines. The Californian only heard of the disaster next morning.

Senator Smith, the chairman of the American Senate's Investigating Committee, announced yesterday that he will detain all the British witnesses in America as long as their presence is required there. This may delay the work of the Special British Wreck Commission under the presidency of Lord Mersey.

One English witness who was about to leave New York has been taken back to Washington in custody.

Criticisms are made in America of the ignorance displayed by the Investigating Committee, whose chairman, Mr Smith, has attracted attention by inquiring "Why the passengers did not take refuge in the watertight compartments," and "whether the Titanic sank by the bows or the head."

19 MILES FROM THE WRECK
STATEMENT BY CALIFORNIAN'S CAPTAIN

From our own correspondent, New York, Wednesday.

The identity of the vessel which is alleged to have been within five miles of the Titanic at the time of her collision is still shrouded in mystery. It is admitted, however, that there were at least two other vessels which were near enough to the scene of the disaster to have saved all the passengers of the great liner had their captains known of its terrible plight.

Captain Lord of the Leyland steamship Californian, which has arrived at Boston, calculates his distance as seventeen or nineteen miles from the Titanic on the fatal Sunday night. "We steamed into an immense field of ice about 10.30pm," he said today, "and immediately I shut down our engines to wait until daylight as a matter of safety. When the engines were stopped the wireless, of course, ceased working, so we did not hear of the Titanic's fate until we received a message from the Virginian. We then started immediately for the scene of the disaster."

Another vessel which passed close to the scene of the disaster was the freight steamer Lena from Fowey. When the Titanic struck, the Lena was not more than thirty miles distant, but as she is not equipped with wireless the officers were quite unconscious of the terrible calamity. They first learned of it on arrival at Portland, Maine.

The Lena reported that three vessels passed her on the day of the tragedy. The first was the tramp Kelvindale of Liverpool, bound for Louisburg, Nova Scotia. She passed the Lena at 4pm. At 8pm the Lena sighted a passenger steamer which appeared to have four masts, and later in the night another freighter was sighted.

SENATOR SMITH
"WE SHALL DETAIN ALL THE BRITISH WITNESSES"

Washington, Wednesday.

Frederick Fleet, the look-out in the crow's-nest at the time of the disaster, was again called when the Senate Committee's inquiry was resumed this morning.

Mr. Burton: When you were in the Titanic were your eyes examined?—Yes, frequently.

Can you distinguish colours?—Yes.

Did you, when you were in the crow's-nest, see a light?—I saw no light until I got into the lifeboat. Then I saw a bright light on our bow. I don't know what it was. Mr Lightoller (the second officer) saw it before we got off the Titanic. He told us to pull towards it. It finally disappeared, and we never made out what it was.

When you have binoculars, what part of

When the Titanic struck, the Lena was not more than thirty miles distant, but as she is not equipped with wireless the officers were quite unconscious of the terrible calamity.

the time do you have the glasses to your eyes while on the look-out?—If we fancy we see anything on the horizon we use the glasses to make sure.

Had you any experience in loading and lowering lifeboats?—All of us do in the White Star. I saw no lifeboats loaded other than No. 6 boat, in which I pulled away with about thirty passengers.

Were there any women left on the decks who did not get into the boat?—I saw none.

Did you call for them?—Yes. There were men on the decks, but none of them tried or even asked to be taken in. There was a stowaway in boat No. 6 an Italian, who had hidden beneath the seat. He was no help because he had injured his arm. Boat No. 6 asked for and got another man from the lifeboat to which we tied up.

Did you hear any cries for help?—Yes but they were very faint.

Did you go back to help?—No. Some of the passengers wanted to, but the quartermaster, who was in command, ordered us to keep on rowing.

How far were you from the Titanic when she sank?—It must have been a mile.

Senator Smith: In view of your experience in trying to estimate how far the Titanic was from the iceberg when you sighted it, I should say that you have not any judgment for distance?

"No more I haven't," answered the witness, whose evidence then concluded.

Senator Smith, as chairman of the Committee, then rose and formally said that he wanted to answer an inquiry which had arisen with regard to the purpose of the Committee.

"It is to get all the facts attending the catastrophe from the surviving officers and men of this ship and the shipbuilders. If we get from them what they know, it is all we can expect. Now a word regarding our plans. It is the intention of the Committee to question all subjects of Great Britain who are in this country and know anything about the disaster. We shall hold them here until we have learned all we can. This course will be pursued until the Committee concludes that it has obtained all accessible, useful information for the proper understanding

RIGHT: Emily Richards, holding her son George, pictured just before they boarded the Titanic. Originally from Penzance, she was emigrating to Ohio to join her husband. Emily was travelling with her two sons and four other members of her family; the women all managed to escape in two of the lifeboats but her brother, Richard George Hocking, went down with the ship.

OPPOSITE PAGE: The women on the Carpathia immediately rallied together to assist the rescued passengers with blankets, spare clothes and wraps.

of the disaster. The Committee will not tolerate any further attempt on the part of anyone to shape its course. We shall proceed in our own way."

Senator Smith delivered this statement with emphasis, punctuating his remarks by pounding his fist on the table. He would give no detailed explanation of what actuated his remarks.

THE FIFTH OFFICER

Mr. Harold J. Lowe, the fifth officer of the Titanic, was then called. He sketched his experiences from the time he ran away to sea at fourteen. He knocked about the world in sailing ships and steamers. He joined the White Star fifteen months ago. Until he shipped in the Titanic he had never been on the North Atlantic.

Did you ever hear of ice, Senator Smith asked, in the vicinity of Newfoundland?—No.

Never hear of any iceberg?—Yes, off Cape Horn. It was the only one I have ever seen until I saw a number at dawn on the day after the collision.

Are you a temperate man, Mr. Lowe?—I am. I say it without fear of contradiction.

I am glad to hear that, because I have just passed had up a note which says that it was reported by a reputable man that you were drinking on the night of the accident—Me drinking! It's impossible. That's rubbish. I am a total abstainer.

He gave this answer indignantly. He did not know when he was awakened. He dressed hurriedly and went on deck.

"I found people with lifebelts on and the boats being prepared. I could feel by my feet that something was wrong. The vessel was tipping by about 15deg. by the head. When I got on deck I began working the lifeboats under Mr. Murdock. Boat No. 5 was the first one we lowered."

SCENE WITH MR ISMAY

Who got into that boat?—I don't know; but there's one man here, and, had he not been here, I would not have known that I ordered Mr. Ismay away from the boat. A steward met me in the Carpathia and said to me, "What did you say to Mr. Ismay that night on deck?" I said that I did not know Mr. Ismay. The steward in the Carpathia said that I had used the strongest language to Mr Ismay. Shall I repeat it? If you want me to I will ; if not I won't. I happened to talk to Mr. Ismay because he appeared to be getting excited. He was saying excitedly, "Lower away! Lower away! Lower away!"

At this juncture the chairman asked Mr. Ismay about the words used. Mr. Ismay suggested that the objectionable language might be written down. This was done, and

"The dangers are that if you overcrowd a boat it will buckle up from the ends. 65.5 is the floating capacity. If you load from the deck to lower I should not like to put more than fifty in a lifeboat."

after the chairman had read what Mr Lowe had written he said:

"Then you said this to Mr Ismay? (showing the witness the writing), Why did you say it?"—Because he was in anxiety to get the boat lowered and was interfering with our work. He was interfering with me. I wanted him to get back, so that we could work. He was not trying to get into the boat. Finally I turned to him and said, "If you'll get to hell out of here we can get this boat away."

Did he step back?—Yes

Did Mr. Ismay make any reply?—No.

How many men were in the boat?—I'm not sure. I should say about ten.

How many men were put in for the purpose of manning her?—Five. I don't know if there was an officer aboard. Possible Mr Pittman was in that boat or in No. 3.

Were there any male passengers?—I think so, because we could find no more women.

The Chairman asked if the lifeboat before it was lowered was loaded to the proper capacity and had some difficulty in obtaining the answer in the form he wanted, having to interrupt the witness. Mr. Lowe, after complaining that the chairman was "pulling him up," finally answered "Yes."

You think it was properly loaded for lowering? What is the official quota for such lifeboats?—65.5

You mean that it can carry 65 adults and, say, a boy or a girl? Then you wish the Committee to understand that a lifeboat with new tackle and equipment under British regulations could not be lowered with safety with more than fifty people aboard?—The dangers are that if you overcrowd a boat it will buckle up from the ends; 65.5 is the floating capacity. If you load from the deck to lower I should not like to put more than fifty in a lifeboat.

Senator Smith : Referring to Mr. Pittman's testimony yesterday. He said there were 35 people in lifeboat No. 5. That being the case, why could not Mr. Pittman have gone to the rescue of the drowning, whose cries he heard plainly, but did not heed? Would he not have been able to accommodate 30 more with safety in that lifeboat?

Mr. Lowe: No. Had he attempted to rescue those in the water, he would have endangered the lives of those with him. I was not in a position to order who was to go into the boats.

WITNESS'S PROTESTS

But you were in a position to tell Mr. Ismay to go to hell?—Yes, because he was interfering with me personally. I wanted him to get away so that I could do something.

He did?—Yes, and I did something.

Is it not true that the reason why the boats were not properly loaded was because the crew were unable to row?—No.

What was the drill at Southampton for?—It was for the Board of Trade.

There were eight men to a boat then, where were those men when the emergency arose? They were all oarsman, Where were they when you were loading lifeboat No. 5?

You must remember that in harbour we had the pick of the men. At the time of the collision the men went down with the bos'n to clear away the gangway and doors to make way for the loading.

Did that take skilled men? Anyone could have done that, and yet skilled men were sent below when they were needed for loading and lowering the lifeboats. Is that the impression you want to give the Committee?

The witness protested against the interpretation of his statement.

> "I then called for volunteers to row back to the wreck. We rowed back and picked up four men struggling in the water. Three of them survived, but the fourth, Mr Hays of New York, died shortly after we took him out of the water."

Mr Lowe said that the discipline was excellent. Only one boat, a collapsible one, overturned. All the remainder of the nineteen boats were scientifically handled. "It takes from eight to ten men to make a lifeboat ready," he said.

What was the number of the crew?—So far as I know there were 903 crew.

And with 903 men on board you did not have enough men to man twenty lifeboats properly? The witness objected to this question, and the chairman criticised the refusal of the witness to make direct replies.

"You mean enough men present at the boats?" said Mr Lowe finally. "No, there were not."

Were any men, women, or children refused admission to the boats or put out of them after they had got in?—None were refused. The only confusion was created by passengers interfering with the lowering gear. Everything was quiet and orderly.

With everything quiet and orderly, who selected the people for the boats?—There was no such thing as selecting. First we took the women and children, and then the others as they came.

As you passed the women into the boats what did you say?—I simply shouted, "Women and children first; Men stand back."

Was there any discrimination as to class?—None whatever.

How about the stewardesses?—It made no difference.

Mr Smith sought in vain to learn the number of women in lifeboat No. 3. The witness thought that men and women were about equally divided, but he knew none of their names. He ventured the belief that the boat contained about forty persons.

Why were there not more?—We could not find anyone who wanted to go. They seemed not to care about getting into the boats. They were free to wander wherever they pleased. There was no effort made by the officers or crew either to restrain or to direct the passengers.

Did you see any of the women there?—Certainly, I saw women there, but I didn't have time to go and drag them away. They didn't respond to our calls.

A COWARD'S DISGUISE

"Afterwards I lowered three boats and walked across the deck and met Moody. We filled lifeboats Nos. 14,15 and 16 on that side with women and children. There was one man passenger in No. 14, an Italian who sneaked in. He was dressed rather like a woman. He had a shawl over his head. We did not find him out until too late."

Mr Lowe told the Committee that there were fifty eight people in his boat and that he tied five lifeboats together and transferred passengers from his boat to other boats.

"I then called for volunteers to row back to the wreck. We rowed back and picked up four men struggling in the water. Three of them survived, but the fourth, Mr Hays of New York, died shortly after we took him out of the water. I did not know the names of the others. There were a number of bodies floating around, but I did not see a single female corpse."

At what time was this?—Dawn was just breaking. it was light enough for me to get a good look round. Then when I sighted the Carpathia I set out for her because mine

> *"We did not dare go into the struggling mass. We remained at the edge of the scene. We would have taken everyone aboard that we could, but it would have been suicide to have gone in."*

was the fastest boat. I was afraid that the Carpathia might miss us.

You said a moment ago that you waited before returning to the wreck for things to quiet down. What did you mean by "quiet down?"—Until the cries had ceased.

The cries of the drowning?—Yes. We did not dare go into the struggling mass. We remained at the edge of the scene. We would have taken everyone aboard that we could, but it would have been suicide to have gone in.

MR ISMAY'S OBSESSION

Mr. Lightoller, the second officer, was recalled. Mr Barton asked him to relate his conversation with Mr. Ismay in the Carpathia.

"My fellow officers and I," said the witness, "talked over sailing in the Cedric, and we agreed that it would be a jolly good idea if we could catch the Cedric. Mr. Ismay asked me if I thought it would be desirable to send a wireless to hold the Cedric, I said 'Most certainly.'

"I will say that at the time, Mr. Ismay was in no mental condition to transact business. He seemed obsessed with the idea that he ought to have gone down with the ship, because there were women who went down. I tried my best to get the idea out of his head, but could not.

"I told him that there was more for him to do on earth, and that he should not let the idea possess him that he had done wrong in not staying behind to drown. The doctor in the Carpathia had trouble with Mr. Ismay on this ground.

"I was told in the Carpathia that when the chief officer, Wild, who was working forward at a collapsible boat, told Mr Ismay that there were no more women to. go, he stood back. Wild, who was a big powerful man, led him to the boat and put him in."

Mr. Smith plied him with questions and asked him to keep to Mr. Ismay, reverting to the questions asked at the previous hearing. "That's all in the previous testimony. You can find it all there." said Mr. Lightoller.

"I know I can find it there, but your memory seems to be better today than it was last week," retorted the chairman.

Did you know, when the telegrams were sent about the Cedric, that the Senate was to hold an investigation?—Most certainly not, or the telegram would never have been sent. Our sole idea was to keep the witnesses together for just such an investigation which we thought would be made at home in England.

Do you always follow the direct track?—When we know that there is ice we have a track which we sometimes use, the extreme southern one going home.

Who changes these routes?—The company. I have never known a commander change his track without orders.

A few minutes before the Titanic sank the pursers came to me. We all shook hands. "Goodbye, old man," they said. I said "Goodbye."

Did none of them survive?—No, all were lost.

Was there any panic on board?—Not the slightest.

The crowds of anxious relatives watched the passengers disembark from the Carpathia. Spotlights were shone on the crowds so survivors could find their relatives. No one was allowed to leave the ship without someone there to greet them.

OPPOSITE PAGE: Thomas Whiteley, a first saloon steward on board the Titanic. His leg was broken after being caught in one of the ropes as lifeboats were lowered. Other survivors had also broken limbs and several were suffering from frost-bite after prolonged periods in the freezing water..

BELOW: The crowds of anxious relatives watched the passengers disembark from the Carpathia. Spotlights were shone on the crowds so survivors could find their relatives. No one was allowed to leave the ship without someone there to greet them.

Blood money aboard Lifeboat No. 1?

Of the many emergency craft that left Titanic undermanned, Lifeboat No. 1 attracted particular comment. It left the sinking ship with 12 occupants – five first-class passengers and seven crewmen – when it could have accommodated 40. At the centre of the controversy were Sir Cosmo Duff Gordon and his wife, who were accused of vetoing the suggestion that they should search for other survivors. Fireman Charles Hendrickson said that having rowed some 200 yards away to escape the suction vortex created by the sinking liner, he suggested they ought to return to the scene to render assistance. The Duff Gordons objected, he said, fearing the boat might be swamped. Duff Gordon offered the crewmen a financial inducement when the subject was raised. The five-pound payment was putatively in reparation for their lost kit, but, given its timing, what might have been seen as a generous gesture invited a somewhat less noble interpretation.

LEFT: Colonel John Jacob Astor IV, the American millionaire lost his life. He had recently divorced his first wife and married 18 year-old Madeleine Talmadge Force, who was a year younger than his son. This caused a huge scandal and the couple had extended their honeymoon in Egypt and Europe to let the gossip die down. She was five months pregnant when they boarded the ship; he had ensured she was helped onto a lifeboat and consequently survived along with their son born exactly four months later.

OPPOSITE PAGE ABOVE: Ismay and his attorney leaving the inquest. Senator William Alden Smith was in charge of the initial American inquiry which began the day after the Carpathia returned to New York. Held in the ballroom at the Waldorf-Astoria Hotel, he was anxious to interview key witnesses before they all dispersed.

OPPOSITE PAGE BELOW: Scenes from the U. S. Senate enquiry. Other key witnesses were Charles Lightoller, the second officer aboard and Harold Bride, one of the wireless operators. Lightoller defended the actions of his superiors and emerged as one of the officers who was proactive in loading passengers onto lifeboats.

THE TITANIC INQUIRY.

CONSTITUTION OF THE BRITISH COURT.

FIRST SITTING

TO TAKE PLACE IN LONDON ON THURSDAY NEXT.

The first sitting of the British Court of Inquiry into the loss of the Titanic will be held on Thursday next at the London Scottish Hall, Buckingham Gate, S.W.

The names of four of the five assessors who will assist Lord Mersey in the conduct of the British inquiry have been announced. They are Rear-Admiral the Hon. S. A. Gough-Calthorpe, Captain A. W. Clarke, Commander F. C. Lyon, R.N.R., and Professor J. H. Biles.

The most interesting part of the evidence given yesterday at the United States inquiry into the loss of the Titanic was that of witnesses from the Californian.

The wireless operator in this vessel stated that before the Titanic struck the iceberg, he, acting on the instructions of his captain, warned the Titanic of the nearness of ice and was told to "Shut up" as he was interfering with messages being sent to Cape Race.

But it was also brought out that the Titanic had previously heard the Californian's warning sent to other ships.

The captain of the Californian spoke of an unknown vessel which lay near him in the icefield on the night of the disaster, and sent up white rockets, but made no reply to inquiries as to who she was.

Senator Smith, the man of the moment, has been invited to lecture at a London music-hall on "Modern Liners."

The Mansion House Relief Fund now amounts to £168,000.

Acting on the instructions of his captain, he warned the Titanic of the nearness of ice and was told to "shut up" as he was interfering with messages being sent to Cape Race.

MR. ISMAY

Told To Stand Back From Boat When Anxious To Get It Lowered.

Another Reuter message states that Mr. Lowe, the fifth officer of the Titanic, said he did not know when he was awakened. He dressed hurriedly and went on deck.

"I found people with lifebelts on and the boats being prepared. I could feel by my feet that something was wrong. The vessel was tipping about 15deg. by the head. When I got on deck I began working the lifeboats under Mr. Murdock. Boat No. 5 was the first one we lowered."

Who got into that boat?—I don't know; but there's one man here, and had he not been here, I would not have known that I ordered Mr. Ismay away from the boat. A steward met me in the Carpathia and said to me, "What did you say to Mr. Ismay that night on deck?" I said that I did not know Mr. Ismay.

The steward in the Carpathia said that I had used the strongest language to Mr. Ismay. Shall I repeat it? If you want me to I will; if not, I won't. I happened to talk to Mr. Ismay because he appeared to be getting excited. He was saying excitedly, "Lower away! Lower away! Lower away!"

At this juncture the chairman asked Mr. Ismay about the words used. Mr. Ismay suggested that the objectionable language might be written down. This was done, and after the chairman had read what Mr. Lowe had written he said:

"Then you said this to Mr. Ismay? (showing the witness the writing). Why did you say it?"—Because he was in anxiety to get the boat lowered and was interfering with our work. He was interfering with me. I wanted him to get back, so that we could work. He was not trying to get into the boat. Finally I turned to him and said, "If you'll get to hell out of here we can get this boat away."

Did he step back?—Yes.

Did Mr. Ismay make any reply?—No.

Senator Smith: Referring to Mr. Pittman's testimony yesterday. He said there were thirty-five people in lifeboat No. 5. That being the case, why could not Mr. Pittman have gone to the rescue of the drowning, whose cries he heard plainly, but did not heed? Would he not have been able to accommodate thirty more with safety in that lifeboat?

Mr. Lowe: No. Had he attempted to rescue those in the water he would have endangered the lives of those with him. I was not in a position to order who was to go into the boats.

THE STORY OF THE UNSINKABLE TITANIC 97

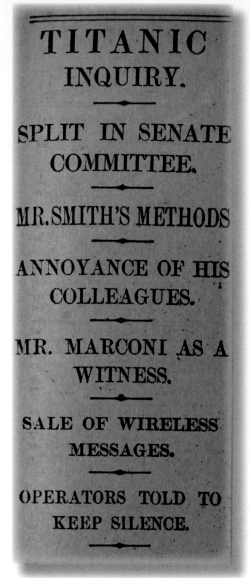

TITANIC INQUIRY.

SPLIT IN SENATE COMMITTEE.

MR. SMITH'S METHODS

ANNOYANCE OF HIS COLLEAGUES.

MR. MARCONI AS A WITNESS.

SALE OF WIRELESS MESSAGES.

OPERATORS TOLD TO KEEP SILENCE.

Dissensions have now arisen in the United States Senate Committee, which has been investigating the loss of the Titanic.

The chairman Senator Smith, has been outvoted by his colleagues.

The committee has now decided to expedite matters "by apportioning the work of examining witnesses to different Members of the Committee".

A character sketch of Senator Smith by our New York correspondent appears on the preceding page.

Mr Marconi was the principal witness yesterday. He was confronted with wireless messages to the Carpathia which had been picked up by an American battleship, and placed by the United States Government at the disposal of the Committee.

MR MARCONI
THE SALE OF WIRELESS NEWS
WASHINGTON, Thursday

The inquiry into the Titanic disaster was continued today. Mr Marconi was called, and questioned regarding a message sent from New York to the wireless operators in the Carpathia asking them to hold the news when they reached port for 'four figures'.

"Yes," said Mr Marconi, "that message was sent by Mr Sammis (chief engineer of the Marconi system). I knew nothing about it until afterwards. The message was not sent until the Carpathia had passed Sandy Hook.

About your official connection with the British Government:— I have no official connection except for consultation. Our company has a contract with the Government for the extension of wireless in the British Empire. The work will take us at least eighteen years.

Have you the exclusive right to equip British wireless stations?—We have the rights so far as the courts protect our patents in England.

Have you such rights in Germany?— No. Germany's ships and stations are controlled by a company which works in harmony with us. Mr Marconi detailed his contracts with the Italian, Canadian, and Newfoundland Governments.

The station at Cape Race could maintain communication with a vessel for 400 or 500 miles by day, and over 1,000 miles by night.

Was there any arrangement which gave the alarm on board a ship when she was called by wireless?—On the old equipment used by ships there was a bell arrangement which did not work well, because it alarmed the operators of all ships as well as the one called.

Then there is no alarm signal on the instruments now?—No.

Unless the operator sat constantly with the receiver on his head he would not get a signal?—That's correct.

What about the operators' pay?—In England the pay ranges from 16s. to 19s. a week. with board and lodging. In America pay is slightly higher.

Did you have any communication with Cape Race on Sunday, April 14th or on any day up to the arrival of the Carpathia at New York?— I had no direct communication. I urged that every means should be tried to get information of the disaster.

On boarding the Carpathia, I went directly to the wireless room and congratulated Mr Bride. Mr Cottam, the Carpathia's operator, was not there. He rang me up later and asked whether he might give out a report of the wreck. I told him he might under the circumstances. There is an ironclad rule of the company's regulations prohibiting operators from acting as reporters.

Under British law it is a penal offence for operators to send out information on their own initiative. This is probably the reason why no reports of the disaster were forthcoming from the Carpathia on her way to New York.

Did you send a wireless to the operator in the Carpathia telling him to meet you and Mr Sammis at the Strand Hotel and to keep his mouth shut?—I did not.

THE TITANIC'S CALL

Mr. Cottam, the wireless operator in the Carpathia, was then recalled. The first message from the Titanic was "come at once, have struck berg. This C.Q.D." He assisted the Titanic to communicate with other ships, the Titanic operator saying that escaping steam on board was interfering with his instruments. Hr told how he got into touch with the Olympic, Californian and Baltic.

Did you receive a wireless from the Chester?—Several, asking for the passenger list. I took the messages to the captain. He replied later stating that names of survivors had already been forwarded. He told the Chester that all but the third-class passengers had been sent and that the Chester could have these if wanted.

Did you know that the message was from the President?—No. It was only signed by the commander of the Chester.

Senator Smith read the "Keep your mouth shut" telegram, but the witness said he did not know of it. He did remember the receipt of a message from Mr Sammis promising operators money in four figures for their stories.

Did you keep your mouth shut as directed?—Certainly. The captain told me to ignore passing ships and to refuse all calls for details. We had passengers to look after.

"Then there is no alarm signal on the instruments now?" – "No." "Unless the operator sat constantly with the receiver on his head he would not get a signal?" – "That's correct."

Cottam said that when he arrived in New York, he went to the Strand Hotel, but he could not find Mr Marconi or anyone connected with the company. He waited about the hotel for a time. An hour later he called up Mr Marconi on the telephone. He sold his story, but had not yet received anything for it. He had only talked to a reporter. He had been told that it would be all right for him to tell his story. He did not talk about money, relying on the message from Mr Sammis.

Is there any rivalry or enmity between Marconi operators and those of other systems?—There is some feeling.

Did any feeling exist between the operators in the Titanic and the one in Frankfurt, who did not reply promptly to the Titanic's C.Q.D? No, The signal C.Q.D. was enough for the operator to have reported immediately the distress of the vessel. I would have answered the operator of the Frankfurt in the same way that the Titanic did – "Keep out, you fool" – if it had been my place to when the Frankfurt answered the Titanic's C.Q.D call. When there are only two hours between life and death, twenty minutes is a long time. I don't know what else but a fool to call a man who is so foolish as to interfere with other communications in answer to the C.Q.D and ask "What's the matter?" twenty minutes later.

BELOW: The Italian inventor Guglielmo Marconi photographed in 1896 with his first wireless receiver. Bride and Phillips were employed by the Marconi International Marine Communication Company rather than White Star. Marconi's station near South Wellfleet in Massachusetts was one of the first to pick up the Titanic's distress signal. At the British enquiry it was widely acknowledged that his invention had helped to save the lives of hundreds of rescued passengers.

SENATOR SMITH'S INQUIRY.

Moreover, strictly speaking, under international law, the officers and men of the Titanic are answerable only to a British court. There is no wish on this side to strain that point, but its cogency is unquestionable. The Titanic sailed under the British flag; she was lost on the high seas. It was, therefore, on British territory that the catastrophe took place. It is of the extremest importance that her loss should be the subject of full and careful inquiry by a court of experts, with legal power to enforce its judgment, at the earliest possible date. For such an inquiry the witnesses must be forthcoming in England. We hope then, that, in Mr. Acland's words, "We may trust to the usual good sense of the American Senate and American people not to desire to detain persons whose attendance may be required by the Statutory Court of Inquiry in this country." Vital issues hang upon the finding of that tribunal. The Board of Trade acknowledges that further precautions are urgently required to give safety at sea. But until the British court has brought expert knowledge to bear and shown what is needed, those precautions cannot be taken. Only less important is the question of compensation to the survivors, which cannot be decided until the court has ascertained whether the disaster was caused by negligence or by what we know as an "act of God."

SHOTS IN THE TITANIC

At the close of last night's sitting Mr. Lowe, the fifth officer, was asked by Senator Smith: Did you hear any pistol shots during the disaster?—He answered:

I fired them. As lifeboat No. 15 was going down the ship's side I feared that many would leap into it as we passed the decks. I thought, "Well, I shall have to see that no one else gets into the boat." I thought that if any more got in something would snap. As we were lowering away I saw a lot of Italians at the ship's rail glaring and ready to spring. I yelled "Look out!" I know I didn't hurt anyone — Reuter's Special.

PEERS AND THE INQUIRY

LORD HALSBURY EMPHATIC Lord Stanhope, in the House of Lords yesterday, raised the question of the jurisdiction of the United States Inquiry into the loss of the Titanic, remarking that it was difficult to see where we should end if the case was to be taken as a precedent. He could imagine nothing more terrible than that the survivors should be dragged about from one country to another to attend inquiries and give evidence.

Lord Morley, who deprecated discussion on the matter, said there was no doubt that any State could institute an inquiry into the wreck of a foreign vessel in which its own citizens had been lost. There had been no communication with the United States upon the point.

Lord Halsbury did not think the national character of the ship a mere technicality. It was a matter of supreme importance. A jurisdiction all over the world would be intolerable.

Lord Morley said the government were in communication with the British Ambassador, and he had had, up till that day at all events, no appeal from any British subjects desiring protection against detention or arrest, or anything else.

Mr Bryce, the British Ambassador, and Mrs Bryce have left Washington for San Francisco, whence they will sail for New Zealand. They will be absent for three months.

205 BODIES FOUND.

DEATH BELIEVED TO HAVE BEEN INSTANTANEOUS.

NEW YORK, Thursday.

The cable ship Mackay Bennett reports that she has picked up 205 bodies. The captain is of the opinion that the majority of the other bodies will never rise to the surface. He says that, with a week's fine weather, he "would pretty well clear up the relics." It is not indicated when the Mackay Bennett will reach Halifax.

According to medical opinion death was instantaneous in the case of those who went down with the Titanic owing to the pressure when the bodies were drawn down into the vortex.—Reuter.

SHIP THAT WAS SEEN FROM THE SINKING LINER.

WASHINGTON, Friday.

Edward J. Baley, able seaman, of Southampton, of the Titanic, testified that another steamer with two lights at her masthead was visible when the Titanic struck.

She passed right by us, he said, and we thought that she was coming to us. If she had everyone could have boarded her. The lifeboats started for those very lights, and it was these lights which kept the boats together. For about three hours the steamer was stationary, and then she made tracks.

Mr. Fletcher: Why could she not see your sky-rockets?—She could not help seeing them. She was close enough to see our lights, and we could see the ship itself.

I saw this steamer before I left the Titanic and told the passengers that it was coming to our assistance. That was what kept the passengers quiet.

The steamer gave no signal whatever, but they must have known the Titanic was in distress for they must have seen our rockets.—Reuter's Special.

Monetary offer

Sir Cosmo and his wife painted a very different picture. There were 'no people visible' on the starboard deck when the lifeboat was lowered, hence there was no breach of the 'women and children first' rule. Once the ship went under, they heard no cries, had no recollection of anyone suggesting they return to the scene and denied being concerned their cutter might be swamped. Asked if he noted that Lifeboat No. 1 had room for many other persons, Sir Cosmo replied: 'There would have been more room if the oars and masts had been thrown away'. He admitted making the monetary offer, an oddly timed goodwill gesture, as one of his inquisitors pointed out: 'Do you suggest that it was more natural to think of offering men five pounds to replace their kit than to think of those screaming people who were drowning?'

The Inquiry, while finding in general terms that more could have been done to rescue those flailing around in the freezing ocean, exonerated the titled couple from the particular allegations levelled against them. Lord Mersey's report said the bribery charge was unfounded, and on the question of returning to help those in need said: 'I do not believe that the men were deterred from making the attempt by any act of Sir Cosmo Duff Gordon's. At the same time I think that if he had encouraged the men to return to the position where the Titanic had foundered they would probably have made an effort to do so and could have saved some lives.'

MAIN PICTURE: The position of the crow's nest on the Titanic is marked by the hole in the mast which held the ship's telephone. On one occasion the scientists sent a video camera down through the space once occupied by the first class staircase where original light fixtures and the carved oak bases of the pillars were still visible.

SENATOR SMITH.

"THERE IS NO BRITISH OPPOSITION."

WASHINGTON, Friday.

The criticism passed in England on the conduct of the Titanic inquiry has received a good deal of attention. Senator Smith, while declining to make any detailed reply to the criticism, said:

"I have had personal assurances from most of the Titanic's officers that they have no criticisms to make on the Committee or the conduct of the inquiry.

"There is no British opposition to this inquiry. I have heard of none from anywhere."

Seaman Samuel Hemming said that he was asleep when the ship struck. He looked out and returned to bed. A boatswain came and said: "Turn out you fellows. You haven't half an hour to live. That's from Mr. Andrews (one of the designers of the ship). Keep it to yourselves. Let no one know." Other members of the crew stated that they got no such warning. Many of them were "sky-larking and joking" after the accident.

Quartermaster Rowe, who was in charge of the lifeboat in which Mr. Ismay left, said that Mr. Ismay did not get into the lifeboat until after the women and children had failed to respond to calls. Mr. Ismay was not ordered from the boat, but stepped into it just before it was lowered. No one asked Mr. Ismay to get in.

The inquiry proper was resumed at a quarter past ten this morning. Mr. Franklin, vice-president of the International Maritime Company (owners of the White Star) was called.

Senator Smith asked Mr. Franklin if he could say if the Naronic was lost at sea (in 1893) near the spot at which the Titanic went down.—The ship was never heard of after the time she left port. No one knows where she went down.

The operator Cottam testified before the Committee in New York that he did not report a message to the captain of the Carpathia because he did not consider it important. The operator in the Titanic refused to take a warning of the presence of ice from the Californian because he was busy with his accounts. I ask you if there should not be rules and regulations governing the operators?—I agree, most emphatically.—Reuter's Special.

THE SHIP NEAREST THE TITANIC.

"WATCHING DISTRESS SIGNALS."

AFFIDAVIT BY A SEAMAN.

CAPTAIN'S DENIAL.

The feature of yesterday's evidence before the American Committee of Inquiry was an affidavit by a seaman of the Californian, who swore that he saw the Titanic's distress signals.

This was denied by the Californian's captain, who said that the "distress signals" were only white rockets sent up by some other ship of which he did not know the name, which lay-to near him and afterwards steamed away.

SEAMAN'S AFFIDAVIT

WATCHING THE ROCKETS FROM THE TITANIC

Ernest Gill, of Liverpool, aged twenty-nine, a donkey-engine man of the Californian, the ship nearest the Titanic when she sank, was called before the Committee.

Senator Smith first read an affidavit made by Gill on Wednesday. He said that he saw the Titanic most plainly. Ten minutes after midnight he saw a white rocket ten miles away. A second rocket went up seven or eight minutes later.

He said to himself, "That must be a vessel in distress." He did not notify the bridge because it was not his business. They could not have helped seeing the rockets.

At 6.40 a.m. he was awakened by orders to turn out to render assistance as the Titanic had gone down. The Californian was then proceeding at full speed. He heard the second officer, Evans, telling the fourth officer, Wooten, that the third officer had reported rockets during his watch. Gill said that he knew then that it must be the Titanic he had seen. Mr. Gibson reported rockets to the captain, who told him to continue Morse to the distressed vessel until he got a reply. No reply was received. Gill said that the next remark he heard Evans make was, "Why the devil don't they wake the wireless man?"

The entire crew, according to Gill, talked among themselves about the disregard of the rockets.

CAPTAIN'S DENIAL

Captain Stanley Lord of the Californian, who was prepared to give a sweeping denial to Gill's statements, then took the stand.

How far were the Californian and Titanic apart when you sent the message to the Titanic telling him that you were blocked in ice? - We were about nineteen and a half miles apart.

Did the Californian receive the Titanic's distress call? - No. We got it from the Virginian about six o'clock in the morning. We made thirteen and a half knots when we were going to the Titanic. We were driving her all we could.

Did you see any of the Titanic's signals or anything of the ship herself? - No.

Was the Titanic beyond your range of vision? - Yes; nineteen and a half or twenty miles away.

On Sunday night, he continued, the watch was doubled. We had reports two or three days before of the presence of ice ahead, and I took precautions.

From whom did you receive those reports? - Captain Barr of the Caronia gave us the report on April 13. The day before he told us that west-bound steamers had reported a field of ice.

What was your next warning? - The Parisian was ahead of us. I asked the Parisian on April 14 in the daytime. She said that she had passed three large icebergs. The New Amsterdam also warned us.

If you had received the distress call on Sunday evening how long would it have taken you to reach her? - At the very least two hours.

Do you know whether your wireless operator was on duty on Sunday night after he sent the warning message? - I think not. I went by his room about 11.45. There was no light, and that would indicate that he had gone to bed.

I did not see any distress signals. When I came on the bridge at 10.30 on Sunday night the officer said he thought he saw a light. It was a peculiar night. We had been having trouble with the stars, mistaking them for lights. Then a ship came up.

I asked the operator if he had heard anything. He replied that he had, from the Titanic, to which he had given the ice message.

ANOTHER SHIP'S ROCKETS

Then this ship came up and lay within four or five miles of us. She lay there all night, but we couldn't hear from her. It was not the Titanic, I am sure of that.

About one o'clock I told the operator to call this ship again. She sent up several rockets, but would not answer. I told him to ask her who she was. I heard him calling her when I went to bed, but she did not answer. I have a faint recollection of hearing the cabin boy about four o'clock saying something about the ship still standing by. Soon after she steamed away.

This boat sent up several white rockets, but they were not distress signals. In the position in which the Californian lay, eighteen miles away from the Titanic, it would have been impossible to see either Morse or distress signals. The ice conditions that night were deceiving.

Cyril Evans, the wireless operator in the Californian, said:

I called the Titanic and said, "Say, old man, we are surrounded by ice." He replied, "Shut up I'm working with Cape Race," and said I jammed him. I did not hear him again direct, but I knew he was sending messages to Cape Race. I didn't take them down.

I went to bed at 11.30. I was awakened at 3.40 by the chief officer, who said he had seen rockets and wanted to get some information.

I called and the Frankfurt answered with the news of the sinking of the Titanic. The Virginian called before I left the key and furnished more information. I have none of the messages which passed because they were merely conversational.

Did anyone tell you about Captain Lord being informed three times that night about a ship sending up rockets? - I think Gibson, the apprentice, told me that the captain was called and told about the rockets. The rockets were talked about in the Ship generally by the crew. While the Californian was on the way to the scene he heard the men say that five rockets had been sent up and that the captain had been roused. The apprentice got out Morse signals and tried to get into communication with the distressed vessel. No effort was made to use rockets in the Californian. -Reuter's Special.

OPPOSITE PAGE: That night the S.S. Californian had decided to stop due to the presence of the ice field. It had radioed a warning to the Titanic about the ice just before the radio operator went to bed. It was not until the morning that the ship picked up messages about the sinking. It immediately headed towards her last known location but did not arrive until around 8.30am. By then the Carpathia had collected the last of the surviving passengers.

"What was your next warning?" - *"The Parisian was ahead of us. I asked the Parisian on April 14 in the daytime. She said that she had passed three large icebergs. The New Amsterdam also warned us."*

"Why the devil don't they wake the wireless man?" The entire crew, according to Gill, talked among themselves about the disregard of the rockets.

Captain Stanley Lord

Captain Stanley Lord, master of the SS Californian, taped his account of the sinking of the Titanic shortly before his death in 1962, confident that his name would somehow one day be cleared.

His statement said: "Californian stopped (by ice) at 10.20. Never moved her engines until after 4 o'clock the next morning.

"Titanic stopped at 11.20. Look-out man and two officers on the bridge said there was nothing in sight.

"One o'clock, a steamer came close to the (Titanic's) lifeboats, then turned around and steamed away.

"How the devil could that have been the Californian when all the evidence proves she never moved."

ABOVE: Captain Stanley Lord of the S.S. Californian was questioned at the inquest. There were claims that another ship was close to the Titanic just prior to the sinking. He acknowledged that he had seen white rockets during the night and instructed a crew member to signal with a Morse lamp. Both enquiries concluded that he should have woken the radio operator to investigate further although more recent studies have claimed that the ship was not as close to the Titanic as originally thought.

"NOT THE TITANIC."

MYSTERY OF A SHIP WHICH SENT UP ROCKETS.

WASHINGTON, Friday.

Ernest Gill, of Liverpool, aged twenty-nine, a donkey-engine man of the Californian, the ship nearest the Titanic when she sank, was called before the Committee.

Senator Smith first read an affidavit made by Gill on Wednesday. He said that he saw the Titanic most plainly. Ten minutes after midnight he saw a white rocket ten miles away. A second rocket went up seven or eight minutes later. He said to himself, "That must be a vessel in distress." He did not notify the bridge, because it was not his business. They could not have helped seeing the rockets.

At 6.40 a.m. he was awakened by orders to turn out to render assistance as the Titanic had gone down. The Californian was then proceeding at full speed. He heard the second officer, Evans, telling the fourth officer, Wooten, that the third officer had reported rockets during his watch. Gill said that he knew then that it must

"CASE OF MR. ISMAY."

ATTACK BY ADMIRAL MAHAN.

From Our Own Correspondent.

NEW YORK, Sunday.

The case of Mr. Ismay, as the newspapers call it, continues to absorb a large share of public discussion of the Titanic disaster. Both in the correspondence columns of the newspapers as in the investigation proceeding at Washington, the fact of Mr. Ismay's escape has formed the basis for persistent comment.

A few days ago criticisms of Mr. Ismay were characterised by Admiral Chadwick as "the acme of emotionalism." This characterisation is the subject of a letter from Admiral Mahan, the famous naval expert, which is to-day widely quoted in the American Press.

After expressing his opinion that "censure and approval had best wait upon the result of the investigations being made here and to be made in England," Admiral Mahan proceeds:

"Certain facts are so notorious that they need no inquiry to ascertain. These are: (1) that before the collision the captain of the Titanic was solely responsible for the management of the ship; (2) that after the collision there were not boats enough to embark more than one-third of those on board; and (3) for that circumstance the White Star Company are solely responsible—not legally, for legal requirements were met, but morally.

"Of this company Mr. Ismay is a prominent, if not the most prominent, member. For all loss of life the company is responsible individually and collectively and Mr. Ismay personally, not only as one of its members. He believed the Titanic was unsinkable. The belief relieves him of moral guilt, but not of responsibility. Men bear the consequences of their mistakes as well as of their faults.

"He and Admiral Chadwick justify his leaving over 1,500 persons, the death of each of whom lay on the company, on the ground that it was the last boat, that it was half-filled, and that Mr. Ismay has said that no one else was to be seen. But was there none to be reached? Mr. Ismay knew there must be many, because he knew the boats could take only a third of all.

"The Titanic was 882 feet long and 92 feet broad. Within this space were congregated over 1,500 souls on several decks. True, to find any one person at such a moment in the intricacies of the vessel were a vain hope, but to encounter some stragglers would not seem to be.

"Mr. Ismay was in no sense responsible for the collision, but when the collision had occurred he was confronted with a wholly new condition for which he was responsible and not the captain—viz., the sinking of a vessel without adequate provision for the saving of life. Did no obligation as to particularity of conduct rest upon him under such a condition? I hold that under that condition so long as there was a soul that could be saved the obligation lay upon Mr. Ismay that that one person and not he should have been in the boat.

"More than 1,500 perished. Circumstances may yet be developed which may justify Mr. Ismay's action completely, but such justification is imperatively required."

POSITION WRONGLY GIVEN.

The Titanic was still calling "C.Q.D." at 1.20 a.m. The Frankfurt replied at 1.35, "Starting for you." Six minutes later the Titanic flashed "C.Q.D. Boilers flooded." Other ships then began calling, but could get no answer. Later the Russian steamer Birma got the Olympic and reported, "All quiet now." The Titanic had not spoken since 1.47 a.m.

The Titanic, said Captain Moore, undoubtedly had not fixed her position properly. She must have been eight miles further east than the spot reported. The fact that he found no evidence of the wreck when he got to the Titanic's position tended to confirm this.

Senator Smith said that he had received scores of telegrams from relatives of the drowned, urging that divers should be sent by the Government to explore the ship. He asked Captain Moore if he did not think that every sea-going vessel should be fitted with a buoy attached to a long cable, which, in case of the ship sinking, would mark the spot. (The depth where the Titanic sank is 12,000 feet.) Captain Moore did not think the idea practicable.

Suppose that you had been advised of ice ahead, would you consider it wise to drive a ship at that speed through the night?—It would be very unwise.

MR. STEAD'S LIFEBELT.

A steward named Cunningham was asked, Was there any emergency alarm call for the passengers in the Titanic?—I do not think so. In time of distress each stateroom steward calls his passengers. At 12.20 all my passengers had gone on deck except one. After that Mr. W. T. Stead asked me to show him how to put on his lifebelt. I put the lifebelt on him. It was the last I put on.

"I put on a lifebelt myself," he added, "and after the passengers had been taken care of, after all the boats had gone, my mate and I jumped into the sea and swam clear of the Titanic. We rested on each other while we were swimming, and after we saw the ship go down we struck out for the boats. Finally I was picked up by lifeboat No. 4."

Another steward named Etches said that as lifeboat No. 5 was being lowered "a man and a woman were standing beside the boat. She had her arms around his neck and was crying. I heard her say, 'I can't leave without you. I can't leave you.' I turned my head away, and the next moment I saw the woman with the man sitting behind her in the boat. A voice said, 'Throw out that man,' but we were already being lowered away, and the man remained. I don't know his name. I never heard it. He was a stoutish man—an American.

"When the Titanic went down I saw a crowd of people on her after-deck. Mr. Pittman (the third officer) wanted to go back to help those in the water, and gave orders to do so. The women pleaded with him not to, asking why they should risk their lives in a hopeless effort."—Reuter's Special.

"When the Titanic went down I saw a crowd of people on her after-deck. Mr Pittman wanted to go back to help those in the water, and gave orders to do so. The women pleaded with him not to, asking why they should risk their lives in a hopeless effort."

The Titanic had not fixed her position properly. She must have been eight miles further east than the spot reported.

OPPOSITE PAGE TOP: The ship's bronze steering pedestal.

MAIN PICTURE: One of the ship's enormous boilers. She was equipped with 25 double-ended and 4 single-ended boilers measuring 15ft 9 in each. These were spread between six separate boiler rooms.

"After the passengers had been taken care of, after all the boats had gone, my mate and I jumped into the sea and swam clear of the Titanic. Finally I was picked up by lifeboat No. 4."

Money matters

Speaking of Titanic's final moments, Second Officer Charles Lightoller said: 'She assumed an absolute perpendicular position.' That high-angle plunge, with the stern rising steeply out of the water, became accepted wisdom, and made for a spectacular death scene in James Cameron's 1997 blockbuster movie. Exactly what happened to Titanic's hull in those final minutes was a critical question, though not one dwelt upon during the original Inquiries. Both concluded that the ship sank intact, supporting the 'Company line' view expressed by Harland & Wolff marine architect Edward Wilding. Others, such as Able Seaman Joseph Scarrott, begged to differ. He testified that 'she broke in two between the third and fourth funnel'. Lookout George Symons described the stern rising out of the water, then righting itself 'without the bow'. He concluded that the ship must have broken in half 'abaft the after expansion plate'. At the British Inquiry, when Wilding was giving testimony, Lord Mersey called a halt to this line of questioning: 'The evidence about this breaking of the ship in two immediately before she founders and the righting of the afterend is unsatisfactory.'

THE TITANIC INQUIRY.

LINER CAPTAIN'S STATEMENT.

TWO SHIPS NEAR.

The American Senate Committee's inquiry into the loss of the Titanic was continued on Saturday, when the captain of the liner Mount Temple related how he hurried to the rescue but arrived too late, and how in his opinion the Titanic gave her position wrongly to the extent of eight miles.

He passed a schooner coming from the direction of the Titanic, and found that a large tramp steamer had also lain not far from the Titanic. He could get no answer by wireless from either vessel.

NO REINSURANCE.

WASHINGTON, Saturday.

Senator Smith asked Mr. Franklin, of the White Star Line, whether after the company learned of the loss of the Titanic it reinsured either the vessel or its cargo. An entire denial was given by the witness.

Captain James H. Moore, of the Mount Temple, said his ship picked up the Titanic's distress call at 12.30 a.m. on April 15 and started for the scene at once. The ship was driven as hard as possible, all the firemen working at once. He met the first ice at 3 a.m. and at 3.25 had to stop, being then about fourteen miles distant from where the Titanic had signalled. Another delay was occasioned by a small schooner, which was nearer the Titanic and which got in the Mount Temple's way. The schooner was coming from the direction of the Titanic and was moving not more than two knots. At three in the morning she would be about twelve miles from the Titanic.

Senator Smith asked if he thought the light of this schooner might have been the light Mr. Boxhall and others in the Titanic saw when the Titanic was firing distress rockets and flashing Morse signals.—It might have been the light of a tramp steamer which was on our port bow and passed to starboard of us.

UNKNOWN FOREIGN SHIP.

How large a ship was it?—About 5,000 tons. I did not get her name, but she was a foreigner. She showed no sign. We tried to raise her by wireless, but I don't believe she had any. She had a black funnel with some device on a band near the top. We reached very close to the Titanic's position as given by the Titanic at 4.30 a.m. I saw no wreckage and no bodies. I saw nothing but ice and the tramp steamer.

The second wireless message picked up by the Mount Temple was from the Titanic to the Carpathia, and read:" We struck iceberg. Come at once our assistance." Another message from the Titanic to the Olympic read: "Get boats ready. We going down fast by head." Another from the Titanic to the Frankfurt said: "We struck iceberg, sinking. Tell captain to come."

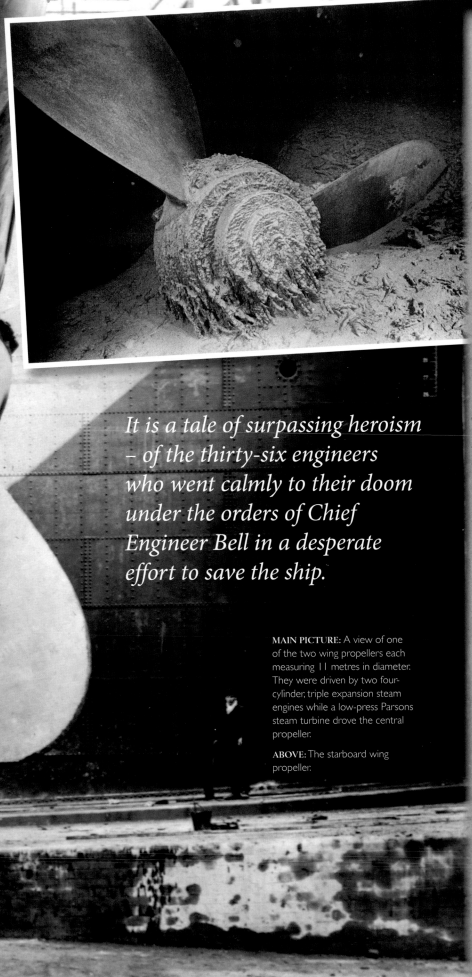

GALLANT ENGINEERS.

WHAT HAPPENED BELOW AFTER THE COLLISION.

We are indebted to a passenger in the Lapland, which brought home the surviving members of the Titanic's crew, for the story of what happened in the ship's engine-rooms and stokeholds after the collision.

It is a tale of surpassing heroism—of the thirty-six engineers who went calmly to their doom under the orders of Chief Engineer Bell in a desperate effort to save the ship, of the oilers and stokers who remained unflinchingly at their posts in a moment of mortal peril.

There was no panic among the "black squad." All did their duty to the last, like Englishmen.

All the watertight doors were in perfect order at the collision. Not one jammed.

Two people on board must have known from the moment the Titanic struck that she was doomed—Mr. Andrews, the constructor, and Chief Engineer Bell. Both went down with her.

Leading Stoker Threlfall states that after the collision his stokehold, No. 4, was dry. "The fires were burning as usual." The watertight doors were closed, but they were opened to bring through an engineer with a broken leg, and were closed after him again. Nos. 1, 2, and 3 stokeholds were also dry. Up to shortly before 2 a.m. "everything was going on just as usual below; the lights were burning and all pumps were working as if nothing had happened."

It was then that the order was given by the chief engineer to the men to go on deck. They found the boats gone, the ship down by the head, her stern up in the air, and her hull with a heavy list to port. The captain ordered all articles that would float to be thrown overboard and gave the command, "Every man for himself."

Threlfall adds that shortly after he took to the water he gained a raft and climbed upon it. There were several firemen standing on it. Chief-Engineer Bell swam up, and they called to him: "Come on, Mr. Bell, we'll pull you on board." He shouted back: "No, men, your raft might capsize. I'll be all right and find something else. Good-bye, men, God bless you."

Oiler A. Whyte states that shortly after the accident the emergency dynamos were started to run the electric light in case the engine-room should be flooded. He was sent on deck by the engineers at 1.40 a.m., saw the last boat leaving, and slid down the falls to her. The engineers were still in the turbine-room.

Leading-Stoker F. Barrett states that at the order of Engineer Harvey he drew thirty-six fires in the boilers. Engineer Shepherd broke his leg by falling in a man-hole. His only sorrow was that he could render no aid to save the ship. Barrett was sent on deck at 1.30 and was ordered to take charge of No. 13 boat. Out of ninety-one men in his watch only sixteen were saved.

It is a tale of surpassing heroism – of the thirty-six engineers who went calmly to their doom under the orders of Chief Engineer Bell in a desperate effort to save the ship.

MAIN PICTURE: A view of one of the two wing propellers each measuring 11 metres in diameter. They were driven by two four-cylinder, triple expansion steam engines while a low-press Parsons steam turbine drove the central propeller.

ABOVE: The starboard wing propeller.

TITANIC SURVIVORS AT NEW YORK AND IN ENGLAND.

(1) Some of the survivors landing at New York from the Carpathia. (2) Mr. Harold Bride, junior "wireless" operator in the Titanic, being carried ashore at New York. His feet were badly injured. (3) Louis and Lolo, the two French children who were rescued and, pending their identification, temporarily adopted by Miss Hays, whose father was lost. (4) A family reunion at Plymouth—one of the rescued seamen with his mother and young brothers. (5) Mr. A. White, who was rescued in the last boat, being greeted by his wife on arrival home at Southampton.

No evidence of negligence

Both Inquiries found that mistakes were made, but there was no evidence of negligence. Even so, claims running into millions of dollars poured in. Irene Harris sought redress to the tune of $1,000,000 for the loss of her theatrical manager husband; Lily May Futrelle claimed $300,000 in compensation for the loss of her husband, author Jacques Futrelle; the widow of artist Francis Davis Millet wanted $100,000. White Star eventually agreed to pay a total of $664,000 to meet all claims in December 1915, a settlement releasing the company from all liability.

70 years later, the discovery of the wreck supported Scarrott and Symons's eyewitness accounts. Titanic had indeed broken in two, opening up a debate as to whether she had a structural weakness. Ismay had insisted on one-inch-thick steel plate for the hull to save weight, sticking rigidly to the minimum Board of Trade requirements. The expansion joints designed by Thomas Andrews also came under suspicion. Perhaps Titanic's back had been broken at a much shallower angle than had been previously thought?

Back in 1912, the reputation of British shipbuilding was at stake and it was in no one's interest to flag up possible design faults — especially when the design conformed to current regulations.

In the year following the disaster, White Star posted record profits.

> *"The first boats left the ship's side half empty because the passengers said they would not leave the Titanic to go in a cockleshell."*

BELOW: Surviving members of the crew of the Titanic at Plymouth Dockyard. As soon as they arrived in New York they were questioned at the enquiry then transferred onto the Lapland, another White Star Line vessel and taken to Plymouth before they were then allowed to go home.

BELOW RIGHT: The insides of a power turbine.

MR. MARCONI.

DEFENCE OF THE COMPANY'S ACTIONS.

WASHINGTON, Monday.

According to an announcement made by Senator Smith, the early conclusion of the Senate's inquiry is assured. He also foreshadows the passing of legislation based upon the Committee's report before the end of the present session of Congress. He said that only a few of the Titanic's passengers would be called.

This morning Mr. Marconi was recalled. He was accompanied by Mr. Sammis, the chief engineer of the Marconi Company; Mr. Bride, the surviving wireless operator of the Titanic; and Mr. John W. Griggs, counsel for the Marconi Company. Mr. Franklin, who has been to New York, and Mr. Ismay were early in attendance.

Mr. Marconi said: "I would like to correct the statement that I did not send any messages to the Carpathia. On my return to New York I found that I had sent one message and immediately wrote a letter to you, senator, enclosing the message. The message was as follows: 'April 18, 1 a.m. To Calvin, wireless Marconi station, Siasconsett.—Send following immediately. Advise us of delivery. Wire news despatches immediately to Siasconsett or naval boats. If this impossible, ask captain to give reason why no news allowed to be transmitted.—GUGLIELMO MARCONI.'"

Mr. Marconi read messages which his company sent to various wireless stations in an endeavour to get information of the disaster.

Mr. Sammis said he could show that personal messages were coming from the Carpathia at the rate of forty or fifty an hour. The captain of the Carpathia would not handle any other business but that of getting news of the survivors to the relatives.

Mr. Bride, the Titanic's second operator, said he received £200 for his story.—Reuter's Special.

MR. ISMAY & THE WOMEN.

STEWARDESSES' NARRATIVES OF THE RESCUES.

From Our Special Correspondent.

PLYMOUTH, Monday.

To-day the stewardesses and stewards of the Titanic told the stories of their escapes. Being more amenable to official control than the trade unionist firemen and sailors, the men had spent the night at the dock station and the women at an hotel, and they were permitted to tell their experience only after making formal depositions of their evidence.

Their statements show very clearly how little the imminence of danger was realised until the ship actually began to tilt downwards for the plunge.

"The first boats left the ship's side half empty because the passengers said they would not leave the Titanic to go in a cockleshell," said Mrs. Gould, a first-class stewardess on B deck. "Mrs. Wallace, the steerage matron, even went back to her cabin after seeing her passengers into their boats and locked herself in, remarking, 'I am going to stay where I am safe.' She was a nervous little woman.

"Mrs. Snape, too, a second-cabin stewardess, a woman of twenty-one, who had left a baby behind in Southampton, shook hands with her passengers as they got in, but would not go in a boat herself."

Among the passengers in Mrs. Gould's section was Mr. Bruce Ismay. She saw him on deck when she went up and he put her into a boat. He was wearing an overcoat over pyjamas. "I saw him again in a boat near to ours when we were rowing up to the Carpathia," said Mrs. Gould. "He was sitting on the gunwale at the stern of the boat. His face was blue with cold and he sat perfectly still, staring straight in front of him, expressionless like a statue."

Mrs. Maclaren was another stewardess whom Mr. Ismay put in a boat. When Mr. Ismay told them to get in the boat they said, "We are not passengers; we are members of the crew." "It doesn't matter," Mr. Ismay replied. "You are women, and I wish you to get in."

Mrs. Martin, a tall, graceful woman, who was a first-saloon stewardess, told how when the steward came to call them to get up and put on lifebelts they thought it was a practical joke.

Curious traits of character were instanced in the story told me by a steward. He told of a woman in his boat who complained that she was unduly crowded and appealed to the officer in charge to prevent her from being crushed. There was a sad tale of a Portuguese bride on her honeymoon who knew no English, and when she saw the Carpathia thought that the boats were returning to the Titanic, in which she had left her husband. An Italian waiter jumped from the top deck into one boat as it was lowered and broke the ankle of a lady, Mrs. Parish.

INDIGNANT REPLY TO SENATOR SMITH'S QUESTIONS.

WASHINGTON, Tuesday.

Mr. Ismay was called before the Senate Committee to-day.

Senator Smith: How many ships has your company lost since you have been managing director?—The only ones I can remember are the Republic and Naronic.

Was a limit in cost placed to the building of the Titanic?—None whatever. The builders were given carte blanche. They were told to go ahead and build on their own plan as passed by us. When the ship is completed they add their percentage of profit, which we pay. In building a ship you begin its construction four or five years before you need her.

What did you say to them when you ordered the ship?—That is difficult to say. It was in conversation with Lord Pirrie. I ordered the Olympic and the Titanic at the same time. I told him that we wanted the very largest and best ships it was possible to produce, irrespective of cost.

Mr. Ismay said although the Titanic had been built for the North Atlantic trade she had not been constructed with specially strengthened bows. Her cost was about £1,500,000 and she was insured for £1,000,000.

Do you know of any attempt to increase the insurance on Monday, April 15?—I cannot imagine anyone connected with the company attempting such a dishonourable act. No one connected with him or his company had made any effort to do it, so far as he knew.

Senator Smith: I don't want you to understand me to assert that such an effort was made.—No, I don't, but the suggestion is horrible.

How did it happen that the Titanic had only twenty lifeboats?—It was a matter for the builders. I suppose she met the requirements of the British Board of Trade, otherwise she would never have left port.

If the Titanic had carried double or treble the number of lifeboats would there not have been more lives saved?—Undoubtedly.

Are you willing to admit that you are in favour of so increasing the number of lifeboats?—Perfectly.

"WHEN YOU LEFT THE SHIP."

Senator Smith: When you left the ship I believe you said that it was in the last collapsible boat on the starboard side?—Yes.

Was it full?—I think there were about forty women there when I got in.

Did you say anything about it to the captain?—No, I did not see him.

Who, if anyone, told you to get into the boat?—No one.

Why did you get in?—Because it was not filled. There was room in it, and there were no women there to get into it. As no one else was there I got in as the boat was being lowered.

Senator Smith then asked Mr. Ismay what he did after he had been picked up by the Carpathia.

Mr. Ismay: I court the fullest inquiry. After I got on board the Carpathia I was standing with my back against a bulkhead. Someone came to me and said, "Go into the saloon and have a bite of something hot or a drink." He repeated it twice, but I told him that I would be happier if I could get off by myself. He took me by the arm and led me to a room, which proved to be the doctor's room. I was not out of it until the Carpathia docked. I was ill and ate no solid food during the run to New York. I want to say that the doctor did not occupy a suite. He had one room in which he slept. He did not occupy it the first night; I was there. He was busy with the Titanic's survivors, but he dressed there. Mr. Jack Thayer was brought into the room the morning we got in the Carpathia. He was there for some time. People were coming and going through this room all the time.

Correspondence between Mr. Ismay and Senator Smith was read. Mr. Ismay wrote on April 25 that he was willing to assist the Committee as much as possible, but was anxious to be excused as soon as was convenient, as he desired to rejoin his family.

Senator Smith in his reply stated that Mr. Ismay would have to remain until the Committee was satisfied that nothing had been overlooked. His letter concluded: "I am working night and day to achieve this result. You should continue to help me, instead of annoying me and delaying my work by personal importunities."

SENATOR SMITH'S APOLOGY.

Before the luncheon adjournment Senator Smith said that he desired to make a statement. During the examination of Mr. Lowe, the fifth officer, a few days ago, he had asked him a question affecting his reputation for sobriety. "I wish to say," Senator Smith continued, "that I had no intention of casting any reflection upon Mr. Lowe. I am very sorry that the misunderstanding arose. The error probably grew out of a remark made by a passenger that Mr. Lowe was 'intemperate'—a word that applied to his temper and not to his habits. He is a teetotaller. I congratulate him."

"Thank you, sir; I can go now," said Mr. Lowe.

Examined after luncheon for the last time, Mr. Ismay said that his captains were not compelled to follow fixed routes or arrive in port on a specified day.

Mr. Ismay was then finally excused, and shook hands with all the members of the committee. He hopes to sail for England in the Adriatic on Thursday.

The Committee adjourned until Friday.
—Reuter's Special.

"How did it happen that the Titanic had only twenty lifebotas?" – "It was a matter for the builders. I suppose she met the requirements of the British Board of Trade, otherwise she would never have left port."

"If the Titanic had carried double or treble the number of lifeboats would there not have been more lives saved? – Undoubtedly."

MAIN PICTURE: One of the Titanic's ship telegraphs, the device which communicated to the engine room the bridge's orders for speed.

By far the greater number of bodies recovered were floating in groups of twenty or more amid the debris. Buoyed up by their cork belts, the bodies at a distance looked like a flock of gulls at rest on the water. Like Mr Astor, they were all in an upright position, as if treading water.

The search for the wreck

Such were the hostile conditions when Titanic went down — air and se temperatures hovering around freezing — that within a matter of hours rescu attempts gave way to a grim recovery operation. Throughout the followir month, White Star commissioned ships that combed the area in search bodies. Over 300 were found quite quickly, but diminishing returns soon set and sightings of life-jacketed corpses became more sporadic. 328 bodies wer recovered by the time the operation was abandoned. Some were identified ar repatriated; others were consigned to the ocean's depths.

Even as that grisly task was being undertaken, there was talk of finding Titan - salvaging it, even. Over the next 70 years there would be a number of attemp to locate the wreckage, all using as their starting point the final distress c ordinates issued: 41 degrees 46' North, 50 degrees 14' West. Titanic was calle the 'Big 'Un' by the crew; finding it was the glittering prize that all wreck-seekir oceanographers dreamed of claiming. Moreover, it would put an end to decad of speculation as to what exactly happened to her hull when it sideswiped th mountain of ice at 11.40 pm on April 14, 1912. At the investigation Harland ar Wolff architect Edward Wilding had posited that a 12 square-foot hole wou have sunk her in the known timescale. That equated to a three-quarter-inch ga: extending some 300 feet. This theory had its proponents and detractors, a lon running argument that could finally be settled if the ship could be found. Steel, the saying goes, doesn't lie.

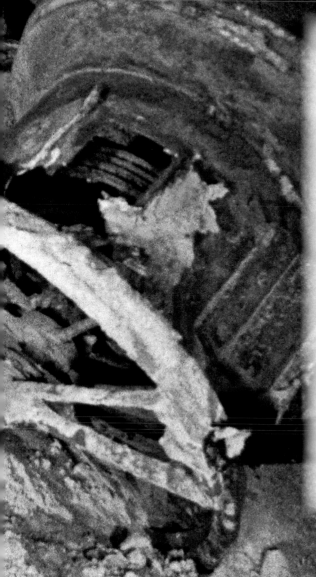

MAN WHO SLEPT TOO LONG

One of the three cooks saved from the Titanic said at Southampton yesterday that after the collision he went to his bunk and had a sleep for an hour.

"When I came on deck," he said naively "I found I had slept too long. All the boats had gone. So I put on a lifebelt and slipped into the water, and after being in the water for nearly an hour I was picked up by one of the boats."

FUNERAL SHIP IN PORT
BODIES FOUND
FLOATING UPRIGHT IN THE SEA

HALIFAX (NOVA SCOTIA) Tuesday

The cable ship Mackay-Bennett returned here today with 190 bodies from the Titanic.

The first man to land from the Mackay-Bennett was Mr. John Snow, who superintended the work of embalming the dead and generally directed the caring for the bodies as they were recovered from the ocean.

"Among the bodies we recovered," he said, "is that of a two-year-old baby boy. He came floating to us with upturned face. His was the only body recovered which had no lifebelt. Nothing I have ever seen at sea made such an impression on me.

"On one day we found 50 bodies all in a group. Near by was a lifeboat which had evidently capsized, all within it being drowned. A red skirt was found tied to a stick, with which, it is supposed, those in the boat sought to attract attention, and, failing to do so, went down to their death.

"We secured about forty miles from the scene of the disaster the bodies of twelve women. It has been stated that there was an explosion in the sinking Titanic, and this probably explains the terribly mutilated condition of many of the bodies. Arms and legs were shattered and faces and bodies mangled. We picked up many lifebelts 170 miles from the wreck.

MAN AT THE WHEEL
THE SCENE ON THE BRIDGE

Survivors of the crew of the Titanic wereagain under examination throughout yesterday's sitting of Lord Mersey's Commission at the London Scottish Hall. Impressive narratives were given of all the incidents at the moment of the collision and immediately afterwards, particularly of the scenes on the bridge and in the stokeholds.

George William Beauchamp, a Titanic fireman, was the first witness called. He is about twenty-five years of age; a lock of curls was pressed down on his forehead. Examined by Mr. Raymond Asquith, he said he was below when the ship struck. There was a slight shock and a sound as of a roll of thunder. The order from the bridge came on the engine-room telegraph to "Stand by" and then "Stop." In less than five minutes after that order the watertight doors closed. A few minutes afterwards an order was given to draw fires.

Did you see any water coming in at that time?—Yes; water was coming in on the plates where the stokers stand.

How long did it take to draw the fires?—About a quarter of an hour. After the fires were drawn I ran up the escape ladder and walked aft and up to the boat deck.

Do you know what your boat station was?—No sir.

The President : Why not?—"A list," the witness replied, "was put up that morning, they said, but I did not see it, That was because I did not look for it."

UNEQUIPPED BOATS

The witness said he helped women and children into Boat 13. Some men also got in. All told there were about 60 or 70.

How were the people chosen?—Women and children first. There were some ladies who would not go into the boat.

How many refused?—I heard two or three say they would not go away in the boat.

Did they give any reason?—No. All the ladies who would come were put into the boat. Some men also got in.

Did the men try and get in or was it orderly?—It was quite calm; everyone obeyed orders.

Was there any compass in your boat?—No.

Any lantern?—No.

Any provisions?—No.

Any waters?—No.

Had you had any boat drill while you were in the Titanic?—No. I did not see any boat drill in the Titanic.

Mr. Scanlon (Seamen and Firemen's Union) : Have you ever had any boat drills in the White Star ships?—Yes, we generally had a boat drill in New York on a Sunday.

The President : Is that the practice of the White Star Company?—I believe so.

Mr. Lewis (British Seafarers' Union) ; Is it the practice to have a boat drill before you leave Southampton?—When you go aboard the ship the names are called out, but there are so many that you do not take much notice.

This witness was confused in his answers, and now told the president that he did not remember whether he was given a number for a boat.

THE CAPTAIN'S QUESTION

Robert Hitchens, a quartermaster of the Titanic, said that on the day of the collision he went on watch at eight o'clock.

By the clock in the wheel-house, the witness said, the vessel struck at twenty minutes to twelve.

Had you been told to do anything to the helm before she struck?—Just as she struck I had the order, "Hard-a-starboard."

Just as she struck?—Not immediately as she struck. The ship had just swung about two points when she struck.

Had you time to get the helm hard-a-starboard before she struck?—Yes.

What was the first notice to you that there was something ahead?—Three gongs from the crow's nest. That was about half a minute before the order, "Hard-a-starboard."

That Attorney-General : Mr. Moody, sixth officer, got a telephone message after the three bells had been struck. You heard him acknowledge this message and say "Thank you"?—Yes. I heard Mr. Moody repeat, "Iceberg right ahead."

To whom did he repeat it?—To Mr. Murdock, first officer.

Then what happened?—I heard Mr. Murdock rush to the telegraph and give the order, "Hard-a-starboard."

How long did you remain at the wheel?—Until 12.23.

Who relieved you?—Quartermaster Perkins.

Can you tell us how long it was after the collision that the ship stopped?—Immediately.

You remained at your post?—Yes sir.

What did you hear?—Just about a minute after the collision Captain Smith rushed out of his room and asked Mr. Murdock, "What was that?" He said, "An iceberg, sir." The captain said, "Close the watertight doors." Mr. Murdock said, "They are already closed."

When the vessel struck did you feel any shock?—Yes. I felt the ship tremble, and felt rather a grinding sensation along the ship's bottom.

Did you see the lists of the stations for the boats on board?—No, sir, I never saw any lists put up anywhere. In every ship I have been in we have always had boat stations—quartermasters, sailors, stewards, firemen, or whatever we were.

LIGHT FIVE MILES AWAY

When the order was given to lower the boat you got the order from Mr. Lightoller, second officer, to steer for a light five miles off on port bow?—That's right sir.

When did you first see that light?—While in the boat taking the passengers on board. We surmised it to be a steamboat. I steered for about a mile in the direction of the light, which was moving and gradually disappearing, and then I could see it no more. Four or five boats rowed towards the light.

STOKER'S VIVID NARRATIVE.

Frederick Barratt, a leading stoker in the Titanic, who said he was on duty in No. 6 Section, was asked by the Attorney-General to state what happened at the time of the collision.

The Witness: There is a clock face in the stokehold, and a red light goes up for "Stop," a white light for "Full speed ahead," and a blue light for "Slow." When the red light came up I shouted, "Shut all the dampers." That order was obeyed, but the crash came before we had them all shut. There came a rush of water into my stokehold. We were standing on plates about 6ft. above the tank tops, and the water came in about 2ft. above the plates; it came in fast through the side of the ship. Together with Mr. Hesketh I jumped through the doorway into No. 5 Section. The watertight door between the section was then open, but it shut just as we jumped through. This door is worked from the bridge. I do not know whether any more of the men in my stokehold were saved. The water was coming in fast enough to flood the place. We got through a coal hole into No. 5 Section. The water was coming in there at about the same level, but not so fast. Mr. Hesketh gave the order, "Every man to his station." I climbed out of No. 5 Section over the bulk head door, and went to the ladder leading down to No. 6 Section, the one I had been working in. I could not get down because there was already 8ft. of water in it. That was less than ten minutes after we had left it. I saw nothing of my mates who had been there.

Shortly afterwards, added the witness, the order came from the engine room to send all the stokers up. Most of them went up through the escape ladder from the section I was in, but I was told to remain with the engineers down there to do any errands. Mr. Harvey, Mr. Wilson, Mr. Shephard, and I waited in No. 5 Section.

Shortly afterwards the lights went out. Mr. Harvey told me to send firemen for lamps. They brought them, but just then the electric light came on again; they must have been changing over the dynamos. The next order given was when Mr. Harvey told me to fetch firemen to draw the furnaces. I fetched about 15 firemen and they drew the 30 furnaces in the section. That occupied about twenty minutes. I looked at the gauge and found there was no water in the boilers. The ship in blowing off steam had blown it out.

After drawing the furnaces the firemen were told to go up again, and they went. Mr. Harvey told me to lift the manhole plate, which I did, and then Mr. Shephard, hurrying across to do something and not noticing the plate had been removed, fell down and broke his leg. We lifted him up and laid him in the pump room. About a quarter of an hour after the fires were drawn there came a rush of water into No. 5 Section and the ship was showing a list.

The court adjourned until this morning.

Many of the bodies were of persons in full evening dress. All the watches worn by the men had stopped at precisely ten minutes past two. There was hardly any variation.

ABOVE: Two lifeboats carry passengers to safety. The Captain had ordered the lifeboats to be prepared but amid the noise and confusion it was a disorganised process. The crew were unfamiliar with the new equipment, there was no public address system and this was coupled with the passengers' reluctance to leave the ship as they were unaware of the true situation.

BELOW: One section of the ship showing some of the three million rivets holding the one-inch thick steel plates together. When the Titanic hit the iceberg the steel buckled causing some of the rivets to pop out, thus allowing water to flood into the forward compartments.

PLAYING " NAP."

William Lucas, a sturdily built A.B., examined by Mr. Rowlatt, said he joined the Titanic after all the gangways had been withdrawn and just as she was on the point of sailing. On the morning of the day preceding the collision he noticed that the cold began to increase.

Did you look at the thermometer?—No; I only put on an extra jersey. (Laughter.) I knew there was ice knocking about.

The shock of the collision, the witness said, nearly knocked him off his feet. It occurred while he was playing " nap." He saw his name in the boat list, which was posted above the fo'c'sle.

After the collision what did you do?—I went down and put on an extra jersey. (Laughter.)

The passengers on the boat deck, so far as he knew, were all of the first class. The boats lowered from that deck were not full by a long way.

Why?—Because there were no women knocking about.

The last boat to get away on the port side was the collapsible boat on that side. He got into it, but Mr. Lightoller ordered him out. He then went to the starboard side to see if there were any boats left there, but there were not, so he came back to the collapsible boat. A lady called out that there were no sailors or plugs in the boat, so he got in. The water was then up to the bridge of the ship. This was about 1½ hours after the collision. With the rising of the water and the tilting of the Titanic the collapsible boat floated off. About fourteen women got in. The men were one quartermaster and two foreigners—third class, he thought. He had to get a couple of women to take oars. They had four oars out altogether. They rowed about a hundred yards before the first explosion in the Titanic. They were about 150 yards away when she sank.

Did you see any wreckage about when the Titanic sank?—Yes, chairs and things like that. He transferred the women from his boat to No. 8 boat, and got in himself, as they wanted a seaman. They went to another collapsible boat which was overturned—36 people were clinging on top of it—and took them on board. Three men were left in the collapsible boat he came away in after they had transferred the women to No. 8. Those men were hanging round in the collapsible boat till morning. That boat and No. 8 rowed back to the scene of the wreck. When they got there, in about a quarter of an hour, the people who had been about to be picked up were dead, and they found nobody alive. No. 8 boat had 40 people on board when she left the ship, and after taking on the people from the collapsible boat she had about 80.

"The watertight door between the section was then open, but it shut just as we jumped through. This door is worked from the bridge. I do not know whether any more of the men in my stokehold were saved".

EVIDENCE OF SEAMEN.

An Iceberg That Looked Like the Rock of Gibraltar.

Some interesting and intelligent evidence was given by two of the crew—a look-out man and an A.B., both of whom reached home last Sunday on the Lapland. The look-out man was a big Cornishman from Bude, named Archie Jewell. He had left the crow's nest about a couple of hours before the smash. He was not, he said, supplied with glasses for the look-out.

The first warning of the possibility of meeting ice seems to have been given him from the bridge at 9-30 in the evening. He passed on the word to the look-out who succeeded him and went to bed until the crash woke him up and sent him on deck again. He was one of the men who helped to get the boats away. When they got the boat into the water they found that there was no biscuits in the locker and no lamp.

This witness told how they saw the ship settling away by the head, the lights shining and people crowding her deck, how at the last moments of all the lights went out and she went down fast with one or two explosions. When daylight came his lifeboat was in among hundreds of icebergs.

The President: Apart from this rush made, was there any panic?—No panic whatever. All the people behaved exceptionally well as far as I could see—both crew and passengers.

Scarrott told a terrible story of how in the darkness his boat found itself in among a "cluster" of wreckage and dead bodies. "We saw across the bodies a man who had climbed on a sort of staircase. He seemed as if praying and at the same time crying for help. The crush of bodies and wreckage was so thick that it took us half an hour to get to him, and then we could only reach him with an oar." They saved this man and one or two others.

Scarrott also threw some light on the statistics of the saved by explaining that the first and second-class passengers had a better chance of getting to the boats, as they had ready access to the boat deck. All barriers were down, but he showed on the model how many staircase and complicated passages a third-class passenger would have to thread before he or she could reach the boats.

Many questions were put to the men designed to obtain information as to the efficiency of the boats, their equipment, and the number of seamen available for handling them.

CALIFORNIAN'S CAPTAIN

LORD MERSEY ON "AWKWARD COINCIDENCES"

The defence by Mr. Dunlop of Captain Lord, of the Californian, was the feature of the Titanic inquiry yesterday. The Californian, which was lying motionless on the night of the wreck, saw rockets which in Lord Mersey's opinion, were the distress signals of the sinking Titanic, but the Californian did not move until the following morning.

Mr. Dunlop submitted that the vessel whose rockets were seen by the Californian was not the Titanic. The Californian was, he said, twenty miles from the place where the Titanic struck.

Lord Mersey: Are you going to say that you saw the signals or that you did not see them? - We saw certain signals.

Are you going to say that they were not distress signals? - If they were distress signals they were not signals from a ship herself in distress, and if they were from a ship herself in distress that vessel was not the Titanic.

Lord Mersey: If they were distress signals, whether they came from the Titanic or not, you ought to have made for them.

Mr. Dunlop declared that what the Californian witness saw was a steamer navigating slowly through ice apparently to a European port. The Titanic was proceeding at twenty-two knots towards America. The rockets seen could not have been those of the Titanic, but of another vessel not before the court.

One theory put forward by Mr. Dunlop was that the rockets seen by the Californian meant "Stand by."

Lord Mersey: What is the use of "Standing by" six miles away when a vessel is going to the bottom? - It comes to this: You saw the same coloured rockets that the Titanic sent up; you saw about the same number as the Titanic sent up; you saw them just about the same time that the Titanic sent them up. Those are awkward coincidences.

Mr. Dunlop said that the Commission was not appointed to inquire to the captain's conduct. Captain Lord had already been sorely and severely punished by public criticism for his inactivity, which counsel urged, was due more to thoughtlessness or an error of judgement than to any wilful disregard of duty.

"It comes to this: You saw the same coloured rockets that the Titanic sent up; you saw about the same number as the Titanic sent up; you saw them just about the same time that the Titanic sent them up. Those are awkward coincidences."

The Titanic inquiry was concluded yesterday, Lord Mersey remarking that he hoped to bring out his report in a reasonable time. The Attorney-General's closing speech dealt mainly with Captain Lord, of the Californian, the ship alleged to have seen the sinking liner's distress signals, and to have remained inactive.

Sir Rufus Isaacs said the reason the Board of Trade had done nothing yet lay in its anxiety to await Lord Mersey's report and the fact that an international conference was proposed.

Lord Mersey: Do you suppose that if the Titanic had been provided with lifeboat accommodation for all on board any more people could have been saved? - The result of the evidence, one may grant, is to the contrary.

Dealing with the Californian, the Attorney-General said: "I am most anxious to help the inquiry to find some possible excuse for the inaction on the part of the Californian. It is a matter of extreme regret that I come to the conclusion that there is no excuse. Whether I am right or wrong is for your lordship's consideration."

Lord Mersey: If Captain Lord saw those signals and neglected reasonable opportunity of going to the vessel in distress it might be that he was guilty of misdemeanour under the Merchant Shipping Act. Am I to try that question?

The Attorney-General: Certainly not. I am asking you to find the fact that they did see distress signals, that they were those of the Titanic, and that the distance of the Titanic from the Californian was only a few miles. I should put it at seven or eight.

Lord Mersey: I think we are of the opinion that the distress rockets seen by the Californian were the distress rockets of the Titanic.

The Attorney-General added that one must come to the conclusion that Captain Lord's evidence was unsatisfactory. It was established quite clearly that he thought that the signal reported to him might have been a distress signal. He had asked for a report to be brought to him. He remained in the chart-room and did nothing.

THE RULE OF HONOUR

If they had established that the "blaze of light" to which reference had been made in the evidence came from the Titanic, that the Captain of the Californian knew of it and did not proceed to the rescue of the vessel or even call up the wireless operator to let him get into communication with the vessel, they had established a state of things which was quite inexplicable. It was the more extraordinary because of the rule which anyone who went to sea could never fail to consider, that if you see a vessel in distress you must do your utmost to help. That was a rule of honour. "That the Californian might have got to the rescue of the Titanic in time to save the passengers is, I'm afraid, the irresistible conclusion of the evidence.

"I can only say that as a result of this inquiry it is to be hoped that no vessel will ever take such utterly unnecessary risks as I submit were taken by the Titanic. Speaking generally, the two causes of the disaster were the failure to keep a good look-out and the proceeding at too great a rate of speed."

Lord Mersey: "I think we are of the opinion that the distress rockets seen by the Californian were the distress rockets of the Titanic."

OPPOSITE PAGE: Officers from the S.S. Californian (L to R) Mr H. Stone, Second Officer, Mr C.V. Groves, third officer, Captain Stanley Lord, and Mr G.F. Stewart, Chief Officer with two passengers.

LEFT: Lord Mersey headed the British Board of Trade's own separate enquiry which began on May 2, 1912 and lasted for two months. Witnesses at the American enquiry were again called and it was widely acknowledged that many of the current safety laws were out of date. As a result new safety measures for ship design, lifeboat and life-vest regulations, practice drills and many others were implemented.

TIDE TURNS FOR THE TITANIC'S SKIPPER OF STONE

WHEN the Titanic went down, nobody wanted the statue of her proud bearded captain.

But the discovery of the wreck of the great liner in the watery depths off Newfoundland has changed all that.

Now two towns look set for a tug-of-war over the stone statue of Edward John Smith, who stood on the bridge as his ship sank shouting 'Be British!' to his crew.

The original plan for the statue to have pride of place outside the town hall in Hanley, Stoke-on-Trent, where he was born, sank with the ship.

The civic fathers, ashamed and embarrassed, disowned one of their most famous sons and gave the carving away.

Reluctant

And for 73 years, arms folded in defiance, the abondoned figure has stood in exile in a Lichfield park 35 miles away, with only flocks of pigeons for company.

Now Stoke councillors think it is time he was rehabilitated.

The idea is to erect the statue outside a new £40 million shopping centre.

But Lichfield, where the carving stands in Beacon Park, may be reluctant to part with it—even though people have forgotten how it came to be there.

Recreation Committee chairman Cllr. Bill Dunsmore said: 'There must have been a reason it was erected in our park.

'Without knowing that reason we wouldn't let it go.'

Trail of the Titanic Iceberg:

Titanic discovered

Human eyes once again gazed upon Titanic on the night of September 1, 1985, during a Franco-American expedition led by Dr Robert Ballard. Since then, numerous teams have visited the ship, which lies over two miles below the surface, its fore and aft sections some 2,000 feet apart. The debris field stretches far beyond and includes all manner of personal effects and fixtures and fittings, from a comb to one of the giant boilers.

The bow section sits upright on the ocean floor but is deeply embedded in bottom mud, obscuring the area of the hull that was opened up with such catastrophic consequences. Even so, a 1996 expedition headed by Dr Ballard revealed that the impact with the berg caused not a single lengthy gash but a series of smaller tears in the steel. The plates in this part of the bow separated, and the fact that these mortal wounds were inflicted in the area where inferior-quality wrought iron rivets were used lent further weight to the theory that here lay the fatal flaw. Had steel rivets been used throughout, or even so-called 'best-best' grade iron rivets in the hull section, perhaps the seams would have held and Titanic would have arrived in New York to great fanfare. As it was, a combination of design weakness, material failure, human error and sheer mischance conspired to bring about an appalling maritime tragedy that will continue to cast a deep shadow long after Nature has taken its course on the physical remains.

Daily Mail, Friday, September 6, 1985

Sea-bed Titanic

OPPOSITE PAGE: Millvina Dean, the last surviving passenger, at the Titanic exhibition held at the National Maritime Museum in Greenwich in 1994. At the time of the collision she was the youngest passenger on board at 2 months and 27 days old. Her family were emigrating to Kansas and she was travelling third class with her parents and brother Bertram. She was loaded onto lifeboat No.10 with her mother and brother but her father perished. She died on the 98th anniversary of the ship's launch.

BELOW: A porthole from the ship.

THIS is the great ship Titanic in her icy grave on the ocean bed.

The dramatic picture, taken 2½ miles below the Atlantic waves, is the first view of the liner for 73 years.

The last people to see her were the survivors of the dreadful disaster when she hit an iceberg and sunk on her maiden voyage in 1912.

The Titanic is almost upright, with her hull and upper rail well preserved. A very small flagpole on the tip of the bows is apparently still standing in 'pristine condition'.

The exploration of the wreck has made a deep impression on the scientists in the joint American-French expedition who located her 500 miles off Newfoundland

Team leader Dr Robert Ballard said that seeing the ship is like going back in time. The fact that she is in total darkness adds to the feeling of eeriness.'

Dr Ballard, said the camera mounted on a robot submarine has now taken 12,000 colour photographs and the mission is to end. But he refused to say precisely where the Titanic is located.

'I would like to keep that confidential, as others are talking about dredging or dragging and damaging it,' he said. 'The Titanic is in beautiful condition and we don't want anyone to come and maul it.'

Dr Ballard, senior marine scientist with the Woods Hole Oceanographic Institute in Massachusetts, said that salvaging the Titanic for any treasures would be a mistake.

Already, a British firm, Wakefield and Imberg, is hoping to agree terms with the scientists for a £100 million plan to raise the ship. It would involve pumping thousands of tonnes of molten wax into the hull. This would solidify and then become buoyant.

" I can only say that as a result of this inquiry it is to be hoped that no vessel will ever take such utterly unnecessary risks as I submit were taken by the Titanic. Speaking generally, the two causes of the disaster were the failure to keep a good lookout and the proceeding at too great a rate of speed."

ay, March 16, 1962

Cleared–the Titanic man

BUT CAPTAIN LORD, SCAPEGOAT FOR A DISASTER, DIED WEEKS TOO SOON

By Daily Mail Reporter

THE stain on sea captain Stanley Lord's reputation is erased today—after 50 years.

But it comes two months too late.

Captain Lord died, aged 84, at his home in Wallasey, Cheshire, in January.

He died still blamed officially for failing to use his 6,223-ton ship Californian to save the 1,500 victims of the Titanic disaster amid the Atlantic icebergs.

Expert opinion

But, actually, he had been told that present expert opinion is that he "may well be considered the victim of the grossest miscarriage of justice in the history of British marine inquiries."

His champion: Mr. Leslie Harrison, general secretary of the Mercantile Marine Service Association, who has re-assessed evidence given at the Titanic inquiry.

He tears to shreds the findings of 73-year-old Lord Mersey, presiding over his first shipping inquiry. This way:

ITEM: Lord Mersey castigated Captain Lord unmercifully for not going to the rescue when he was "only eight to ten" miles away.

FACT: Mr. Harrison says it is clear he was "at least 19 and probably between 25 and 30 miles away" and another ship, the Mount Temple, was nearer the disaster.

ITEM: Captain Lord was accused by implication of not going to the rescue because he was in his cabin, drunk.

FACT: He never drank.

No chance

ITEM: Captain Lord was called only as an ordinary witness—never warned that he might be criticised—and the Mount Temple's officers were not called.

FACT: He never had a chance to reply to accusations and he lost his job with the Californian's owners.

"On top of that," said Mr. Harrison, "Captain Lord had stopped that night to avoid running on into an iceberg, but the Titanic went on. Poor Lord became the official scapegoat."

FLOOR SHOW

AFTER 80 YEARS...

CAPTAIN STILL CURSED BY TITANIC

For 80 years, one man has been seen as the villain of the Titanic disaster.

And yesterday, after a new report into the sinking, it appeared that Captain Stanley Lord's name would remain tarnished.

His liner Californian was the nearest ship when the Titanic hit an iceberg off Newfoundland on April 14 1912.

The report by the Department of Transport said Lord failed to take proper action to respond to distress signals from the Titanic.

But it added that even if he had acted differently, he was too far away to save the 1,500 passengers who died.

CAMPAIGN

The re-examination of the files on the tragedy was ordered two years ago by then Transport Secretary Cecil Parkinson following a long campaign by Captain Lord's supporters, who claim he was blameless.

The report by Captain Thomas Barnett, former principal nautical surveyor at the department confirms Lord's belief that the Californian was between 17 and 20 miles from the Titanic but ruled that 'distress signals were seen and proper action was not taken'.

He said others would continue to speculate on the tragedy, but he hoped they would do so with regard to the 'simple fact that there are no villains in this story – just human beings with human characteristics'.

Accusations against Captain Lord hinge on a 1912 inquiry ruling that the Californian had seen distress rockets and was close enough to have saved everybody. The captain countered that his ship, Boston-bound from London with 47 passengers, had been so far away that no-one could possibly have seen the Titanic or her rockets.

Books and films have fuelled rumours that Captain Lord had been drinking on the night of the disaster and ended up an alcoholic. In fact he went back to sea, served in World War I and retired in 1927. He died in 1962, aged 84.

His 83-year-old son, also called Stanley, claimed yesterday that the new report vindicated his father.

'He was confident he would be cleared when he died, and I have always stood by his belief and knew he would eventually be proved right,' said Mr Lord, of Wallasey, Merseyside.

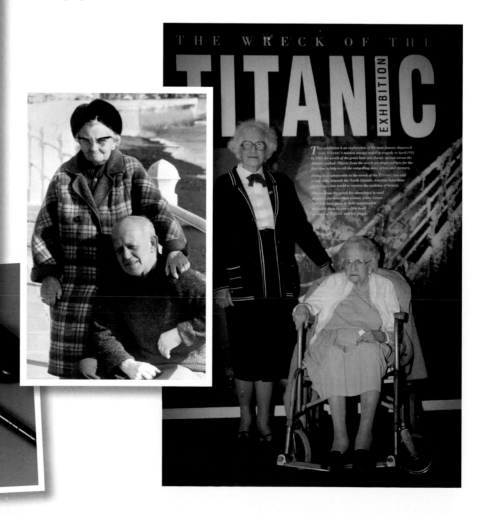

AFTER THE FANTASTIC FIND THAT ENDED A 73-YEAR SEARCH

THE TITANIC SCRAMBLE!

Diamonds to dinner plates, it could all sell for a fortune

About 500 miles off the coast of Newfoundland, and 13,200ft. below the icy waters of the Atlantic the remains of the Titanic lie in a featureless plain of mud.

A gigantic 300ft. section of completely intact bow towers over a trail of debris. China plates and passengers' luggage labelled 'not wanted on voyage' are strewn across an area of about a third of a mile amid rusting pipes and torn steel plates.

This was the scene French and American scientists viewed through remote control cameras when they solved one of the greatest of maritime mysteries—the last resting place of what was once the world's most luxurious liner.

An unmanned robot craft, called Argo, about the size of a small car, found the wreckage at around 2am on Sunday and its cameras zeroed in on a massive boiler.

'It is unbelievably fantastic,' said Dr Roberts Ballard, who heads the joint U.S.-French expedition. 'Suddenly we were there, right bang on top of it and the first thing we saw was that gorgeous boiler.'

SURVIVOR

Jim Freeman, a crewman aboard the U.S. navy research ship, Knorr, said : 'At first it was just a large object and then it came into focus. You could see the rivets and the cut-out plates, the three boiler doors ... every detail.'

So ended the long search for the liner and now begins the scramble for her riches. The Titanic, which sailed from Southampton on its maiden voyage 73 years ago, had 11 millionaires on board and a cargo of diamonds that were worth £7 million in 1912.

She hit an iceberg on the night of April 14-15 and 1,500 people died after water rushed through a 300-foot gash in the side. The ship the makers claimed was unsinkable filled with water and nosedived to the bottom.

Marshall Drew, 81, is one of the 21 survivors still alive. He was eight when he was lowered 70ft. down from the Titanic's deck to a lifeboat.

He was returning to his home after a holiday in Cornwall with an aunt and an uncle. His uncle went down with the ship.

His last memory of the great liner was : 'A huge explosion with steam, sparks and smoke as the boilers blew. Then there were just the cries and the screams of the people in the water.'

Books, films and plays have been made of the final hours of the Titanic. Its sinking spawned a host of maritime safety laws, especially after it was revealed that there were only enough lifeboats for half the 2,200 passengers.

The last resting place of the 46,328 ton liner has intrigued treasure hunters for decades. It inspired films such as Raise the Titanic, but the real life search has had to wait for the coming of sophisticated, hi-tech underwater search equipment.

Texas oilman Jack Grinn poured millions into expeditions in 1980, 1981 and 1983. A division of Walt Disney Productions put more than £2 million into a search.

After the 1981 search Grinn claimed that shadowy video tapes showed a giant propeller from the Titanic.

He said yesterday : 'We have the rights to the Titanic. We have staked our claim. We gave them all the benefits of our information and this is confirmation of our discovery.'

Today's estimated value of the diamonds alone is £146 million. Crockery, pieces of deck or anything authenticated as being recovered from the wreckage could sell for a fortune.

This year a French government organisation, the Institute for Research and Exploitation of the Sea and the American oceanographic survey ship Knorr, financed by the National Geographic Society, began what has now become the final search.

PRESSURE

A French made submarine sonar system and American-made under water cameras began a systematic search of the area in which it had been generally accepted the Titanic lay.

The French research ship, the Suroit, started working the area on June 28 and on August 5 the Knorr and the Argo, joined the hunt.

According to the French government : 'Those on board the Suroit were almost sure they had pinned down the Titanic. The cameras of the American Argo system came in the past few days and confirmed the discovery.'

The operation was code named White Star after the line which owned the ship. An agreement specifies that anything recovered from the wreckage will be jointly owned.

The use of the Argo in the search provided the first practical test of a new generation of unmanned, deep-sea submarines and 'swimming eyeballs' that can survive the crushing pressure and see through miles of darkness on the ocean floor.

Dr Ballard said the Titanic's hull was in such good condition that it could be a museum piece.

The first film of the Titanic was yesterday being flown back by helicopter for showing on TV in the United States and Canada. Photographs were being auctioned off.

Despite theories that ocean currents had broken up the Titanic and scattered it over miles of ocean floor the scientists found it in a fairly compact area.

Meanwhile the two governments may ask the United Nations to declare the site an international memorial and thwart the ambitions of hundreds of treasure hunters.

Marshall Drew, speaking at his home on Long Island, said : 'They should leave the dead in peace. Maybe just knowing where the Titanic sank might put the matter to rest.'

September 4, 1985

OPPOSITE PAGE LEFT: A selection of the 6,000 artefacts removed from the wreck. They have since been exhibited in various locations.

OPPOSITE PAGE MIDDLE: Emily Richards and her son George photographed in 1972 for the 60th anniversary of the disaster. He was ten months old when the ship sank.

OPPOSITE PAGE RIGHT: Millvina Dean and Barbara West Dainton, the two oldest surviving passengers from the ship, at the exhibition in Greenwich. Dainton, who was also emigrating to the States, was 10 months and 18 days old at the time of the collision. She survived along with her mother and sister but her father went down with the ship.

CREW

Officers:
MOODY, Mr James Paul *6th. Officer*
MURDOCH, Mr William McMaster *1st. Officer*
SMITH, Captain Edward John *Master*
WILDE, Mr Henry Tingle *Chief Officer*

Deck crew:
BRADLEY, Mr F. *Able Seaman*
CLENCH, Mr George *Able Seaman*
COUCH, Mr Frank *Able Seaman*
DAVIS, Mr Stephen James *Able Seaman*
HOLMAN, Mr Harry *Able Seaman*
HUTCHINSON, Mr John Hall *Carpenter/Joiner*
KING, Mr Thomas W. *Master-at-arms*
MATHERSON, Mr David *Able Seaman*
MATHIAS, Mr Montague Vincent *Mess Steward*
MAXWELL, Mr John *Carpenter/Joiner*
NICHOLS, Mr Alfred *Boatswain*
O'LOUGHLIN, Dr William Francis Norman *Surgeon*
SAWYER, Mr Robert James *Window Cleaner*
SIMPSON, Dr John Edward *Assistant Surgeon*
SMITH, Mr William *Seaman*
TAMLYN, Mr Frederick *Mess Steward*
TAYLOR, Mr C. *Able Seaman*
TERRELL, Mr Bertram *Seaman*

Engine crew:
ABRAHAM, Mr C. *Fireman/Stoker*
ADAMS, Mr R. *Fireman/Stoker*
ALLEN, Mr Henry *Fireman/Stoker*
ALLSOP, Mr Alfred Samuel *Electrician*
BAILEY, Mr George W. *Fireman/Stoker*
BAINES, Mr Richard *Greaser*
BANNON, Mr John *Greaser*
BARLOW, Mr Charles *Fireman/Stoker*
BARNES, Mr Charles *Fireman/Stoker*
BARNES, Mr J. *Fireman/Stoker*
BARRETT, Mr Frederick William *Fireman/Stoker*
BEATTIE, Mr Joseph *Greaser*
BELL, Mr Joseph *Chief Engineer*
BENDELL, Mr T. *Fireman/Stoker*
BENNETT, Mr George Alfred *Fireman/Stoker*
BENVILLE, Mr E. *Fireman/Stoker*

BESSANT, Mr William Edward *Fireman/Stoker*
BEVIS, Mr Joseph Henry *Trimmer*
BIDDLECOMBE, Mr Charles *Fireman/Stoker*
BIGGS, Mr Edward Charles *Fireman/Stoker*
BILLOWS, Mr J. *Trimmer*
BLACK, Mr Alexander *Fireman/Stoker*
BLACK, Mr D. *Fireman/Stoker*
BLACKMAN, Mr H. *Fireman/Stoker*
BLAKE, Mr Percival Albert *Trimmer*
BLAKE, Mr Seaton *Mess Steward*
BLAKE, Mr Thomas *Fireman/Stoker*
BLANEY, Mr James *Fireman/Stoker*
BLANN, Mr Eustace Horatius *Fireman/Stoker*
BOTT, Mr W. *Greaser*
BRADLEY, Mr Patrick Joseph *Fireman/Stoker*
BREWER, Mr Henry ("Harry") *Trimmer*
BRIANT, Mr Albert *Greaser*
BROOKS, Mr J. *Trimmer*
BROWN, Mr John *Fireman/Stoker*
BROWN, Mr Joseph James *Fireman/Stoker*
BURROUGHS, Mr Arthur *Fireman/Stoker*
BURTON, Mr Edward John *Fireman/Stoker*
BUTT, Mr William John *Fireman/Stoker*
CALDERWOOD, Mr Hugh *Trimmer*
CANNER, Mr J. *Fireman/Stoker*
CARR, Mr Richard Stephen *Trimmer*
CARTER (BALL), Mr James (W.) *Fireman/Stoker*
CASEY, Mr T. *Trimmer*
CASTLEMAN, Mr Edward *Greaser*
CHERRETT, Mr William Victor *Fireman/Stoker*
CHISNALL, Mr George Alexander *Boilermaker*
CHORLEY, Mr John *Fireman/Stoker*
COE, Mr Harry *Trimmer*
COLEMAN, Mr John *Mess Steward*
COOPER, Mr Harry *Fireman/Stoker*
COOPER, Mr James *Trimmer*
COPPERTHWAITE, Mr B. *Fireman/Stoker*
CORCORAN, Mr Denny *Fireman/Stoker*
COTTON, Mr A. *Trimmer*
COUCH, Mr Joseph Henry *Greaser*
COY, Mr Francis Ernest George *Junior Assistant 3rd. Engineer*
CRABB, Mr H. *Trimmer*
CREESE, Mr Henry Philip *Deck Engineer*
CROSS, Mr W. *Fireman/Stoker*
CUNNINGHAM, Mr B. *Fireman/Stoker*
CURTIS, Mr Arthur *Fireman/Stoker*
DAVIES, Mr Thomas *Leading Fireman*
DAWSON, Mr Joseph *Trimmer*
DICKSON, Mr W. *Trimmer*
DODD, Mr Edward Charles *Junior 3rd. Engineer*
DODDS, Mr Henry Watson *Junior Assistant 4th Engineer*
DOYLE, Mr Laurence *Fireman/Stoker*
DUFFY, Mr William Luke *Writer/Engineer's Clerk*
DYER, Mr Henry Ryland *Senior Assistant 4th. Engineer*
EAGLE, Mr A. J. *Trimmer*
EASTMAN, Mr Charles *Greaser*
ELLIOTT, Mr Everett Edward *Trimmer*
ERVINE, Mr Albert George *Electrician*
EVANS, Mr William *Trimmer*
FARQUHARSON, Mr William Edward *Senior 2nd. Engineer*
FAY, Mr Thomas Joseph *Greaser*
FERRARY, Mr Anton *Trimmer*
FERRIS, Mr W. *Leading Fireman*

FITZPATRICK, Mr Hugh J. *Junior Boilermaker*
FORD, Mr H. *Trimmer*
FORD, Mr Thomas *Leading Fireman*
FOSTER, Mr Albert C. *Storekeeper*
FRASER, Mr J. *Fireman/Stoker*
FRASER, Mr James *Junior Assistant 3rd. Engineer*
GARDNER, Mr F. *Greaser*
GEER, Mr Alfred Ernest *Fireman/Stoker*
GODWIN, Mr Frederick Walter *Greaser*
GOLDER, Mr M. W. *Fireman/Stoker*
GORDON, Mr J. *Trimmer*
GOREE, Mr Frank *Greaser*
GOSLING, Mr Bertram James *Trimmer*
GOSLING, Mr S. *Trimmer*
GREEN, Mr George *Trimmer*
GREGORY, Mr David *Greaser*
GRODIDGE, Mr Ernest Edward *Fireman/Stoker*
GUMERY, Mr George *Mess Steward*
HAGAN, Mr John *Fireman/Stoker*
HALL, Mr J. *Fireman/Stoker*
HALLETT, Mr George *Fireman/Stoker*
HANDS, Mr Bernard *Fireman/Stoker*
HANNAM, Mr George *Fireman/Stoker*
HARRIS, Mr Amos Fred *Trimmer*
HARRIS, Mr Edward *Fireman/Stoker*
HARRISON, Mr Norman E. *Junior 2nd. Engineer*
HART, Mr James *Fireman/Stoker*
HARVEY, Mr Herbert Gifford *Junior Assistant 2nd. Engineer*
HASGOOD, Mr Roland *Fireman/Stoker*
HASLIN, Mr James *Trimmer*
HEAD, Mr A. *Fireman/Stoker*
HESKETH, Mr John Henry *Engineer*
HILL, Mr James *Trimmer*
HINTON, Mr Stephen William *Trimmer*
HODGE, Mr Charles *Senior Assistant 3rd. Engineer*
HODGES, Mr W. *Fireman/Stoker*
HODGKINSON, Mr Leonard *Senior 4th. Engineer*
HOSGOOD, Mr Richard *Fireman/Stoker*
HOSKING, Mr George Fox *Senior 3rd. Engineer*
HUNT, Mr Tom *Fireman/Stoker*
HURST, Mr Charles John *Fireman/Stoker*
INGRAM, Mr Charles *Trimmer*
INSTANCE, Mr T. *Fireman/Stoker*
JACOBSON, Mr John *Fireman/Stoker*
JAGO, Mr Joseph *Greaser*
JAMES, Mr Thomas *Fireman/Stoker*
JARVIS, Mr Walter *Fireman/Stoker*
JOAS, Mr N. *Fireman/Stoker*
JUKES, Mr James *Greaser*
JUPE, Mr Boykett Herbert *Electrician*
KEARL, Mr Charles Henry *Greaser*
KEARL, Mr G. *Trimmer*
KEEGAN, Mr James *Leading Fireman*
KELLY, Mr James *Greaser*
KELLY, Mr William *Assistant Electrician*
KEMP, Mr Thomas Hulman *Extra Assistant 4th Engineer (Refrigeration)*
KENCHENTEN, Mr Frederick *Greaser*
KENZLER, Mr Augustus *Storekeeper*
KERR, Mr Thomas *Fireman/Stoker*
KINSELLA, Mr L. *Fireman/Stoker*
KIRKHAM, Mr J. *Greaser*
LAHY, Mr T. E. *Fireman/Stoker*
LEE, Mr H. *Trimmer*
LIGHT, Mr Christopher William *Fireman/Stoker*
LIGHT, Mr W. *Fireman/Stoker*

LLOYD, Mr W. *Fireman/Stoker*
LONG, Mr F. *Trimmer*
LONG, Mr W. *Trimmer*
MACKIE, Mr William Dickson *Junior 5th. Engineer*
MARRETT, Mr G. *Fireman/Stoker*
MARSH, Mr Frederick Charles *Fireman/Stoker*
MASKELL, Mr Leopold Adolphus *Trimmer*
MASON, Mr J. *Leading Fireman*
MAY, Mr Arthur *Fireman/Stoker*
MAY, Mr Arthur William *Fireman Messman*
MAYO, Mr William Peter *Leading Fireman*
MCANDREW, Mr Thomas *Fireman/Stoker*
MCANDREWS, Mr William *Fireman/Stoker*
MCCASTLEN, Mr W. *Fireman/Stoker*
MCGARVEY, Mr Edward Joseph *Fireman/Stoker*
MCGAW, Mr Eroll V. *Fireman/Stoker*
MCGREGOR, Mr J. *Fireman/Stoker*
MCINERNEY, Mr Thomas *Greaser*
MCQUILLAN, Mr William *Fireman/Stoker*
MCRAE, Mr William Alexander *Fireman/Stoker*
MCREYNOLDS, Mr William *Junior 6th. Engineer*
MIDDLETON, Mr Alfred Pirrie *Electrician*
MILFORD, Mr George *Fireman/Stoker*
MILLAR, Mr Robert *Extra 5th Engineer*
MILLAR, Mr Thomas *Deck Enginer*
MINTRAM, Mr William *Fireman/Stoker*
MITCHELL, Mr Lawrence *Trimmer*
MOORE, Mr Ralph William *Trimmer*
MOORES, Mr Richard Henry *Greaser*
MORGAN, Mr Arthur Herbert *Trimmer*
MORGAN, Mr Thomas A. *Fireman/Stoker*
MORRELL, Mr R. *Trimmer*
MORRIS, Mr Arthur *Greaser*
MORRIS, Mr W. *Trimmer*
MOYES, Mr William Young *Senior 6th. Engineer*
NETTLETON, Mr George *Fireman/Stoker*
NEWMAN, Mr Charles Thomas *Assistant Storekeeper*
NOON, Mr John *Fireman/Stoker*
NORRIS, Mr J. *Fireman/Stoker*
NOSS, Mr Bertram Arthur *Fireman/Stoker*
NOSS, Mr Henry *Fireman/Stoker*
OLIVE, Mr Charles *Greaser*
PAINTER, Mr Charles *Fireman/Stoker*
PAINTER, Mr Frank Frederick *Fireman/Stoker*
PALLES, Mr Thomas *Greaser*
PARSONS, Mr Frank Alfred *Senior 5th. Engineer*
PERRY, Mr H. *Trimmer*
PHILLIPS, Mr A. G. *Greaser*
PITFIELD, Mr William James *Greaser*
POND, Mr George *Fireman/Stoker*
PRESTON, Mr Thomas Charles Alfred *Trimmer*
PROUDFOOT, Mr Richard *Trimmer*
PUGH, Mr Percy *Leading Fireman*
READ, Mr J. *Trimmer*
READ, Mr Robert *Trimmer*
REEVES, Mr F. *Fireman/Stoker*
RICHARDS, Mr Joseph James *Fireman/Stoker*
RICKMAN, Mr George Albert *Fireman/Stoker*
ROBERTS, Mr Robert George *Fireman/Stoker*
ROUS, Mr Arthur J. *Plumber*
RUDD, Mr Henry *Assistant Storekeeper*
RUTTER (GRAVES), Mr Sidney Frank *Fireman/Stoker*
SANGSTER, Mr Charles *Fireman/Stoker*
SAUNDERS, Mr T. *Fireman/Stoker*
SAUNDERS, Mr W. *Fireman/Stoker*
SAUNDERS, Mr Walter Edward *Trimmer*

SELF, Mr Alfred Henry *Greaser*
SENIOR, Mr Harry *Fireman/Stoker*
SHEA, Mr Thomas *Fireman/Stoker*
SHEPHERD, Mr Jonathan *Junior Assistant 2nd. Engineer*
SHILABEER, Mr Charles Frederick *Trimmer*
SKEATS, Mr William *Trimmer*
SLOAN, Mr Peter *Chief Electrician*
SMALL, Mr William *Leading Fireman*
SMITH, Mr Emest George *Trimmer*
SMITH, Mr James M. *Junior 4th. Engineer*
SMITHER, Mr Harry John *Fireman/Stoker*
SNELLGROVE, Mr G. *Fireman/Stoker*
SNOOKS, Mr W. *Trimmer*
STAFFORD, Mr. M. *Greaser*
STANBROOK, Mr Alfred Augustus *Fireman/Stoker*
STEEL, Mr Robert Edward *Trimmer*
STOCKER, Mr H. *Trimmer*
STUBBS, Mr James Henry *Fireman/Stoker*
SULLIVAN, Mr S. *Fireman/Stoker*
TAYLOR, Mr T. *Fireman/Stoker*
THOMAS, Mr Joseph *Fireman/Stoker*
TIZARD, Mr Arthur *Fireman/Stoker*
TOZER, Mr James *Greaser*
TURLEY, Mr Richard *Fireman/Stoker*
VAN DER BRUGGE, Mr Wessel Adrianus *Fireman/Stoker*
VEAL, Mr Arthur *Greaser*
VEAR, Mr H. *Fireman/Stoker*
VEAR, Mr William *Fireman/Stoker*
WARD, Mr Arthur *Junior Assistant 4th. Engineer*
WARD, Mr J. *Leading Fireman*
WARDNER, Mr Albert *Fireman/Stoker*
WATERIDGE, Mr Edward Lewis *Fireman/Stoker*
WATSON, Mr W. *Fireman/Stoker*
WATTS, Mr F *Trimmer*
WEBB, Mr S. *Trimmer*
WEBBER, Mr Francis Albert *Leading Fireman*
WHITE, Mr Alfred *Greaser*
WHITE, Mr Frank Leonard *Trimmer*
WILLIAMS, Mr E. *Fireman/Stoker*
WILSON, Mr Bertie *Senior Assistant 2nd. Engineer*
WILTON, Mr William *Trimmer*
WITCHER, Mr Albert Ernest *Fireman/Stoker*
WITT, Mr Henry Dennis *Fireman/Stoker*
WOODFORD, Mr Frederick *Greaser*
WOODS, Mr Henry *Trimmer*
WYETH, Mr James *Fireman/Stoker*
YOUNG, Mr Francis James *Fireman/Stoker*

Musicians:

BRAILEY, Mr W. Theodore Ronald *Musician*
BRICOUX, Mr Roger Marie *Musician*
CLARKE, Mr John Frederick Preston *Musician*
HARTLEY, Mr Wallace Henry *Musician*
HUME, Mr John Law *Musician*
KRINS, Mr Georges Alexandre *Musician*
TAYLOR, Mr Percy Cornelius *Musician*
WOODWARD, Mr John Wesley *Musician*

Victualling crew:

ABBOTT, Mr Ernest Owen *Lounge Pantry Steward*
AHIER, Mr Percy Snowden *Saloon Steward*
AKERMAN, Mr Albert *Steward*
AKERMAN, Mr Joseph Francis *Assistant Pantryman Steward*
ALLAN, Mr Robert Spencer *Bed Room Steward*

ALLARIA, Sig Baptiste *Assistant Waiter*
ALLEN, Mr Frederick *Lift Steward*
ALLEN, Mr George *Scullion*
ALLSOP, Mr Frank Richard *Saloon Steward*
ANDERSON, Mr Walter J. *Bed Room Steward*
ASHCROFT, Mr Austin Aloysius *Clerk*
ASHE, Mr Henry Wellesley *Glory Hole Steward*
ASPESLAGH, Mr Georges *Assistant Plateman*
AYLING, Mr George Edwin *Assistant Vegetable Cook*
BACK, Mr Charles Frederick *Assistant Lounge Steward*
BAGLEY, Mr Edward Ernest *Saloon Steward*
BAILEY, Mr George Francis *Saloon Steward*
BANFI, Sig Ugo *Waiter*
BARKER, Mr Albert Vale *Baker*
BARKER, Mr Ernest T. *Saloon Steward*
BARKER, Mr Reginald Lomond *Purser*
BARLOW, Mr George *Bed Room Steward*
BARNES, Mr Frederick *Baker*
BARRETT, Mr Arthur *Bell Boy*
BARRINGER, Mr Arthur William *Saloon Steward*
BARROW, Mr Harry *Butcher*
BARROWS, Mr William *Saloon Steward*
BARTON, Mr Sidney John *Steward*
BASILICO, Sig Giovanni *Waiter*
BAXTER, Mr Harry Ross *Steward*
BAXTER, Mr Thomas Ferguson *Linen Steward*
BAZZI, Sig N. *Waiter*
BEDFORD, Mr William Barnet *Assistant Roast Cook*
BEEDMAN, Mr George Arthur *Bed Room Steward*
BEERE, Mr William *Kitchen Porter*
BENHAM, Mr Frederick *Saloon Steward*
BERNARDI, Sig Battista *Assistant Waiter*
BERTOLDI, Sig Florentini *Scullion*
BESSANT, Mr Edward William *Baggage Steward*
BEST, Mr Alfred Edwin *Saloon Steward*
BEUX, Mr David *Assistant Waiter*
BIETRIX, Mr George Baptiste *Cook*
BISHOP, Mr Walter Alexander *Bed Room Steward*
BLUMET, Mr Jean Baptiste *Pantryman*
BOCHET, Sig Pierre Giuseppe *Waiter*
BOCHETEZ, Mr Alexis Joseph *Chef*
BOGIE, Mr Norman Leslie *Bed Room Steward*
BOLHUIS, Hendrik *Cook*
BOND, Mr William John *Bed Room Steward*
BOOTHBY, Mr W. *Bed Room Steward*
BOSTON, Mr William John *Deck Steward*
BOUGHTON, Mr B. *Saloon Steward*
BOYD, Mr John *Saloon Steward*
BOYES, Mr John Henry *Saloon Steward*
BRADSHAW, Mr J. A. *Plate Steward*
BREWSTER, Mr George H. *Bed Room Steward*
BRISTOW, Mr Harry *Saloon Steward*
BRISTOW, Mr Robert Charles *Steward*
BROOKMAN, Mr John *Steward*
BROOM, Mr H. *Bath Steward*
BROOME, Mr Athol Frederick *Verandah Steward*
BROWN, Mr Walter James *Saloon Steward*
BUCKLEY, Mr H. E. *Assistant Vegetable Cook*
BULL, Mr W. *Scullion*
BULLEY, Mr Henry Ashburnham *Boots*
BUNMELL, Mr Wilfred *Plate Steward*
BURKE, Mr Richard Edward *Lounge Steward*
BURR, Mr Ewart Sydenham *Saloon Steward*
BUTT, Mr Robert Henry *Saloon Steward*
BUTTERWORTH, Mr John *Saloon Steward*

BYRNE, Mr J. E. *Bed Room Steward*
CAMPBELL, Mr Donald S. *3rd Class Clerk*
CARNEY, Mr William *Lift Steward*
CARTWRIGHT, Mr James Edward *Saloon Steward*
CASALI, Sig Giulio *Waiter*
CASSWILL, Mr Charles *Saloon Steward*
CAUNT, Mr William Ewart *Grill Cook*
CAVE, Mr Herbert *Saloon Steward*
CECIL, Mr C. *Steward*
CHABOISSON, Mr Adrien *Roast Cook*
CHARMAN, Mr John *Saloon Steward*
CHEVERTON, Mr William Edward *Saloon Steward*
CHITTY, Mr Archibald George *Steward*
CHITTY, Mr George Henry *Baker*
CHRISTMAS, Mr H. *Assistant Saloon Steward*
CLARK, Mr T. *Bed Room Steward*
COLEMAN, Mr Albert Edward *Saloon Steward*
CONWAY, Mr P. W. *Saloon Steward*
COOK, Mr George *Saloon Steward*
COOMBS, Mr Augustus Charles *Cook*
CORBEN, Mr Ernest Theodore *Assistant Printer Steward*
CORNAIRE, Mr Marcel Raymond André *Roast Cook*
COUTIN, Mr Auguste *Entreé Cook*
COX, Mr William Denton *Steward*
CRISP, Mr Albert Hector *Saloon Steward*
CRISPIN, Mr William *Glory Hole Steward*
CROSBIE, Mr J. Bertram *Turkish Bath Attendant*
CROVELLA, Sig Louis *Assistant Waiter*
CRUMPLIN, Mr Charles *Bed Room Steward*
DASHWOOD, Mr William George *Saloon Steward*
DAVIES, Mr Gordon Raleigh *Bed Room Steward*
DAVIES, Mr John James *Extra 2nd Baker*
DAVIES, Mr Robert J. *Saloon Steward*
DE BREUCQ, Mr Maurice *Assistant Waiter*
DE MARSICO, Sig Giovanni *Assistant Waiter*
DEAN, Mr George H. *Assistant Saloon Steward*
DEEBLE, Mr Alfred Arnold *Saloon Steward*
DERRETT, Mr Albert *Saloon Steward*
DESLANDS, Mr Percival Stainer *Saloon Steward*
DESVERNINE, Sig Louis Gabriel *Assistant Pastry Chef*
DINENAGE, Mr James Richard *Saloon Steward*
DODD, Mr George Charles *Steward*
DOLBY, Mr Joseph *Reception Room Steward*
DONATI, Sig Italo *Assistant Waiter*
DONOGHUE, Mr Frank *Bed Room Steward*
DORNIER, Mr Louis Auguste *Assistant Fish Cook*
DOUGHTY, Mr W. *Saloon Steward*
DUNFORD, Mr William *Hospital Steward*
DYER, Mr William *Saloon Steward*
EDBROOKE, Mr F. *Steward*
EDE, Mr George B. *Steward*
EDGE, Mr Frederick William *Deck Steward*
EDWARDS, Mr Clement *Assistant Pantryman Steward*
EGG, Mr W. H. *Steward*
ENNIS, Mr Walter *Turkish Bath Attendant*
EVANS, Mr George Richard *Saloon Steward*
FAIRALL, Mr Henry *Saloon Steward*
FARRENDON, Mr Ernest John *Confectioner*
FELLOWS, Mr Alfred J. *Boots*
FELTHAM, Mr G. *Vienna Baker*
FEY, Sig Carlo *Scullion*
FINCH, Mr Harry *Steward*
FIORAVANTE, Sig Giuseppe *Assistant Scullion*

FLETCHER, Mr Peter W. *Bugler Steward*
FORD, Mr Ernest *Steward*
FORD, Mr F. *Bed Room Steward*
FOX, Mr William Thomas *Steward*
FRANKLIN, Mr Alan Vincent *Saloon Steward*
FREEMAN, Mr Ernest Edward Samuel *Deck Steward*
GATTI, Sig Gaspare *Restaurant Manager*
GEDDES, Mr Richard Charles *Bed Room Steward*
GILARDINO, Sig Vincenzo *Waiter*
GILES, Mr John Robert *Baker*
GILL, Mr Joseph Stanley *Bed Room Steward*
GILL, Mr Patrick *Ship's Cook*
GOLLOP, Mr F. *Assistant Passage Cook*
GOSHAWK, Mr Arthur James *3rd Saloon Steward*
GROSCLAUDE, Gérald *Waiter*
GUNN, Mr Joseph Alfred *Assistant Saloon Steward*
GWYNN, Mr William Logan *Postal Clerk*
HALFORD, Mr Richard *Steward*
HALL, Mr F. A. J. *Scullion*
HAMBLYN, Mr Ernest William *Bed Room Steward*
HAMILTON, Mr Ernest *Assistant Smoke Room Steward*
HARDING, Mr A. *Assistant Pantry Steward*
HARRIS, Mr Charles William *Saloon Steward*
HARRIS, Mr Clifford Henry *Bell Boy*
HARRIS, Mr Edward *Assistant Pantryman Steward*
HATCH, Mr Hugh *Scullion*
HAWKESWORTH, Mr James *Saloon Steward*
HAWKESWORTH, Mr William Walter *Deck Steward*
HAYTER, Mr Arthur *Bed Room Steward*
HEINEN, Mr Joseph *Saloon Steward*
HENDY, Mr Edward Martin *Saloon Steward*
HENSFORD, Mr Herbert George *Butcher*
HEWETT, Mr Thomas *Bed Room Steward*
HILL, Mr H. P. *Steward*
HILL, Mr James Colston *Bed Room Steward*
HINCKLEY, Mr George *Bath Steward*
HINE, Mr William Edward *Baker*
HISCOCK, Mr S. *Plate Steward*
HOARE, Mr Leonard James *Saloon Steward*
HOGG, Mr Charles William *Bed Room Steward*
HOGUE, Mr E. *Plate Steward*
HOLLAND, Mr Thomas *Reception Steward*
HOLLOWAY, Mr Sidney *Clothes Presser*
HOPKINS, Mr F. *Plate Steward*
HOUSE, Mr William *Saloon Steward*
HOWELL, Mr Arthur Albert *Saloon Steward*
HUGHES, Mr William Thomas *Steward*
HUMBY, Mr Frederick *Plate Steward*
HUMPHREYS, Mr Thomas Humphrey *Assistant Saloon Steward*
HUTCHINSON, Mr James *Vegetable. Cook*
IDE, Mr Harry John *Bed Room Steward*
INGROUVILLE, Mr Henry *Steward*
INGS, Mr William Ernest *Scullion*
JACKSON, Mr Cecil *Boots*
JAILLET, Mr Henri Marie *Pastry Chef*
JANAWAY, Mr William Frank *Bed Room Steward*
JANIN, Mr Claude Marie *Soup Chef*
JEFFERY, Mr William Alfred *Controller*
JENNER, Mr Harry *Saloon Steward*
JENSEN, Mr Charles Valdemar *Saloon Steward*
JOHNSON, Mr Harry *Assistant Ship's Cook*
JONES, Mr Albert *Saloon Steward*
JONES, Mr Arthur Ernest *Plate Steward*

JONES, Mr H. *Roast Cook*
JONES, Mr Reginald V. *Saloon Steward*
JOUANMAULT, Mr George *Sauce Chef*
KELLAND, Mr Thomas *Library Steward*
KENNELL, Mr Charles *Hebrew Cook*
KERLEY, Mr William Thomas *Assistant Saloon Steward*
KETCHLEY, Mr Henry *Saloon Steward*
KIERAN, Mr James W. *Chief 3rd Class Steward*
KIERAN, Mr Michael *Storekeeper*
KING, Mr Alfred *Lift Steward*
KING, Mr Ernest Waldron *Clerk*
KING, Mr G. *Scullion*
KINGSCOTE, Mr William Ford *Saloon Steward*
KIRKALDY, Mr Thomas *Bedroom Steward*
KITCHING, Mr Arthur Alfred *Saloon Steward*
KLEIN, Mr Herbert *Barber*
KNIGHT, Mr Leonard George *Steward*
LACEY, Mr Bert W. *Assistant Saloon Steward*
LAKE, Mr William *Saloon Steward*
LANE, Mr Albert Edward *Saloon Steward*
LATIMER, Mr Andrew L *Chief Steward*
LAWRENCE, Mr Arthur *Saloon Steward*
LEADER, Mr Archie *Confectioner*
LEFEBVRE, Mr Paul Georges *Saloon Steward*
LEONARD, Mr Matthew *Steward*
LEVETT, Mr George Alfred *Assistant Pantryman Steward*
LIGHT, Mr C. *Plate Steward*
LLOYD, Mr Humphrey *Saloon Steward*
LOCKE, Mr A. *Scullion*
LONGMUIR, Mr John Dickson *Assistant Pantry Steward*
LOVELL, Mr John *Grill Cook*
LYDIATT, Mr Charles *Saloon Steward*
MABEY, Mr J. *Steward*
MACKIE, Mr George William *Bed Room Steward*
MAJOR, Mr Thomas Edgar *Bath Steward*
MANTLE, Mr Roland Frederick *Steward*
MARCH, Mr John Starr *Postal Clerk*
MARKS, Mr J. *Assistant Pantryman Steward*
MARRIOTT, Mr J. W. *Assistant Pantryman Steward*
MATTMAN, Mr Adolf *Ice Man*
MAYTUM, Mr Alfred *Chief Butcher*
MCCARTHY, Mr Frederick J. *Bed Room Steward*
MCCAWLEY, Mr Thomas W. *Gymnasium Steward*
MCELROY, Mr Hugh Walter *Purser*
MCGRADY, Mr James *Saloon Steward*
MCMULLEN, Mr James *Saloon Steward*
MCMURRAY, Mr William Ernest *Bed Room Steward*
MELLOR, Mr Arthur *Saloon Steward*
MIDDLETON, Mr M. V. *Saloon Steward*
MISHELLANY, Mr Abraham *Printer Steward*
MONTEVERDI, Sig Giovanni *Entreé Cook*
MOORE, Mr Alfred Ernest *Saloon Steward*
MORGAN (BIRD), Mr Charles Frederick *Assistant Storekeeper*
MOSS, Mr William *1st. Saloon Steward*
MOUROS, Mr Jean *Assistant Waiter*
MULLEN, Mr Thomas A. *Steward*
MÜLLER, Mr L. *Interpreter Steward*
NANNINI, Sig Francesco *Head Waiter*
NICHOLLS, Mr Sidney *Saloon Steward*
NICHOLS, Mr A.D. *Steward*
O'CONNOR, Mr Thomas Peter *Bed Room Steward*
OLIVE, Mr Ernest Roskelly *Clothes Presser Steward*
ORPET, Mr Walter Hayward *Saloon Steward*

ORR, Mr J. *Assistant Vegetable Cook*
OSBORNE, Mr William Edward *Saloon Steward*
OWEN, Mr Lewis *Assistant Saloon Steward*
PACEY, Mr Reginald lvan *Lift Steward*
PACHERAT, Mr Jean Baptiste *Assistant Larder Cook*
PAINTIN, Mr James Arthur *Captain's Steward (Tiger)*
PARSONS, Mr Edward *Chief Storekeeper*
PARSONS, Mr Richard *Saloon Steward*
PEARCE, Mr Alfred Emest *Steward*
PEDRINI, Sig Alex *Assistant Waiter*
PENNAL, Mr Thomas Francis *Bath Steward*
PENNY, Mr William Farr *Assistant Saloon Steward*
PENROSE, Mr John Poole *Bed Room Steward*
PERACCHIO, Sig Alberto *Waiter*
PERACCHIO, Sig Sebastiano *Waiter*
PERKINS, Mr Laurence Alexander *Telephone Steward*
PEROTTI, Sig Alfonsi *Assistant Waiter*
PERRIN, Mr William Charles *Boots*
PERRITON, Mr Hubert Prouse *Saloon Steward*
PETTY, Mr Edwin Henry *Bed Room Steward*
PHILLIPS, Mr John George *Telegraphist*
PHILLIPS, Mr Walter John *Storekeeper*
PIATTI Sig, Louis *Waiter*
PIAZZA, Sig Pompeo *Waiter*
PLATT, Mr W. *Scullion*
POGGI, Emilio *Waiter*
POOK, Mr P. *Assistant Pantry*
PORTEUS, Mr Thomas *Butcher*
PRICE, Mr Ernest *Barman*
PRIDEAUX, Mr John "Jack" Arthur *Steward*
PROCTOR, Mr Charles *Chef*
PRYCE, Mr Charles William *Saloon Steward*
PUSEY, Mr John E. *Saloon Steward*
RANDALL, Mr Frank Henry *Saloon Steward*
RANSOM, Mr James *Saloon Steward*
RATTI, Sig Enrico *Waiter*
RATTONBURY, Mr William Henry *Boots*
REED, Mr Charles S. *Bed Room Steward*
REVELL, Mr William *Saloon Steward*
RICALDONE, Sig Rinaldo Renato *Assistant Waiter*
RICE, Mr John Reginald *Clerk*
RICE, Mr Percy *Steward*
RICKS, Mr Cyril G. *Storekeeper*
RIDOUT, Mr W. *Saloon Steward*
RIGOZZI, Sig Abele *Assistant Waiter*
RIMMER, Mr Gilbert *Saloon Steward*
ROBERTON, Mr George Edward *Assistant Saloon Steward*
ROBERTS, Mr Frederick (Frank John?) *Third Butcher*
ROBERTS, Mr Hugh H. *Bed Room Steward*
ROBINSON, Mr James William *Saloon Steward*
ROGERS, Mr Edward James William *Assistant Storekeeper*
ROGERS, Mr Michael *Saloon Steward*
ROSS, Mr Horace Leopold *Scullion*
ROTTA, Sig Angelo *Waiter*
ROUSSEAU, Mr Pierre *Chef*
ROWE, Mr Edward M. *Saloon Steward*
RUSSELL, Mr Boysie Richard *Saloon Steward*
RYAN, Mr Tom *Steward*
SACCIGGI, Sig Giovanni *Assistant Waiter*
SALUSSOLIA, Sig Govanni *Glass man*
SAMUEL, Mr Owen Wilmore *Saloon Steward*
SARTORI, Sig Lazar *Assistant Glass Man*

SAUNDERS, Mr D. E. *Saloon Steward*
SCAVINO, Sig Candido *Carver*
SCOTT, Mr John *Boots*
SCOVELL, Mr Robert *Saloon Steward*
SEDUNARY, Mr Sidney Francis *Steward*
SESIA, Sig Giacomo *Waiter*
SEVIER, Mr William *Steward*
SHAW, Mr Henry *Kitchen Porter*
SHEA, Mr John *Saloon Steward*
SIEBERT, Mr Sidney Conrad *Bed Room Steward*
SIMMONS, Mr Frederick C. *Saloon Steward*
SIMMONS, Mr W. *Passage Cook*
SKINNER, Mr Edward *Saloon Steward*
SLIGHT, Mr Harry John *Steward*
SLIGHT, Mr William H. *Larder Cook*
SMILLIE, Mr John *Saloon Steward*
SMITH, Mr Charles *Kitchen Porter*
SMITH, Mr Charles Edwin *Bed Room Steward*
SMITH, Mr F. *Assistant Pantryman Steward*
SMITH, Mr J. *Baker*
SMITH, Mr John Richard Jago *Postal Clerk*
SMITH, Mr Robert G. *Saloon Steward*
SNAPE, Mrs Lucy Violet *Stewardess*
STAGG, Mr John Henry *Saloon Steward*
STEBBING, Mr Sydney Frederick *Chief Boots Steward*
STONE, Mr Edmond J. *Bed Room Steward*
STONE, Mr Edward Thomas *Bed Room Steward*
STROUD, Mr Edward Alfred Orlando *Saloon Steward*
STROUD, Mr Harry John *Saloon Steward*
STRUGNELL, Mr John H. *Saloon Steward*
STUBBINGS, Mr Harry Robert *2nd. Class Cook*
SWAN, Mr W. *Bed Room Steward*
SYMONDS, Mr J. *Saloon Steward*
TALBOT, Mr George Frederick Charles *Steward*
TAYLOR, Mr Bernard Cuthbert *Steward*
TAYLOR, Mr George Frederick *Stenographer*
TAYLOR, Mr Leonard *Turkish Bath Attendant*
TAYLOR, Mr William John *Saloon Steward*
TESTONI, Sig Ercole *Assistant Glass man*
TEUTON, Mr Thomas Moore *Saloon Steward*
THALER, Mr Montague Donald *Steward*
THOMPSON, Mr Herbert Henry *2nd (Assistant) Storekeeper*
THORLEY, Mr William *Cook*
TIETZ, Sig Carlo *Kitchen Porter*
TOPP, Mr Thomas Frederick *Butcher*
TOSHACK, Mr James Adamson *Saloon Steward*
TUCKER, Mr B. *2nd Pantry Steward*
TURNER, Mr L. *Saloon Steward*
TURVEY, Charles *Page boy*
URBINI, Sig Roberto *Waiter*
VALVASSORI, Sig Ettero *Waiter*
VEAL, Mr Thomas Henry Edom *Saloon Steward*
VICAT, Mr Alphonse *Cook*
VILLVARLANGE, Mr Pierre *Soup Chef*
VINE, Mr H. *Assistant Restaurant Controller*
VIONI, Sig Roberto *Waiter*
VOEGELIN, Mr Johannes *Waiter*
WAKE, Mr Percy *Baker*
WALLIS, Mrs Catherine Jane *Matron*
WALPOLE, Mr James *Chief Pantryman Steward*
WALSH, Miss Catherine *Stewardess*
WARD, Mr Edward *Bed Room Steward*
WARD, Mr Percy Thomas *Bed Room Steward*
WAREHAM, Mr Robert Arthur *Bed Room Steward*

WARWICK, Mr Tom *Saloon Steward*
WATSON, Mr W. A. *Bell Boy*
WEATHERSTONE, Mr Thomas Herbert *Saloon Steward*
WEBB, Mr Brooke Holding *Smoke Room Steward*
WELCH, Mr W. H. *Cook*
WHITE, Mr Arthur *Barber*
WHITE, Mr J. W. *Glory Hole Steward*
WHITE, Mr Leonard Lisle Oliver *Saloon Steward*
WHITFORD, Mr Alfred Henry *Saloon Steward*
WILLIAMS, Mr Arthur J. *Storekeeper*
WILLIAMSON, Mr James Bertram *Postal Clerk*
WILLIS, Mr W. *Steward*
WILTSHIRE, Mr William Audrey *Butcher*
WINSER, Mr Rowland *Steward*
WITTMAN, Mr Henry *Bed Room Steward*
WOOD, Mr James Thomas *Assistant Saloon Steward*
WOODY, Mr Oscar Scott *Postal Clerk*
WORMALD, Mr Frederick William *Saloon Steward*
WRAPSON, Mr Frederick Bernard *Assistant Pantryman Steward*
WRIGHT, Mr Frederick *Sports Instructor*
ZANETTI, Sig Minio *Assistant Waiter*
ZARRACCHI, Sig L. *Wine butler*

FIRST CLASS VICTIMS
ALLISON, Miss Helen Loraine
ALLISON, Mr Hudson Joshua Creighton
ALLISON, Mrs Bessie Waldo
ANDREWS, Mr Thomas
ARTAGAVEYTIA, Mr Ramon
ASTOR, Colonel John Jacob
BAUMANN, Mr John D.
BAXTER, Mr Quigg Edmond
BEATTIE, Mr Thomson
BIRNBAUM, Mr Jakob
BLACKWELL, Mr Stephen Weart
BOREBANK, Mr John James
BRADY, Mr John Bertram
BRANDEIS, Mr Emil
BREWE, Dr Arthur Jackson
BUTT, Major Archibald Willingham
CAIRNS, Mr Alexander (Manservant to Mr Carter)
CARLSSON, Mr Frank Olof
CARRAU, Mr Francisco M.
CARRAU, Mr José Pedro
CASE, Mr Howard Brown
CAVENDISH, Mr Tyrell William
CHAFFEE, Mr Herbert Fuller
CHISHOLM, Mr Roderick Robert Crispin
CLARK, Mr Walter Miller
CLIFFORD, Mr George Quincy
COLLEY, Mr Edward Pomeroy
COMPTON, Mr Alexander Taylor jr
CRAFTON, Mr John Bertram
CROSBY, Captain Edward Gifford
CUMINGS, Mr John Bradley
DAVIDSON, Mr Thornton
DOUGLAS, Mr Walter Donald
DULLES, Mr William Crothers
EVANS, Miss Edith Corse
FARTHING, Mr John (Servant to Mr Straus)
FOREMAN, Mr Benjamin Laventall
FORTUNE, Mr Charles Alexander
FORTUNE, Mr Mark
FRANKLIN, Mr Thomas Parnham

FRY, Mr John Richard (Valet to Mr Ismay)
FUTRELLE, Mr Jacques Heath
GEE, Mr Arthur H.
GIGLIO, Mr Victor
GOLDSCHMIDT, Mr George B.
GRAHAM, Mr George Edward

GUGGENHEIM, Mr Benjamin
HARRINGTON, Mr Charles Henry (Manservant to Mr Moore)
HARRIS, Mr Henry Birkhardt
HARRISON, Mr William Henry
HAYS, Mr Charles Melville
HEAD, Mr Christopher
HILLIARD, Mr Herbert Henry
HIPKINS, Mr William Edward
HOLVERSON, Mr Alexander Oskar
ISHAM, Miss Ann Elizabeth
JAKOB, Mr Birnbaum
JONES, Mr Charles Cresson
JULIAN, Mr Henry Forbes
KEEPING, Mr Edwin Herbert (Valet to Mr Widener)
KENT, Mr Edward Austin
KENYON, Mr Frederick R.
KLABER, Mr Herman
LAMBERT-WILLIAMS, Mr Fletcher Fellows
LEWY, Mr Ervin G.
LINDEBERG-LIND, Mr Erik Gustaf
LONG, Mr Milton Clyde
LORING, Mr Joseph Holland
MAGUIRE, Mr John Edward
MARVIN, Mr Daniel Warner
MCCAFFRY, Mr Thomas Francis
MCCARTHY, Mr Timothy J.
MEYER, Mr Edgar Joseph
MILLET, Mr Francis Davis
MINAHAN, Dr William Edward
MOLSON, Mr Harry Markland
MOORE, Mr Clarence Bloomfield
NATSCH, Mr Charles
NEWELL, Mr Arthur Webster
NICHOLSON, Mr Arthur Ernest
OSTBY, Mr Engelhart Cornelius
OVIES Y RODRIGUEZ, Mr Servando Jose Florentino
PARR, Mr William Henry Marsh
PARTNER, Mr Austin

PAYNE, Mr Vivian Ponsonby
PEARS, Mr Thomas Clinton
PEÑASCO Y CASTELLANA, Mr Victor
PORTER, Mr Walter Chamberlain
REUCHLIN, Mr Jonkheer Johan George
RIGHINI, Mr Sante (Manservant to Mrs White)
ROBBINS, Mr Victor (Manservant to Colonel Astor)
ROEBLING, Mr Washington Augustus II
ROOD, Mr Hugh Roscoe
ROSENSHINE, Mr George
ROSS, Mr John Hugo
ROTHSCHILD, Mr Martin
ROWE, Mr Alfred G.
RYERSON, Mr Arthur Larned
SILVEY, Mr William Baird
SMART, Mr John Montgomery
SMITH, Mr James Clinch
SMITH, Mr Lucian Philip
SMITH, Mr Richard William
SPENCER, Mr William Augustus
STEAD, Mr William Thomas
STEWART, Mr Albert A.
STRAUS, Mr Isidor
STRAUS, Mrs Rosalie Ida
SUTTON, Mr Frederick
TAUSSIG, Mr Emil
THAYER, Mr John Borland
URUCHURTU, Don. Manuel E.
VAN DER HOEF, Mr Wyckoff
WALKER, Mr William Anderson
WARREN, Mr Frank Manley
WEIR, Colonel John
WHITE, Mr Percival Wayland
WHITE, Mr Richard Frasar
WICK, Mr George Dennick
WIDENER, Mr George Dunton
WIDENER, Mr Harry Elkins
WILLIAMS, Mr Charles Duane
WRIGHT, Mr George

SECOND CLASS VICTIMS
ABELSON, Mr Samuel
ALDWORTH, Mr Charles Augustus
ANDREW, Mr Edgar Samuel
ANDREW, Mr Frank Thomas
ANGLE, Mr William A.
ASHBY, Mr John
BAILEY, Mr Percy Andrew
BAINBRIGGE, Mr Charles Robert
BANFIELD, Mr Frederick James
BATEMAN, Fr Robert James
BEAUCHAMP, Mr Henry James
BERRIMAN, Mr William John
BOTSFORD, Mr William Hull
BOWENUR, Mr Solomon
BRACKEN, Mr James H.
BRITO, Mr José Joaquim de
BROWN, Mr Thomas William Solomon
BRYHL, Mr Kurt Arnold Gottfrid
BUTLER, Mr Reginald Fenton
BYLES, Fr Thomas Roussel Davids
BYSTRÖM, Mrs Karolina
CAMPBELL, Mr William Henry
CARBINES, Mr William
CARTER, Fr Ernest Courtenay
CARTER, Mrs Lilian

CHAPMAN, Mr Charles Henry
CHAPMAN, Mr John Henry
CHAPMAN, Mrs Sara Elizabeth
CLARKE, Mr Charles Valentine
COLERIDGE, Mr Reginald Charles
COLLANDER, Mr Erik Gustaf
COLLYER, Mr Harvey
CORBETT, Mrs Irene
COREY, Mrs Mary Phyllis Elizabeth
COTTERILL, Mr Henry "Harry"
CUNNINGHAM, Mr Alfred Fleming
DAVIES, Mr Charles Henry
DEACON, Mr Percy William
DEL CARLO, Mr Sebastiano
DENBUOY, Mr Albert ("Herbert")
DIBDEN, Mr William
DOUTON, Mr William Joseph
DREW, Mr James Vivian
EITEMILLER, Mr George Floyd
ENANDER, Mr Ingvar
FAHLSTRØM, Mr Arne Joma
FAUNTHORPE, Mr Harry Bartram
FILLBROOK, Mr Joseph Charles
FOX, Mr Stanley Hubert
FROST, Mr Anthony Wood
FUNK, Miss Annie Clemmer
FYNNEY, Mr Joseph J.
GALE, Mr Harry
GALE, Mr Shadrach
GASKELL, Mr Alfred
GAVEY, Mr Laurence
GILBERT, Mr William
GILES, Mr Edgar
GILES, Mr Frederick Edward
GILES, Mr Ralph
GILL, Mr John William
GILLESPIE, Mr William Henry
GIVARD, Mr Hans Kristensen
GREENBERG, Mr Samuel
HALE, Mr Reginald
HARBECK, Mr William H.
HARPER, Rev. John
HARRIS, Mr Walter
HART, Mr Benjamin
HERMAN, Mr Samuel
HICKMAN, Mr Leonard Mark
HICKMAN, Mr Lewis
HICKMAN, Mr Stanley George
HILTUNEN, Miss Marta
HOCKING, Mr Richard George
HOCKING, Mr Samuel James Metcalfe
HODGES, Mr Henry Price
HOLD, Mr Stephen
HOOD, Mr Ambrose Jr
HOWARD, Mr Benjamin
HOWARD, Mrs Ellen Truelove
HUNT, Mr George Henry
JACOBSOHN, Mr Sidney Samuel
JARVIS, Mr Denzil John
JEFFERYS, Mr Clifford Thomas
JEFFERYS, Mr Ernest Wilfred
JENKIN, Mr Stephen Curnow
KANTOR, Mr Sinai
KARNES, Mrs Claire
KEANE, Mr Daniel
KIRKLAND, Rev Charles Leonard
KNIGHT, Mr Robert J.

KVILLNER, Mr Johan Henrik Johannesson
LAHTINEN, Mrs Anna Amelia
LAHTINEN, Fr William
LAMB, Mr John Joseph
LAROCHE, Mr Joseph Philippe Lemercier
LÉVY, Mr René Jacques
LEYSON, Mr Robert William Norman
LINNANE, Mr John
LOUCH, Mrs Alice Adelaide
LOUCH, Mr Charles Alexander
MACK, Mrs Mary
MALACHARD, Mr Jean-Noël
MALLET, Mr Albert
MANGIAVACCHI, Mr Serafino Emilio
MATTHEWS, Mr William John
MAYBERY, Mr Frank Hubert
MCCRAE, Mr Arthur Gordon
MCCRIE, Mr James Matthew
MCKANE, Mr Peter David
MEYER, Mr August
MILLING, Mr Jacob Christian
MITCHELL, Mr Henry Michael
MONTVILA, Rev. Juozas
MORAWECK, Dr Ernest
MORLEY, Mr Henry Samuel
MUDD, Mr Thomas Charles
MYLES, Mr Thomas Francis
NASSER, Mr Nicholas
NAVRATIL, Mr Michel
NESSON, Mr Israel
NICHOLLS, Mr Joseph Charles
NORMAN, Mr Robert Douglas
OTTER, Mr Richard
PAIN, Dr Alfred
PARKER, Mr Clifford Richard
PARKES, Mr Francis "Frank"
PENGELLY, Mr Frederick William
PERNOT, Mr René
PERUSCHITZ, Rev Josef
PHILLIPS, Mr Escott Robert
PONESELL, Mr Martin
PULBAUM, Mr Frank
REEVES, Mr David
RENOUF, Mr Peter Henry
RICHARD, Mr Emile Phillippe
ROGERS, Mr Reginald Harry
SCHMIDT, Mr August
SEDGWICK, Mr Charles Frederick Waddington
SHARP, Mr Percival James R.
SJÖSTEDT, Mr Ernst Adolf
SLEMEN, Mr Richard James
SOBEY, Mr Samuel James Hayden
STANTON, Mr Samuel Ward
STOKES, Mr Philip Joseph
SWANE, Mr George
SWEET, Mr George Frederick
TROUPIANSKY, Mr Moses Aaron
TURPIN, Mrs Dorothy Ann
TURPIN, Mr William John Robert
VEAL, Mr James
WARE, Mr John James
WARE, Mr William Jeffery
WATSON, Mr Ennis Hastings
WEISZ, Mr Leopold
WEST, Mr Edwy Arthur
WHEADON, Mr Edward H.
WHEELER, Mr Edwin Charles "Fred" (Valet to

George W. Vanderbilt)
YVOIS, Miss Henriette

THIRD CLASS VICTIMS

ABBING, Mr Anthony
ABBOTT, Mr Eugene Joseph
ABBOTT, Mr Rossmore Edward
ÅDAHL, Mr Mauritz Nils Martin
ADAMS, Mr John
AHLIN, Mrs Johanna Persdotter
ALEXANDER, Mr William
ALHOMÄKI, Mr Ilmari Rudolf
ALI, Mr Ahmed
ALI, Mr William
ALLEN, Mr William Henry
ALLUM, Mr Owen George
ANDERSEN, Mr Albert Karvin
ANDERSSON, Mrs Alfrida Konstantia Brogren
ANDERSSON, Mr Anders Johan
ANDERSSON, Miss Ebba Iris Alfrida
ANDERSSON, Miss Ellis Anna Maria
ANDERSSON, Miss Ida Augusta Margareta
ANDERSSON, Miss Ingeborg Constanzia
ANDERSSON, Mr Johan Samuel
ANDERSSON, Miss Sigrid Elisabeth
ANDERSSON, Master Sigvard Harald Elias
ANDREASSON, Mr Paul Edvin
ANGHELOFF, Mr Minko
ARNOLD-FRANCHI, Mr Josef
ARNOLD-FRANCHI, Mrs Josephine
ARONSSON, Mr Ernst Axel Algot
ASIM, Mr Adola
ASPLUND, Master Carl Edgar
ASPLUND, Mr Carl Oscar Vilhelm Gustafsson
ASPLUND, Master Clarence Gustaf Hugo
ASPLUND, Master Filip Oscar
ASSAM, Mr Ali
ATTALA, Mr Solomon
ATTALAH, Miss Malaka
AUGUSTSSON, Mr Albert
BACCOS, Mr Rafoul
BACKSTRÖM, Mr Karl Alfred
BADT, Mr Mohamed
BALKIC, Mr Cerin
BARBARA, Mrs Catherine David
BARBARA, Miss Saude
BARRY, Miss Julia
BARTON, Mr David John
BEAVAN, Mr William Thomas
BENGTSSON, Mr Johan Viktor
BERGLUND, Mr Karl Ivar Sven
BETROS, Mr Tannous
BIRKELAND, Mr Hans Martin Monsen
BJÖRKLUND, Mr Ernst Herbert
BOSTANDYEFF, Mr Guentcho
BOULOS, Master Akar
BOULOS Miss Nourelain
BOULOS, Mrs Sultana
BOURKE, Mrs Catherine
BOURKE, Mr John
BOURKE, Miss Mary
BOWEN, Mr David John "Dai"
BRAF, Miss Elin Ester Maria
BRAUND, Mr Lewis Richard
BRAUND, Mr Owen Harris
BROBECK, Mr Karl Rudolf
BROCKLEBANK, Mr William Alfred

BUCKLEY, Miss Katherine
BURKE, Mr Jeremiah
BURNS, Miss Mary Delia
CACIC, Mr Grego
CACIC, Mr Luka
CACIC, Miss Manda
CACIC, Miss Marija
CALIC, Mr Jovo
CALIC, Mr Peter
CANAVAN, Miss Mary
CANAVAN, Mr Patrick
CANN, Mr Ernest Charles
CARAM, Mr Joseph
CARAM, Mrs Maria Elias
CARLSSON, Mr August Sigfrid
CARLSSON, Mr Carl Robert
CARR, Miss Jane
CARVER, Mr Alfred John
CELOTTI, Mr Francesco
CHARTERS, Mr David
CHEHAB/SHIHAB, Mr Emir Farres
CHRISTMANN, Mr Emil
CHRONOPOULOS, Mr Apostolos M.
CHRONOPOULOS, Mr Dimitrios M.
COELHO, Mr Domingos Fernandeo
COLBERT, Mr Patrick
COLEFF, Mr Fotio
COLEFF, Mr Peyo
CONLIN, Mr Thomas Henry
CONNAGHTON, Mr Michael
CONNOLLY, Miss Kate
CONNORS, Mr Patrick
COOK, Mr Jacob
COR, Mr Bartol
COR, Mr Ivan
COR, Mr Liudevit
CORN, Mr Harry
COXON, Mr Daniel
CREASE, Mr Ernest James
CRIBB, Mr John Hatfield
CULUMOVIC, Mr Jeso
DAHER, Mr Tannous
DAHLBERG, Miss Gerda Ulrika
DAKIC, Mr Branko
DANBOM, Mrs Anna Sigrid Maria
DANBOM, Mr Ernst Gilbert
DANBOM, Master Gilbert Sigvard Emanuel
DANOFF, Mr Yoto
DANTCHOFF, Mr Khristo
DAVIES, Mr Alfred J.
DAVIES, Mr Evan
DAVIES, Mr John Samuel
DAVIES, Mr Joseph
DAVISON, Mr Thomas Henry
DE PELSMAEKER, Mr Alfons
DEAN, Mr Bertram Frank
DELALIC, Mr Redjo
DENKOFF, Mr Mito
DENNIS, Mr Samuel
DENNIS, Mr William
DIBO, Mr Elias
DIKA, Mr Mirko
DIMIC, Mr Jovan
DINTCHEFF, Mr Valtcho
DONOHOE, Miss Bridget
DOOLEY, Mr Patrick
DOUGHERTY, Mr William John

DOYLE, Miss Elizabeth
DRAZENOVIC, Mr Jozef
DUANE, Mr Frank
DYKER, Mr Adolf Fredrik
EDVARDSSON, Mr Gustaf Hjalmar
EKLUND, Mr Hans Linus
EKSTRÖM, Mr Johan
ELIAS, Mr Dibo
ELIAS, Mr Joseph
ELIAS, Mr Tannous
ELSBURY, Mr William James
ESTANISLAU, Mr Manuel Gonçalves
EVERETT, Mr Thomas James
FARRELL, Mr James "Jim"
FISCHER, Mr Eberhard Thelander
FLEMING, Miss Honora
FLYNN, Mr James
FLYNN, Mr John
FOLEY, Mr Joseph
FOLEY, Mr William
FORD, Mr Arthur
FORD, Mr Edward Watson
FORD, Miss Doolina Margaret
FORD, Mrs Margaret Ann Watson
FORD, Miss Robina Maggie
FORD, Mr William Neal Thomas
FOX, Mr Patrick
FRANKLIN, Mr Charles ("Charles Fardon")
GALLAGHER, Mr Martin
GARFIRTH, Mr John
GERIOS THAMAH, Mr Assaf
GHEORGHEFF, Mr Stanio
GILINSKI, Mr Leslie
GOLDSMITH, Mr Frank John
GOLDSMITH, Mr Nathan
GOODWIN, Mrs Augusta
GOODWIN, Mr Charles Edward
GOODWIN, Mr Frederick Joseph
GOODWIN, Master Harold Victor
GOODWIN, Miss Jessie Allis
GOODWIN, Miss Lillian Amy
GOODWIN, Master Sidney Leslie
GOODWIN, Master William Frederick
GREEN, Mr George Henry
GRØNNESTAD, Mr Daniel Danielsen
GUEST, Mr Robert
GUSTAFSSON, Mr Alfred Ossian
GUSTAFSSON, Mr Anders Vilhelm
GUSTAFSSON, Mr Johan Birger
GUSTAFSSON, Mr Karl Gideon
HAAS, Miss Aloisia
HAGLAND, Mr Ingvald Olai Olsen
HAGLAND, Mr Konrad Mathias Reiersen
HAKKARAINEN, Mr Pekka Pietari
HAMPE, Mr Léon Jérome
HANNA, Mr Boulos
HANNA, Mr Mansour
HANSEN, Mr Claus Peter
HANSEN, Mr Henry Damsgaard
HANSEN, Mr Henrik Juul
HARGADON, Miss Catherine "Kate"
HARKNETT, Miss Alice Phoebe
HART, Mr Henry
HASSAN ABILMONA, Mr Houssein Mohamed
HEGARTY, Miss Hanora "Nora"
HEININEN, Miss Wendla Maria
HENDEKOVIC, Mr Ignjac

HENRIKSSON, Miss Jenny Lovisa
HENRY, Miss Bridget Delia
HOLM, Mr John Fredrik Alexander
HOLTHEN, Mr Johan Martin
HORGAN, Mr John
HUMBLEN, Mr Adolf Mathias Nicolai Olsen
IBRAHIM SHAWAH, Mr Yousseff
ILIEFF, Mr Ylio
ILMAKANGAS, Miss Ida Livija
ILMAKANGAS, Miss Pieta Sofia
IVANOFF, Mr Kanio
JARDIM, Mr José Neto
JENSEN, Mr Hans Peder
JENSEN, Mr Niels Peder ("Rasmus")
JENSEN, Mr Svend Lauritz
JOHANSON, Mr Jakob Alfred
JOHANSSON, Mr Erik
JOHANSSON, Mr Gustaf Joel
JOHANSSON, Mr Karl Johan
JOHANSSON, Mr Nils
JOHNSON, Mr Alfred
JOHNSON, Mr Malkolm Joackim
JOHNSON, Mr William Cahoone Jr.
JOHNSTON, Mr Andrew Emslie
JOHNSTON, Miss Catherine Nellie
JOHNSTON, Mrs Elizabeth
JOHNSTON, Master William Andrew
JONKOFF, Mr Lalio
JÖNSSON, Mr Nils Hilding
JUSSILA, Miss Katriina
JUSSILA, Miss Mari Aina
KALLIO, Mr Nikolai Erland
KALVIK, Mr Johannes Halvorsen
KARAJIC, Mr Milan
KARLSSON, Mr Julius Konrad Eugen
KARLSSON, Mr Nils August
KASSEM HOUSSEIN, Mr Fared
KATAVELOS, Mr Vasilios G
KEANE, Mr Andrew "Andy"
KEEFE, Mr Arthur
KELLY, Mr James
KELLY, Mr James
KHALIL, Mr Betros
KHALIL, Mrs Zahie "Maria"
KIERNAN, Mr John
KIERNAN, Mr Philip
KILGANNON, Mr Thomas
KINK, Miss Maria
KINK, Mr Vincenz
KLASÉN, Miss Gertrud Emilia
KLASÉN, Mrs Hulda Kristina Eugenia
KLASÉN, Mr Klas Albin
KRAEFF, Mr Theodor
KUTSCHER, Mr Simon
LAHOUD, Mr Sarkis
LAITINEN, Miss Kristina Sofia
LALEFF, Mr Kristo
LAM, Mr Len
LANE, Mr Patrick
LARSSON, Mr August Viktor
LARSSON, Mr Bengt Edvin
LARSSON-RONDBERG, Mr Edvard A.
LEFEBRE, Mrs Frances Marie
LEFEBRE, Master Henry
LEFEBRE, Miss Ida
LEFEBRE, Miss Jeannie
LEFEBRE, Miss Mathilde

LEINONEN, Mr Antti Gustaf
LENNON, Mr Denis
LENNON, Mrs Mary
LEONARD, Mr Lionel
LESTER, Mr James
LIEVENS, Mr René Aimé
LINDAHL, Miss Agda Thorilda Viktoria
LINDBLOM, Miss Augusta Charlotta
LINDELL, Mr Edvard Bengtsson
LINDELL, Mrs Elin Gerda
LINEHAN, Mr Michael
LING, Mr Lee
LINHART, Mr Wenzel
LIVSHIN, Mr David (Abraham Harmer)
LOBB, Mrs Cordelia K.
LOBB, Mr William Arthur
LOCKYER, Mr Edward Thomas
LOVELL, Mr John Hall ("Henry")
LUNDAHL, Mr Johan Svensson
LYMPEROPOULOS, Peter
LYNTAKOFF, Mr Stanko
MACKAY, Mr George William
MÄENPÄÄ, Mr Matti Alexanteri
MAHON, Miss Bridget Delia
MAISNER, Mr Simon
MÄKINEN, Mr Kalle Edvard
MANGAN, Miss Mary
MARDIROSIAN, Mr Sarkis
MARINKO, Mr Dmitri
MARKOFF, Mr Marin
MARKUN, Mr Johann
MATINOFF, Mr Nicola
MCEVOY, Mr Michael
MCGOWAN, Miss Katherine
MCMAHON, Mr Martin
MCNAMEE, Mrs Eileen
MCNAMEE, Mr Neal
MCNEILL, Miss Bridget
MEANWELL, Mrs Marian
MEEHON, Mr John
MEEK, Mrs Annie Louise Rowley
MEO (MARTINO), Mr Alfonzo
MERNAGH, Mr Robert
MIHOFF, Mr Stoytcho
MILES, Mr Frank
MINEFF, Mr Ivan
MINKOFF, Mr Lazar
MITKOFF, Mr Mito
MOEN, Mr Sigurd Hansen
MOORE, Mr Leonard Charles
MORAN, Mr Daniel James
MORLEY, Mr William
MORROW, Mr Thomas Rowan
MOUSSA, Mrs Mantoura Boulos
MOUTAL, Mr Rahamin Haim
MURDLIN, Mr Joseph
MYHRMAN, Mr Pehr Fabian Oliver Malkolm
NAIDENOFF, Mr Penko
NAKHLI, Mr Toufik
NANCARROW, Mr William Henry
NANKOFF, Mr Minko
NASR ALMA, Mr Mustafa
NASSR, Mr Saade
NAUGHTON, Miss Hannah
NENKOFF, Mr Christo
NIEMINEN, Miss Manta Josefina
NIKLASSON, Mr Samuel

NILSSON, Mr August Ferdinand
NIRVA, Mr Iisakki Antino Äijö
NOFAL, Mr Mansouer
NOSWORTHY, Mr Richard Cater
NYSVEEN, Mr Johan Hansen
O'BRIEN, Mr Timothy
O'BRIEN, Mr Thomas
O'CONNELL, Mr Patrick Denis
O'CONNOR, Mr Maurice
O'CONNOR, Mr Patrick
O'SULLIVAN, Miss Bridget Mary
ÖDAHL, Mr Nils Martin
OLSEN, Mr Henry Margido
OLSEN, Mr Karl Siegwart Andreas
OLSEN, Mr Ole Martin
OLSSON, Miss Elina
OLSSON, Mr Nils Johan Göransson
OLSVIGEN, Mr Thor Anderson
ORESKOVIC, Mr Jeko
ORESKOVIC, Mr Luka
ORESKOVIC, Miss Marija
OSÉN, Mr Olaf Elon
PÅLSSON, Mrs Alma Cornelia
PÅLSSON, Master Gösta Leonard
PÅLSSON, Master Paul Folke
PÅLSSON, Miss Stina Viola
PÅLSSON, Miss Torborg Danira
PANULA, Master Eino Viljami
PANULA, Mrs Maija Emelia Abrahamintytar
PANULA, Mr Ernesti Arvid
PANULA, Master Jaako Arnold
PANULA, Master Juha Niilo
PANULA, Master Urho Abraham
PASIC, Mr Jakob
PATCHETT, Mr George
PAVLOVIC, Mr Stefo
PEACOCK, Master Alfred Edward
PEACOCK, Mrs Edith
PEACOCK, Miss Treasteall
PEARCE, Mr Ernest
PECRUIC, Mr Mate
PECRUIC, Mr Tome
PEDERSEN, Mr Olaf
PEDUZZI, Mr Giuseppe
PEKONIEMI, Mr Edvard
PELTOMÄKI, Mr Nikolai Johannes
PERKIN, Mr John Henry
PETERS, Miss Katie
PETERSEN, Mr Marius
PETRANEC, Miss Matilda
PETROFF, Mr Nedeca
PETROFF, Mr Pentcho
PETTERSSON, Miss Ellen Natalia
PETTERSSON, Mr Johan Emil
PLOTCHARSKY, Mr Vasil
PULNER, Mr Uscher
RADEFF, Mr Alexander
RAIBID, Mr Razi
RASMUSSEN, Mrs Lena Jakobsen (née Solvang)
REED, Mr James George
REKIC, Mr Tido
REYNOLDS, Mr Harold J.
RICE, Master Albert
RICE, Master Arthur
RICE, Master Eric
RICE, Master Eugene Francis
RICE, Master George Hugh

RICE, Mrs Margaret
RIIHIVUORI, Miss Susanna Juhantytär "Sanni"
RINTAMÄKI, Mr Matti
RISIEN, Mrs Emma
RISIEN, Mr Samuel Beard
ROBINS, Mr Alexander A.
ROBINS, Mrs Grace Charity
ROGERS, Mr William John
ROMMETVEDT, Mr Karl Kristian Knut
ROSBLOM, Mrs Helena Wilhelmina
ROSBLOM, Miss Salli Helena
ROSBLOM, Mr Viktor Richard
ROUSE, Mr Richard Henry
RUSH, Mr Alfred George John
RYAN, Mr Patrick
SAAD, Mr Amin
SAAD, Mr Khalil
SADLIER, Mr Matthew
SADOWITZ, Mr Harry
SÆTHER, Mr Simon Sivertsen
SAGE, Mrs Annie Elizabeth
SAGE, Master Anthony William
SAGE, Miss Constance Gladys
SAGE, Miss Dorothy
SAGE, Mr Douglas Bullen
SAGE, Miss Elizabeth Ada
SAGE, Mr Frederick
SAGE, Mr George John
SAGE, Mr John George
SAGE, Miss Stella Anne
SAGE, Master Thomas Henry
SALANDER, Mr Karl Johan
SALONEN, Mr Johan Werner
SAMAAN, Mr Elias
SAMAAN, Mr Hanna Elias
SAMAAN, Mr Youssef ("Joseph")
SAUNDERCOCK, Mr William Henry
SAWYER, Mr Frederick Charles
SCANLAN, Mr James
SDYCOFF, Mr Todor
SEMAN, Master Betros
SEROTA, Mr Maurice
SHAUGHNESSY, Mr Patrick
SHEDID, Mr Daher
SHELLARD, Mr Frederick William Blainey
SHORNEY, Mr Charles Joseph
SIMMONS, Mr John
SIRAYANIAN, Mr Orsen
SIVIC, Mr Husen
SIVOLA, Mr Antti Wilhelm
SKOOG, Mrs Anna Bernhardina
SKOOG, Master Harald
SKOOG, Master Karl Thorsten
SKOOG, Miss Mabel
SKOOG, Miss Margit Elizabeth
SKOOG, Mr Wilhelm ("William Johansson")
SLABENOFF, Mr Petco
SLOCOVSKI, Mr Selman Francis
SMILJANIC, Mr Mile
SMYTH, Mr Thomas
SØHOLT, Mr Peter Andreas Lauritz Andersen
SOMERTON, Mr Francis William
SPECTOR, Mr Woolf
SPINNER, Mr Henry John
STANEFF, Mr Ivan
STANKOVIC, Mr Jovan
STANLEY, Mr Edward Roland

STOREY, Mr Thomas
STOYTCHEFF, Mr Ilia
STRANDBERG, Miss Ida Sofia
STRILIC, Mr Ivan
STRÖM, Miss Elna Matilda
STRÖM, Miss Telma Matilda
SUTEHALL, Mr Henry Jr
SVENSSON, Mr Johan
SVENSSON, Mr Olof
TANNOUS, Mr Elias Nasrallah
THEOBALD, Mr Thomas Leonard
THOMAS, Mr Charles R'ad.
THOMAS/TANNOUS, Mr John
THOMAS/TANNOUS, Mr Tannous
THOMSON, Mr Alexander Morrison
THORNEYCROFT, Mr Percival
TIKKANEN, Mr Juho
TOBIN, Mr Roger
TODOROFF, Mr Lalio
TOMLIN, Mr Ernest Portage
TÖRBER, Mr Ernst Wilhelm
TORFA, Mr Assad
TURCIN, Mr Stefan
UZELAS, Mr Jovo
VAN BILLIARD, Mr Austin Blyler
VAN BILLIARD, Master James William
VAN BILLIARD, Master Walter John
VAN DE VELDE, Mr Johannes Joseph
VAN DEN STEEN, Mr Leo Peter
VAN IMPE, Miss Catharina
VAN IMPE, Mr Jean Baptiste
VAN IMPE, Mrs Rosalie Paula
VAN MELCKEBEKE, Mr Philemon
VANDERCRUYSSEN, Mr Victor
VANDERPLANKE, Miss Augusta Maria
VANDERPLANKE, Mrs Emelie Maria
VANDERPLANKE, Mr Julius
VANDERPLANKE, Mr Leo Edmondus
VANDEWALLE, Mr Nestor Cyriel
VENDEL, Mr Olof Edvin
VESTRÖM, Miss Hulda Amanda Adolfina
VOVK, Mr Janko
WAELENS, Mr Achille
WARE, Mr Frederick
WARREN, Mr Charles William
WAZLI, Mr Yousif Ahmed
WEBBER, Mr James
WENZEL, Mr Linhart
WIDEGREN, Mr Carl / Charles Peter
WIKLUND, Mr Jakob Alfred
WIKLUND, Mr Karl Johan
WILLER, Mr Aaron
WILLEY, Mr Edward
WILLIAMS, Mr Howard Hugh "Harry"
WILLIAMS, Mr Leslie
WINDELØV, Mr Einar
WIRZ, Mr Albert
WISEMAN, Mr Phillippe
WITTENRONGEL, Mr Camilius Aloysius
YASBECK, Mr Antoni
YOUSEFF (SAM'AAN), Mr Gerios
YOUSSEFF (ABI SAAB), Mr Gerios
ZABOUR, Miss Hileni
ZABOUR, Miss Thamine
ZAKARIAN, Mr Mapriededer
ZAKARIAN, Mr Ortin
ZIMMERMANN, Mr Leo

Length: 882 feet, 8 inches
Beam: 92.5 feet
Height: 60.5 feet waterline to Boat Deck, 175 feet keel to top of funnels
Draft: 59.5 feet
Gross Tonnage: 46,328 tons
Top Speed: 23 knots
Total Capacity: 3547 passengers and crew
Decks: 9 in all (including the Orlop Deck)- the Boat Deck, A, B, C, D, E, F, G, and boiler rooms below G.
Fuel Requirement: 825 tons of coal per day
Boilers: 29 (24 double ended boilers and 5 single ended boilers)
Furnaces: 159 providing a total heating surface of 144,142 sq. feet
Watertight compartments: 16, extending up to F deck

The Titanic only had 20 life boats, enough for 1178 people.
Lifeboat capacity –
Lifeboats 1 and 2: 40 people
Lifeboats 3-16: 65 people
Lifeboats A-D: 47 people
Lifeboat 7 left with only 21 people in it, and Lifeboat 1 left with only 12.
There were 3560 lifejackets on board.

The Titanic was a Royal Mail Ship and had a Post Office on board, with five postal clerks.
328 bodies were recovered from the wreck, but 119 were too badly damaged and so were buried at sea.
The Titanic cost $7.5m to build
Two dogs were among the survivors.
There were 13 couples celebrating their honeymoons on board.
The stopping distance for the ship was about half a mile.
Among Titanic cargo claimed as lost were four cases of opium.

Ticket prices were as follows:
First Class (parlor suite) £870/$4,350 (about £49,642 today)
First Class (berth) £30/$150 (about £1712 today)
Second Class £12/$60 (about £684 today)
Third Class £3 to £8/$40 (£171-£456 today)

ABOVE: The bow of the ship on the ocean bed.
The Titanic is gradually being consumed by iron-eating microbes and will eventually disintegrate.